DISCOVER JAVA™

DISCOVER JAVA™

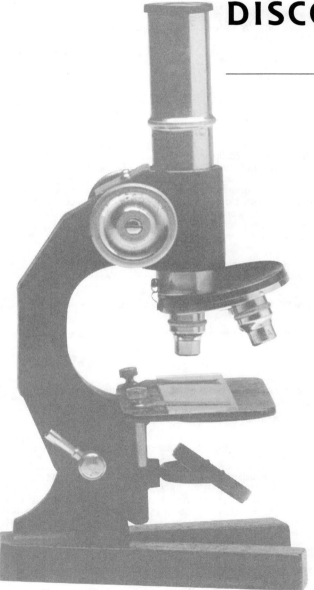

BY ED TITTEL AND
BILL BROGDEN

IDG BOOKS WORLDWIDE, INC.

AN INTERNATIONAL
DATA GROUP COMPANY

FOSTER CITY, CA • CHICAGO, IL •
INDIANAPOLIS, IN • SOUTHLAKE, TX

Discover Java™

Published by
IDG Books Worldwide, Inc.
An International Data Group Company
919 E. Hillsdale Blvd., Suite 400
Foster City, CA 94404

http://www.idgbooks.com (IDG Books Worldwide Web site)

Library of Congress Catalog Card No.: 96-79750

ISBN: 0-7645-8024-8

Printed in the United States of America

10 9 8 7 6 5 4 3 2 1

1IPC/RU/QT/ZX/FC

Distributed in the United States by IDG Books Worldwide, Inc.

Distributed by Macmillan Canada for Canada; by Contemporanea de Ediciones for Venezuela; by Distribuidora Cuspide for Argentina; by CITEC for Brazil; by Ediciones ZETA S.C.R. Ltda. for Peru; by Editorial Limusa SA for Mexico; by Transworld Publishers Limited in the United Kingdom and Europe; by Academic Bookshop for Egypt; by Levant Distributors S.A.R.L. for Lebanon; by Al Jassim for Saudi Arabia; by Simron Pty. Ltd. for South Africa; by Pustak Mahal for India; by The Computer Bookshop for India; by Toppan Company Ltd. for Japan; by Addison Wesley Publishing Company for Korea; by Longman Singapore Publishers Ltd. for Singapore, Malaysia, Thailand, and Indonesia; by Unalis Corporation for Taiwan; by WS Computer Publishing Company, Inc. for the Philippines; by WoodsLane Pty. Ltd. for Australia; by WoodsLane Enterprises Ltd. for New Zealand. Authorized Sales Agent: Anthony Rudkin Associates for the Middle East and North Africa.

For general information on IDG Books Worldwide's books in the U.S., please call our Consumer Customer Service department at 800-762-2974. For reseller information, including discounts and premium sales, please call our Reseller Customer Service department at 800-434-3422.

For information on where to purchase IDG Books Worldwide's books outside the U.S., please contact our International Sales department at 415-655-3172 or fax 415-655-3295.

For information on foreign language translations, please contact our Foreign & Subsidiary Rights department at 415-655-3021 or fax 415-655-3281.

For sales inquiries and special prices for bulk quantities, please contact our Sales department at 415-655-3200 or write to the address above.

For information on using IDG Books Worldwide's books in the classroom or for ordering examination copies, please contact our Educational Sales department at 800-434-2086 or fax 817-251-8174.

For press review copies, author interviews, or other publicity information, please contact our Public Relations department at 415-655-3000 or fax 415-655-3299.

For authorization to photocopy items for corporate, personal, or educational use, please contact Copyright Clearance Center, 222 Rosewood Drive, Danvers, MA 01923, or fax 508-750-4470.

is a trademark under exclusive license to
IDG Books Worldwide, Inc.,
from International Data Group, Inc.

ABOUT IDG BOOKS WORLDWIDE

Welcome to the world of IDG Books Worldwide.

IDG Books Worldwide, Inc., is a subsidiary of International Data Group, the world's largest publisher of computer-related information and the leading global provider of information services on information technology. IDG was founded more than 25 years ago and now employs more than 8,500 people worldwide. IDG publishes more than 275 computer publications in over 75 countries (see listing below). More than 60 million people read one or more IDG publications each month.

Launched in 1990, IDG Books Worldwide is today the #1 publisher of best-selling computer books in the United States. We are proud to have received eight awards from the Computer Press Association in recognition of editorial excellence and three from *Computer Currents'* First Annual Readers' Choice Awards. Our best-selling *...For Dummies®* series has more than 30 million copies in print with translations in 30 languages. IDG Books Worldwide, through a joint venture with IDG's Hi-Tech Beijing, became the first U.S. publisher to publish a computer book in the People's Republic of China. In record time, IDG Books Worldwide has become the first choice for millions of readers around the world who want to learn how to better manage their businesses.

Our mission is simple: Every one of our books is designed to bring extra value and skill-building instructions to the reader. Our books are written by experts who understand and care about our readers. The knowledge base of our editorial staff comes from years of experience in publishing, education, and journalism — experience we use to produce books for the '90s. In short, we care about books, so we attract the best people. We devote special attention to details such as audience, interior design, use of icons, and illustrations. And because we use an efficient process of authoring, editing, and desktop publishing our books electronically, we can spend more time ensuring superior content and spend less time on the technicalities of making books.

You can count on our commitment to deliver high-quality books at competitive prices on topics you want to read about. At IDG Books Worldwide, we continue in the IDG tradition of delivering quality for more than 25 years. You'll find no better book on a subject than one from IDG Books Worldwide.

John J. Kilcullen

John Kilcullen
CEO
IDG Books Worldwide, Inc.

**Eighth Annual
Computer Press
Awards ≥1992**

**Ninth Annual
Computer Press
Awards ≥1993**

**Tenth Annual
Computer Press
Awards ≥1994**

**Eleventh Annual
Computer Press
Awards ≥1995**

IDG Books Worldwide, Inc., is a subsidiary of International Data Group, the world's largest publisher of computer-related information and the leading global provider of information services on information technology. International Data Group publishes over 275 computer publications in over 75 countries. Sixty million people read one or more International Data Group publications each month. International Data Group's publications include: **ARGENTINA:** Buyer's Guide, Computerworld Argentina, PC World Argentina; **AUSTRALIA:** Australian Macworld, Australian PC World, Australian Reseller News, Computerworld, IT Casebook, Network World, Publish, Webmaster; **AUSTRIA:** Computerwelt Osterreich, Networks Austria, PC Tip Austria; **BANGLADESH:** PC World Bangladesh; **BELARUS:** PC World Belarus; **BELGIUM:** Data News; **BRAZIL:** Annuário de Informática, Computerworld, Connections, Macworld, PC Player, PC World, Publish, Reseller News, Supergamepower; **BULGARIA:** Computerworld Bulgaria, Network World Bulgaria, PC & MacWorld Bulgaria; **CANADA:** CIO Canada, Client/Server World, ComputerWorld Canada, InfoWorld Canada, NetworkWorld Canada, WebWorld; **CHILE:** Computerworld Chile, PC World Chile; **COLOMBIA:** Computerworld Colombia, PC World Colombia; **COSTA RICA:** PC World Centro America; **THE CZECH AND SLOVAK REPUBLICS:** Computerworld Czechoslovakia, Macworld Czech Republic, PC World Czechoslovakia; **DENMARK:** Communications World Danmark, Computerworld Danmark, Macworld Danmark, PC World Danmark, Techworld Denmark; **DOMINICAN REPUBLIC:** PC World Republica Dominicana; **ECUADOR:** PC World Ecuador; **EGYPT:** Computerworld Middle East, PC World Middle East; **EL SALVADOR:** PC World Centro America; **FINLAND:** MikroPC, Tietoverkko, Tietoviikko; **FRANCE:** Distributique, Hebdo, Info PC, Le Monde Informatique, Macworld, Reseaux & Telecoms, WebMaster France; **GERMANY:** Computer Partner, Computerwoche, Computerwoche Extra, Computerwoche FOCUS, Global Online, Macwelt, PC Welt; **GREECE:** Amiga Computing, GamePro Greece, Multimedia World; **GUATEMALA:** PC World Centro America; **HONDURAS:** PC World Centro America; **HONG KONG:** Computerworld Hong Kong, PC World Hong Kong, Publish in Asia; **HUNGARY:** ABCD CD-ROM, Computerworld Szamitastechnika, Internetto online Magazine, PC World Hungary, PC-X Magazin Hungary; **ICELAND:** Tolvuheimur PC World Island; **INDIA:** Information Communications World, Information Systems Computerworld, PC World India, Publish in Asia; **INDONESIA:** InfoKomputer PC World, Komputek Computerworld, Publish in Asia; **IRELAND:** ComputerScope, PC Live!; **ISRAEL:** Macworld Israel, People & Computers/Computerworld; **ITALY:** Computerworld Italia, Macworld Italia, Networking Italia, PC World Italia; **JAPAN:** DTP World, Macworld Japan, Nikkei Personal Computing, OS/2 World Japan, SunWorld Japan, Windows NT World, Windows World Japan; **KENYA:** PC World East African; **KOREA:** Hi-Tech Information, Macworld Korea, PC World Korea; **MACEDONIA:** PC World Macedonia; **MALAYSIA:** Computerworld Malaysia, PC World Malaysia, Publish in Asia; **MALTA:** PC World Malta; **MEXICO:** Computerworld Mexico, PC World Mexico; **MYANMAR:** PC World Myanmar; **NETHERLANDS:** Computer! Totaal, LAN Internetworking Magazine, LAN World Buyers Guide, Macworld Netherlands, Net, WebWereld; **NEW ZEALAND:** Absolute Beginners Guide and Plain & Simple Series, Computer Buyer, Computer Industry Directory, Computerworld New Zealand, MTB, Network World, PC World New Zealand; **NICARAGUA:** PC World Centro America; **NORWAY:** Computerworld Norge, CW Rapport, Datamagasinet, Financial Rapport, Kursguide Norge, Macworld Norge, Multimediaworld Norge, PC World Ekspress Norge, PC World Nettverk, PC World Norge, PC World ProduktGuide Norge; **PAKISTAN:** Computerworld Pakistan; **PANAMA:** PC World Panama; **PEOPLE'S REPUBLIC OF CHINA:** China Computer Users, China Computerworld, China InfoWorld, China Telecom World Weekly, Computer & Communication, Electronic Design China, Electronics Today, Electronics Weekly, Game Software, PC World China, Popular Computer Week, Software Weekly, Software World, Telecom World; **PERU:** Computerworld Peru, PC World Profesional Peru, PC World SoHo Peru; **PHILIPPINES:** Click!, Computerworld Philippines, PC World Philippines, Publish in Asia; **POLAND:** Computerworld Poland, Computerworld Special Report Poland, Cyber, Macworld Poland, Networld Poland, PC World Komputer; **PORTUGAL:** Cerebro/PC World, Computerworld/Correio Informático, Dealer World Portugal, Mac*In/PC*In Portugal, Multimedia World; **PUERTO RICO:** PC World Puerto Rico; **ROMANIA:** Computerworld Romania, PC World Romania, Telecom Romania; **RUSSIA:** Computerworld Russia, Mir PK, Publish, Seti; **SINGAPORE:** Computerworld Singapore, PC World Singapore, Publish in Asia; **SLOVENIA:** Monitor; **SOUTH AFRICA:** Computing SA, Network World SA, Software World SA; **SPAIN:** Communicaciones World España, Computerworld España, Dealer World España, Macworld España, PC World España; **SRI LANKA:** Infolink PC World; **SWEDEN:** CAP&Design, Computer Sweden, Corporate Computing Sweden, Internetworld Sweden, it.branschen, Macworld Sweden, MaxiData Sweden, MikroDatorn, Nätverk & Kommunikation, PC World Sweden, PCAktiv, Windows World Sweden; **SWITZERLAND:** Computerworld Schweiz, Macworld Schweiz, PCtip; **TAIWAN:** Computerworld Taiwan, Macworld Taiwan, NEW ViSiON/Publish, PC World Taiwan, Windows World Taiwan; **THAILAND:** Publish in Asia, Thai Computerworld; **TURKEY:** Computerworld Turkiye, Macworld Turkiye, Network World Turkiye, PC World Turkiye; **UKRAINE:** Computerworld Kiev, Multimedia World Ukraine, PC World Ukraine; **UNITED KINGDOM:** Acorn User UK, Amiga Action UK, Amiga Computing UK, Apple Talk UK, Computing, Macworld, Parents and Computers UK, PC Advisor, PC Home, PSX Pro, The WEB; **UNITED STATES:** Cable in the Classroom, CIO Magazine, Computerworld, DOS World, Federal Computer Week, GamePro Magazine, InfoWorld, I-Way, Macworld, Network World, PC Games, PC World, Publish, Video Event, THE WEB Magazine, and WebMaster; online webzines: JavaWorld, NetscapeWorld, and SunWorld Online; **URUGUAY:** InfoWorld Uruguay; **VENEZUELA:** Computerworld Venezuela, PC World Venezuela; and **VIETNAM:** PC World Vietnam.   2/14/97

Welcome to the Discover Series

Do you want to discover the best and most efficient ways to use your computer and learn about technology? Books in the Discover series teach you the essentials of technology with a friendly, confident approach. You'll find a Discover book on almost any subject — from the Internet to intranets, from Web design and programming to the business programs that make your life easier.

We've provided valuable, real-world examples that help you relate to topics faster. Discover books begin by introducing you to the main features of programs, so you start by doing something *immediately*. The focus is to teach you how to perform tasks that are useful and meaningful in your day-to-day work. You might create a document or graphic, explore your computer, surf the Web, or write a program. Whatever the task, you learn the most commonly used features, and focus on the best tips and techniques for doing your work. You'll get results quickly, and discover the best ways to use software and technology in your everyday life.

You may find the following elements and features in this book:

Discovery Central: This tearout card is a handy quick reference to important tasks or ideas covered in the book.

Quick Tour: The Quick Tour gets you started working with the book right away.

Real-Life Vignettes: Throughout the book you'll see one-page scenarios illustrating a real-life application of a topic covered.

Goals: Each chapter opens with a list of goals you can achieve by reading the chapter.

Side Trips: These asides include additional information about alternative or advanced ways to approach the topic covered.

Bonuses: Timesaving tips and more advanced techniques are covered in each chapter.

Discovery Center: This guide illustrates key procedures covered throughout the book.

Visual Index: You'll find real-world documents in the Visual Index, with page numbers pointing you to where you should turn to achieve the effects shown.

Throughout the book, you'll also notice some special icons and formatting:

A Feature Focus icon highlights new features in the software's latest release, and points out significant differences between it and the previous version.

Web Paths refer you to Web sites that provide additional information about the topic.

Tips offer timesaving shortcuts, expert advice, quick techniques, or brief reminders.

The X-Ref icon refers you to other chapters or sections for more information.

Pull Quotes emphasize important ideas that are covered in the chapter.

Notes provide additional information or highlight special points of interest about a topic.

The Caution icon alerts you to potential problems you should watch out for.

The Discover series delivers interesting, insightful, and inspiring information about technology to help you learn faster and retain more. So the next time you want to find answers to your technology questions, reach for a Discover book. We hope the entertaining, easy-to-read style puts you at ease and makes learning fun.

Credits

ACQUISITIONS EDITOR
John Osborn

DEVELOPMENT EDITOR
Bill Sullivan

SENIOR COPY EDITOR
Barry Childs-Helton

COPY EDITOR
Kyle Looper

TECHNICAL EDITOR
Jeff Bankston

PRODUCTION COORDINATOR
Katy German

GRAPHICS AND PRODUCTION SPECIALISTS
Laura Carpenter
Jude Levinson
Ed Penslien
Chris Pimentel
Dina F Quan
Andreas F. Schueller
Mark Schumann

QUALITY CONTROL SPECIALIST
Mick Arellano

PROOFREADERS
Desne Border
Andrew Davis
Stacey Lynn
Candace Ward
Anne Weinberger

INDEXER
Elizabeth Cunningham

BOOK DESIGN
Seventeenth Street Studios
Phyllis Beaty
Kurt Krames

About the Authors

Ed Tittel has contributed to over 30 computing-related books. He is the co-author of three ...*For Dummies* books: *Windows NT Networking For Dummies* (with Mary Madden and Earl Follis), *HTML For Dummies*, now it its second edition (with Stephen N. James), and *NetWare For Dummies*, currently in its third edition (co-authored with Deni Connor and Earl Follis). Most recently he's co-authored *Building Windows NT Web Servers* (with Mary Madden and David B. Smith), plus *CGI Bible*, *Web Programming SECRETS*, and two *60 Minute Guides* on Java and VRML, with Mark Gaither, Sebastian Hassinger, and Mike Erwin, all for IDG Books.

In a past life, Ed was the Director of Technical Marketing for Novell, Inc., where he worked in a variety of networking-related technical positions between 1988 and 1994. Ed has been a regular contributor to the computer trade press since 1987, with a decided emphasis on networking technology. These publications include *Computerworld, Datamation, InfoWorld, LAN Times, LAN Magazine, BYTE, Iway, NetGuide, Windows NT Magazine*, and *Computer Shopper*. At present, Ed is a weekly columnist for *Interop Online*.

You can reach Ed by e-mail at `etittel@lanw.com`, or through his Web page at `http://www.lanw.com/etbio.htm`.

Bill Brogden lives in the country with his wife, several computers, and a variable number of dogs, mostly basset hounds. He has been programming computers in a variety of languages since the late seventies. Computer software consulting is his third career; the first two were natural products chemistry and chemical oceanography. He has really enjoyed exploring the new possibilities Java has opened up.

You can reach Bill by e-mail at `wbrogden@bga.com`

Acknowledgments

I'd like to start by thanking my co-author, Bill Brogden, who not only represents the brains behind this book, but who also carried this project through from start to finish. His encyclopedic knowledge, boundless enthusiasm, and hard work are revealed in nearly every page you'll read here. I'd also like to thank the rest of my team at LANWrights, Inc., especially Dawn Rader and Louise Leahy, who pulled these materials together and made them into the book you now hold in your hands. Finally, thanks to my family, near and far, for putting up with the occasional inattention that writing books will sometimes cause. I'd like to conclude with some very special thanks to my mother, Ceceilia Katherine Kociolek Tittel, who taught me to love language, and to pick my words with care and discrimination.

— *Ed Tittel*

I would like to acknowledge the support of my wife and family. Thanks for putting up with my odd hours and uneven income stream. I would also like to thank the Java community as a whole. The mutual support and sharing of ideas has helped to make the last year a very exciting time.

— *Bill Brogden*

CONTENTS AT A GLANCE

PART THREE—ADVANCED JAVA APPLICATIONS AND DEVELOPMENT TOPICS

CONTENTS

2 JAVA SYNTAX AND SEMANTICS, 43

PART THREE—ADVANCED JAVA APPLICATIONS AND DEVELOPMENT TOPICS, 179

8   WRITING A JAVA APPLICATION, 181

9   JAVA APPLICATION MANAGEMENT, 189

JAVA QUICK TOUR

This quick tour of Java is designed around the questions we get asked all the time. We hope these answers will inspire you to get going with Java.

What Is Java?

Java is a new, full-featured computer language that incorporates the best of modern thinking about object-oriented (OO) programming. Java is simpler and more robust than other computer languages and combines features which make it ideal for programs which must deal with networks. The designers of Java emphasized security, ease of programming and independence from any particular hardware. These features brought Java near-instant acclaim in the programming world and a meteoric rise in public consciousness.

The sudden success of Java could not have happened without the Internet. Because Java can be used to create tiny programs (called applets) which can live on a Web page and interact with users, thousands of Web pages incorporating Java appeared within a few months of Java's initial release. The early adoption of Java by Netscape for the Navigator browser set the course for a revolution in people's expectations of what could be accomplished on a Web page. However, note that the Netscape scripting language, called JavaScript, actually has very little to do with the Java language.

Java is not limited to applets, many people feel that there will be major applications downloaded over networks and running the same code on many different combinations of hardware and operating systems. Write once/run anywhere is the Java rallying cry.

How Is Java Different?

By starting with a clean slate, Java designers were able to create a simple language which combined the best of modern thinking about object-oriented design. An OO language uses "objects" to enclose the various parts of a program and protect them from inadvertent modification. Java also performs many "housekeeping" functions automatically, thus removing many causes of software bugs. Unlike most other common computer languages, Java was designed from the start to multitask and be network-aware.

What Do I Need to Run Java?

Java requires a hardware and operating system capable of 32-bit operations, so you won't be able to run it on your old 286 system. There are Java development systems for Windows 95 and NT, OS/2, Macintosh, and many UNIX systems. Work is being done on getting Java to run under Windows 3.1, but it will probably never be happy there. Java development systems generally expect a color monitor and a mouse, but do not require a huge amount of memory, or disk space.

What Do I Have to Buy?

You can accomplish an amazing amount without buying anything if you can get on the Internet. The Java Developers Kit (JDK) can be downloaded for free from www.javasoft.com and there are many other free resources which are discussed in the book. For cheap technical support, try asking questions on the Java-related newsgroups.

If you want a more sophisticated programming environment, there are many software companies who will be glad to sell you development environments integrated with Java compilers and class libraries. Some of these include "visual" interface design systems and support for linking Java programs with databases.

How Can I Learn Java?

Your computer programming background will determine what you find easiest and hardest to learn about Java. In general, all programmers will be pleased with the built-in networking capabilities and the strict type checking, which lets the compiler catch many common errors. The easy availability of multitasking in Java will come as a pleasant surprise, because in other languages, multitasking is impossible or is heavily tied to a specific operating system.

Here is our estimate as to how different backgrounds might condition your approach to learning Java.

* **No programming background**. Without any preconceived notions to unlearn, you may have an advantage. Be sure you understand the basics of the different variable types and operators before jumping into classes and objects.

* **C programmer**. The Java syntax will be familiar, but you will have to work at converting from the procedural techniques of C to the object techniques of Java and the event orientation of typical Java Graphical User Interfaces (GUIs). Instead of structures, you will be dealing with classes. You may find the absence of pointers to be frustrating at first, but think of all the bugs you will be avoiding.

* **C++ programmer**. Like the C programmer, you will find the syntax familiar and the absence of pointers frustrating. Many of the complexities of C++ were left out of Java for the sake of simplicity. Some C++ programmers get annoyed at the absence of some of these complexities, such as multiple inheritance, but you will find that Java has ways to accomplish all you need to do.

* **Visual Basic programmer**. You will find the creation of user interfaces using Java components to be similar to Visual Basic, but you will have to work harder at creating the connections between components and code. Java does not yet have the huge list of component vendors that you have enjoyed with Visual Basic, but the true object-oriented nature of Java will make it easier to derive your own components.

What Do People Do with Java?

In the following subsections, we examine some of the more common uses of the Java programming language.

JAZZ UP A WEB PAGE

Here are some of the simple Java applets we have seen in use to simply jazz up an otherwise static Web page:

* Scrolling "ticker tape" text messages
* Animated text that wanders around the screen
* Animated characters that respond to the user's mouse movements
* A random "slide show" of images

REAL-TIME DATA

Java applets can be used to present complex data from real-time events. Our favorite example (because we helped program it) is the Instant Ballpark applet which shows an animated view of major league baseball games using data delivered from a Web server within a minute or two of the actual play. Other examples include stock market data delivery systems (not nearly as much fun).

MEDICAL DATA

Some of the most impressive Java applications on the Internet today are in the medical field. One of the first allowed users to select images of human body cross sections using a mouse. There are several examples of Java-driven user interfaces to huge databases of DNA sequences. Only Java can provide the same user friendly interface to scientists all over the world using a variety of computer hardware.

EDUCATION

Educators were very quick to catch on to the possibilities of using Java to create online demonstrations and simulations. Here are some of the educational Java programs we found in recent Web surfing:

* A graphic simulation of electrons moving in a plasma
* Several viewers for 3-D molecular models
* A simulation of the thermodynamics of a Stirling cycle engine
* An online neural network training demonstration
* Graphic presentation of the evolution of artificial life forms
* A simulation of flocking behavior in birds, wildebeests, and gnats

CLIENT/SERVER APPLICATIONS

In a client/server application, a Java applet provides the user's interface to a program running on an Internet server. Java can be used to create both applets and server programs because the standard Java library of classes include many which facilitate network connections. Complete Web servers have been created entirely in Java, so adding special Java functions to a Web site may easier than you would expect. Here are some of the client/server applications we have seen:

* Chat systems. Both plain-text and graphical chat programs with both the user interface and server implemented in Java
* Online games. A wide variety of online games, both single-player and multi-player, have been created with Java
* Databases. Many database vendors have announced Java compatibility for their products so this area of activity is really booming

In this part of the book, we introduce some Java basics and explore its background and origin. We also provide a detailed review of Java syntax and semantics, including a quick trip through its reserved words and predefined terms as well as its declaration and variable handling mechanisms. Here too, the structure and function of the Java run-time system are explored and explained in some detail. This part concludes with a comprehensive overview of Java's Base Classes and predefined objects and a discussion of the techniques and approaches most recommended for extending and enhancing existing object definitions.

DJ: What was your Web site like before Java?

DB: During the 1995 baseball season, Instant Sports provided live, pitch-by-pitch coverage of every Major League Baseball game in a textual format. Our pages included detailed information about the current situation, such as the pitcher, batter, runners, and count of balls and strikes, as well as one-line descriptions of every play. The pages were generally updated within about 30 to 60 seconds of the live action in the ballparks. It gave fans the information they wanted, but the form was pretty static.

DJ: What does your Java applet do?

DB: Our Java applet, Instant Ballpark(TM), provides live animated coverage of Major League Baseball games. The animation shows the path of the ball and the actions of the fielders and runners. In addition, there is a VCR-like control panel which gives the fan complete control over the pace and flow of the game. For example, the fan can stop the action, back up and watch a play again, and then resume with live coverage. The applet also includes a scrolling scoreboard with the current situation of every game on the schedule, allowing the fan to switch games

DJ: How much effort did it take to create the Java-ized Web site?

DB: All told, it took between six and twelve person-months, once the central database and raw data feed from the ballparks were in place. A lot of the work involved ensuring that the right data was ready for use by the applet at the right time.

DJ: What kind of problems did you have?

DB: The biggest problem was testing, aggravated by the fact that Java was still an immature technology, and that our applet was probably the most complex that had been written up to that time. So when something went wrong, it was very hard to isolate the cause. We were constantly asking ourselves: was it the Java implementation on the browser, was it the compiler, was it our source code, was it the data feed from our database, or a combination?

DJ: What has the response of the viewers been?

DB: Response from fans has been very positive. The animation gives them a much more enjoyable way to follow their favorite teams and players. On the other hand, many fans were also very disappointed that their browsers did not support Java. Java's promise of platform independence is very enticing, but during 1996, the availability of good Java implementations didn't match the promise. We hope that situation will be better in 1997.

DJ: Where can we see it online?

DB: Take a look at `http://www.InstantSports.com/baseball.html` and follow the links to the Java applet.

CHAPTER ONE

ORIGINS AND
USES OF JAVA

IN THIS CHAPTER YOU LEARN THESE KEY SKILLS

Java is a hot, crucial language that brings a multitude of uses to both the programming community and the World Wide Web at large. Although there's an island in Indonesia and a ubiquitous stimulant that share its name, the language's creator (Sun Microsystems) defines this flavor of Java as "a simple, robust, object-oriented, platform-independent, multithreaded, dynamic, general-purpose programming environment." Keep reading for an explanation of what those impressive adjectives actually mean!

The buzz surrounding Java is phenomenal: in May, 1996, over 100 books on Java hit the shelves. And in an unprecedented move, Microsoft licensed the software without licensing its creator company as well — a first-time occurrence. There's no question that Java has been recognized as a crucial part of the computing future. As a language (ultimately) created with the World Wide Web in mind, it comes already primed for Web use, a characteristic that few languages can boast. Its importance to the world of object-oriented programming can't be overlooked, either — it was carefully crafted to glean the best parts of C and C++, while striving to redefine what constitutes a solid, well-constructed, object-oriented language (OOL). In essence, Java was custom-designed to fit the programming needs that have emerged as distributed computing has been recognized as the direction of the future.

Java has the power to distribute information in a radical new manner, one that pushes the Web into unprecedented realms of interactivity and communication. Its platform-independence and strong industry support translate into a positive future, and Sun, armed with impressive marketing and research funds, is doggedly committed to making Java a ubiquitous language. The company has stated its goal as follows at the Javasoft Web site (`http://www.javasoft.com/java.sun.com/`): "To promote open systems, open architectures, and consistent versions of the Java language."

 WEB PATH If you want to get a whiff of Java before diving into this book, there are plenty of online references available. Sun's "Getting Started With Java" is a good place to begin:

`http://java.sun.com/starter.html`

The Java Tools site is also an excellent resource for late-breaking Java news:

`http://www.cybercom.net/~frog/javaide.html`

Here's a great page of Java links:

`http://www.nebulex.com/URN/devel.html`

Investigate IDG's JavaWorld page for exhaustive Java information:

`http://www.javaworld.com/cgi-bin/w3com/start?JW+main`

Rusty Elliotte's Java tutorial contains lots of interesting background information on Java:

`http://sunsite.unc.edu/javafaq/javatutorial.html`

What Makes Java So Very Sexy

In the bygone days of mainframe computers, people used individual terminals but actually shared one gargantuan computer. If one person wanted to send some information to another, the data simply had to change locations within the machine ("simply," of course, being a relative term, since computing was seriously user-*un*friendly in those days). This paradigm was shattered by the desktop computer, which brought computers into the control of individuals. Although this system was an improvement over the mainframe system, which required users to timeshare their computer use, it removed the automatic connectivity that came with joint use of a single machine. A communication protocol was needed to reestablish the benefit of connectivity, and Ethernet was developed to address this problem. Ethernet provided a system for linking computers and permitting the exchange of geographically separated information. Java takes this control one step farther by not only bringing the computer onto the desktop, but also downloading all the code that's necessary to run its applications to the desktop.

Now here's Java's seductive appeal: It exploits both the networked states of computers and the power of the desktop. Through the structure of the Web, you can connect to anything, anywhere, and use Java in your travels across the wires. When you find something that's Javafied, it's downloaded to your desktop, where it runs with excellent speed and security. And since you don't have to be connected to a Web server to run your Java apps, the bandwidth drain that normally plagues big Web sites (especially those loaded with extensive multimedia content) is no longer an issue. It ties up the wires while you're downloading, but can then run your Java apps for hours without needing to occupy bandwidth (of course, if you're dealing with information that needs to be updated, like stock market quotes or avatar positions in an interactive chat room, connectivity needs to be maintained).

There's another technology brewing that may well make Java a ubiquitous detail of daily life: In May 1996, Sun licensed four companies to manufacture "Java chips" that introduce Java's power to silicon. The chips, which eliminate the need for Java interpretation, make Java run many times faster on the devices it inhabits, and could revolutionize the way we use communication devices like cellular phones and VCRs. Look for the inclusion of these chips in a stunning array of communication devices beginning in 1997.

Java's Dual Identity: The Lingua Franca of the Web

Java is a language of two identities. One of them revolves around its use on the World Wide Web, where it has been oft-heralded as the most important creation since the Web itself (of course, the same catch phrase has been applied to VRML). Java's Web-related strengths lie in its ability to create applets and applications for complex, distributed networks, including both the Internet and intranets. Java is truly architecture-independent, meaning that the minute you write a program on one computer, you can immediately run it on any other computer architecture that has the Java run-time environment installed; there's no need to port code between machines.

The brilliant blaze of applets — miniapplications written in Java that run inside Web pages — appearing across the Web's wires has been responsible for much of Java's attention (even though most applets on the Web fall far short of their potential). Web users need only a Java-savvy browser to see Java content; therefore, they don't have to exert effort to be exposed to the functionality that Java brings to the Web's mass of information. The first Java browser was Sun's

HotJava. It was soon followed by Netscape Navigator 2.0 and Microsoft's Internet Explorer, with many more choices hot on their heels.

The applets that Java-enabled Web browsers support have a practically unlimited (and wildly underexploited) ability to open up unexplored corridors of cyberspace by unleashing a wave of interactivity and live contact. They bring a new precedent of dynamism to Web pages that will fundamentally alter the way the Web is perceived and used. And by literally downloading its executable content to the user's computer, Java's an important tool in reducing the mass info-jam limitations that plague the Web today.

The inclusion of Java code into Web pages has fundamentally altered the way that content is displayed. Pre-Java Web pages had little hope of presenting true interactivity or live action on them; they were static displays of information (except for a few fill-in forms and check boxes). Imbuing a Web page with the power of Java changes all that, making such staid sites from the past look placid and boring. When Java is gracing your page, it can present information at a much greater level of stimulation — applets can be running live video, juicy sounds, colorful animations, networked games, and many more fascinating diversions. Java's being heavily explored by Web sites for its interactive uses, such as discussion forums; its combination with Moving Worlds VRML 2.0 will unleash a new standard of real-time interactivity in 3D space.

Just as the advent of the World Wide Web made the Internet explode in accessibility and therefore in popularity, so Java can make the Web explode with dynamic content. With an emphasis on interactivity and animation, Java can transform Web pages. There's no reason that a Java page has to be visually static or predefined in its interactions. Instead, the information that it contains can be transformed into a forum that is ripe for spontaneity. The Java-enabled Web browser changes according to what transpires as it functions, actively shaping the information that's on the Web.

Java's executable content is another key to its success. When a non-Java-enabled Web browser comes across information for download, it's defined in terms of MIME (Multipurpose Internet Mail Extensions) specifications. MIME specifications include a variety of multimedia document formats, the content of which is displayed in the browser once it's downloaded. To display images, sound, and video, the browser may request the assistance of a helper application, and it's necessary to configure the browser for each type of helper app used.

A Java-enabled browser functions in much the same way, but features an additional, essential step. When a user requests content, it is downloaded as defined by the MIME specification and then displayed. However, when the browser spots an <APPLET> tag in the page that it's downloading, it's alerted to the fact that the page is Javafied. The <APPLET> tag has an attribute written in bytecode that tells the browser how the applet should be executed.

Java and the Web's future

Java is set to become *the* language for transferring dynamic, executable content over the Web. Although applets are still Java's most obvious contribution to the Web, the union of Java with the Web heralds great things. For example, it will no longer be necessary to create different versions of applications for every single platform that exists (of course, this means that lots of programmers have to find different work!). This fact will have a positive impact upon individual programmers and small development groups that lack the resources to port applications to multiple platforms.

Java brings a whole new level of seamless use to Web surfing as well. The days of worrying about which helper application to download are over, because Java takes care of those concerns for you. Through the grace of encapsulation, Java applications download whatever handlers you need, making your Web-surfing experience much smoother.

Java browsers have the capacity to extend their abilities on the fly, which allows them to dynamically adapt to new types of information. This is a wonderful attribute, because it means that Java browsers are designed to handle formats that haven't yet been developed. When a Java-aware browser encounters a new form of information, it updates itself automatically to handle the fresh format and can process all future information it encounters in that format. This ability to update goes beyond Web pages as well — it also includes the potential to update software and implement new protocols.

Keep an eye out for Java's use with intelligent agents as well. The Internet is the ideal forum for their use, and Java's the ideal language for performing a multitude of "intelligent" tasks, such as pulling up the latest weather, dealing with travel itineraries, watching stocks on the market, and so on. In the future, Java's abilities of this type will be combined with consumer electronic devices, and before you know it, you'll be running your VCR from your flip phone, controlling your AC from your computer, and programming your dog to walk itself (just kidding about that last one).

Java's Dual Identity: OOL Supreme

The Web is not the only arena that is primed for a juicy experiment with Java's power — programming at large is going to hugely benefit from this language's strength. Pro-Java programmers are quick to point out that Java's halcyon days are still in the future. As a full-fledged programming language, Java's power extends far beyond what you see exhibited in the current star shower of applets gracing the Web. Although C++ is still the grande dame of programming, it faces stiff competition from Java. Java's just as competent as Pascal or C++ in running normal programs (although not yet as speedy — its speed will come with just-in-time compilation) and it runs impressively as a stand-alone development environment. In fact, Java was carefully designed to mimic C and C++, with the idea that familiarity would ensure a quick acceptance among the programming community.

However, Java's potential is much greater than that of its monolithic competitors. Java eliminates many of C/C++'s negative characteristics (pointers for one), and includes positive ones that C/C++ can't touch (more on those later in this chapter). Mix into the brew the fact that Java has been enthusiastically received by a multitude of important companies, as well as the US university computing brain banks, and the language's future success seems pretty clinched.

Java is responsible for forging ahead with a new vision of distributed software, one that allows an entirely new approach to software distribution. At the current time, there are hundreds of languages that prevent computer programmers from forming a united coalition. Java has the powerful potential to make traditional applications disappear — they will be replaced by a framework of objects and classes that are united through open APIs. The users will finally have the power to create their own interfaces, from whatever pieces are desirable for their purposes. This new development will revolutionize software distribution — you'll pay minuscule amounts for just the parts of software that you use through a system of microaccounting.

For this vision to succeed, Java has to be everywhere, though. With the proper commitment from the developer community (which seems to exist), the vision may well become a reality.

Sun has played its hand well by maintaining a common API (application programming interface) for all the platforms it services with its JDK (Java Developer's Kit). This commonality ensures a conformity and consistency that will aid Java's future development, especially since Microsoft and Apple are willing to remain compliant with the API as it moves forward.

 WEB PATH **You'll find a timeline of Java's evolution at this site:**

http://ils.unc.edu/blaze/java/javahist.html

Java's popularity has only continued to grow. A list of Java's current licensees is kept here:

http://java.sun.com/java.sun.com/licensee-list.html

 TIP **Sun still provides (e-mail) technical support on Java and say they will continue to do so as long as it doesn't become inappropriately used (or too overwhelming to handle).**

Java's Essence

Here's a breakdown of the components that, by Sun's definition, make Java what it is.

Object-oriented

Java's pure object-orientation clearly sets it apart from its predecessors. Object-oriented languages like Java describe the interactions that occur among objects, requiring users to think about how an application's data is manipulated, and not just the procedures running the program. Java's objects are software bundles of data whose behavior is based upon functions (called *methods*) that operate on those data elements. Object-oriented programming's perspective is similar to that of the "real world," because it lets you both manipulate objects and represent problems through those objects. No prior language in common use, including C++, is as fully object-oriented as Java, because Java was fundamentally designed as an object-oriented language. For this reason, you'll have the most success with Java if you think about it from a different angle than previous languages, and recognize the new slant it takes on design issues.

Programming in Java is all about defining classes and making objects. As an OOL, Java uses classes in its programs. Classes, the fundamental units of object-oriented programming, are collections of code that display the behavior of objects in software. They're like templates that indicate how objects should be created. Classes bring the benefit of reusability — programmers can repeatedly use a class to create many objects. Although each of these objects will have its own data, they share the method implementation.

Java's pristine object-orientation means that it thoroughly employs *encapsulation* and *reuse*, which make it a stronger language. Encapsulation — the process of bundling an object's data with its methods — lets you protect your object's definition by making only its necessary parts accessible to the outside world. So when you use encapsulation, you're preventing others from knowing exactly how your object is put together; encapsulation's secretive side ensures that while your promised goal is accomplished, it's not necessarily anyone's business how your programming realizes that goal (this protection is called *implementation hiding*). Through encapsulation, an object groups data into a single unit, which makes it easier to examine it for flaws, isolate the effects of changes, and recognize data dependencies. This independent object maintenance is called *modularity*.

The following code is a simple example of a Java class encapsulating the X and Y coordinates of a point. The user of a DPoint object does not know or care how the data is stored; the internal storage could be in polar coordinates, for instance.

```
class DPoint extends Object {
    double  X;
    double  Y;
    public DPoint( double x, double y ) { // constructor
      X = x ; Y = y ;
    }
    public void setX(double x) {
        X = x;
    }
    public void setY(double y) {
        Y = y;
    }
    public double x() {
        return X;
    }
    public double y() {
        return Y;
    }
}
```

Another Java advantage that comes from its object-oriented essence is that it is reusable just like in C++. In Java, when you create a design, it's easy to pull it out of your program and reuse it in another program, because each of its objects are self-contained. Although this feat is sometimes possible in languages like Pascal and C, it's not as accurate because you often have to make assumptions about the code, which usually engenders syntax errors. Java's facile ability to isolate code in this manner makes programming easier and cleaner — it's much more obvious where you must venture to fix program errors or make important changes. In addition, its manner of interaction is more solid and tangible.

Distributed

Client/server applications are said to be *distributed* — they distribute their processing workload as well as their information for sharing and collaboration. Because Java supports applications on networks (and was designed to do so), it's defined as a distributed language. Java sees no difference between opening a local file and a remote file — the process is equally easy. Java's *socket* class also supports reliable stream network connections, which provides the ability to create distributed clients and servers.

Interpreted and compiled

Java has a compiler that converts Java source code it encounters into a machine-independent format called *bytecodes*. This conversion gives the source the ability to run on any computer that has the "Java Virtual Machine" (the hypothetical machine for which all Java programs are compiled), and lets Java code be created independent of platform constraints. Because the Java Virtual Machine interprets the compiled bytecode, it's classified as an interpreted language. When you compile a Java program into independent binary bytecode form, it's then interpreted by a platform-specific Java runtime environment. This combination is what defines Java as both an interpreted and a compiled language.

Because it is compiled for a standard "Virtual Machine," Java eliminates platform concerns that detract from other languages. It's only necessary to maintain a single source of Java code to run the compiled bytecode on a multitude of platform-specific Java environments.

Architecture-neutral

Java's architecture independence is one of its most wonderful characteristics. Java is truly architecture-neutral, which means that any Java application can run on any system containing the Java Virtual Machine. Java can run on the full gamut of the Internet's systems.

Java's architectural neutrality is useful not only for networks, but also for software development. The number of possible platforms continues to swell, which means that creating software for every platform is becoming more difficult. However, Java can transcend those differences, because an application written in it can run on all platforms. Under the JDK (Java Developer's Kit) or the Java Virtual Environment, UNIX, Apple, Microsoft, and the Java appliance world are all united, so Java development should move ahead cohesively, and hopefully, coherently.

Portable

Java's portability comes largely from the neutral construction of its architecture. The way that the hardware interprets arithmetic operations also affects portability — while C and C++ platforms can implement arithmetic operations slightly differently, Java's consistency ensures that a result on one computer with Java can be exactly replicated on another. Java's platform-neutral architecture is the first element of its portability — the second is the fact that it won't include "implementation-dependent" aspects of the language specification. The Java environment itself can also be ported to new operating systems and hardware platforms.

Multithreaded

Multitasking occurs when an operating system runs more than one program simultaneously. When those applications are equipped to have more than one thread of execution at a time, that's when *multithreading* occurs. Having multithreading capabilities simply means that Java is able to run multiple tasks within the context of one large application. Java's multithreading opens the door to a superior level of interactive performance, and makes real-time performance much more exciting. Java can prioritize its threads so that threads of low importance (like garbage collection) are delegated to a low-priority mode. Because people are often not as fast as computers, Java's ability to carry out tasks while waiting is very valuable.

Java's multithreading is also exciting because it's included at every level. The first level is the syntactical level, where synchronization modifiers are included in the language. The second level is the object level, where class libraries inherit classes, thereby allowing the creation of threaded applications. At the third level, the Java run-time environment employs multithreading in the background in ways that increase quality and speed while staying fully usable. When you write a program in the Java interpreter, it automatically multi-threads.

Dynamic

Java is dynamic because it can adapt to an evolving environment. Java programs are able to allow for new instance variables and methods in a library's objects without affecting the dependent client objects. Through its series of interfaces, Java relieves the dependency of complete reconciliation when a parent class is changed, a dependency that C++ code has. Java makes it easier to make adjustments, since lots of its linkage manipulation can be deferred until run time. Even from across a network, Java's dynamic abilities will permit the loading of classes.

Robust

Robust software isn't prone to "breaking" from logic errors or programming bugs: Java's elimination of pointer manipulation from the language imbues it with its robust qualities. One of the reasons that it's so robust is because of its early background as a language for consumer devices, which demand a highly reliable, high-quality language. Java's pointer elimination increases its robust flavor — although pointer manipulation in languages like C and C++ can be useful for veteran programmers, it's also an enormous source of run-time errors and memory loss. By doing away with the pointer (and therefore eliminating bugginess), Java is a much more robust language than C++. The chance of bringing in a bug is also minimized through Java's automatic garbage collection and automatic memory management.

Secure

One of Java's most hyped advantages is its excellent security. Its security system has four levels, and each of them is armed to prevent corruption. Although security issues have arisen with JavaScript and applet execution, they don't change the fact that Java is an inherently secure language. There are three features in Java's runtime environment that make it secure:

1. Runtime memory layout.

2. Bytecode verifier.

3. File access restrictions.

The need for greater security on the Net was one of the motivations for the inception of Java, and Java was definitely designed with security at its forefront. Java's client-side operation is its most forceful security defense; its programs are downloaded from a host machine to your computer, and all incoming Java bytecodes are inspected by the runtime system. Anything that is identified as unsafe is unequivocally rejected. Because of Java's oh-so-many security sensitivities, it's not as fast as some other languages right now; the time that it devotes to ferreting improprieties isn't devoted to running your program. Although it's easy to argue that there are plenty of things that C++ does just as well as Java, it's also easy to point out that C++ provides hackers with a much better-lit path to undertaking their nefarious business.

Java provides additional protection because the programmer isn't able to touch the system's actual memory pointers or change the system through Java programs (and therefore erase hard drives, and so on). Java also pays lots of attention to what's going on in a program — it's constantly checking to make sure that everything is operating as it should — and it's quick to scout out any suspicious action.

WARNING: BAD APPLETS

The garden of Eden had a bad apple, and the Elysian etherworld has been cursed with some bad applets. The fact that Java's security was so highly touted obviously made it a very juicy target for hackers and computer science students. Furthermore, Sun took the unusual step of making the complete source code public. The result was a flurry of discovery of weaknesses revealed in public discussion on the Net. Although alarming to many people, each discovery of a weakness and subsequent fix by Sun and the browser manufacturers has made Java a more secure language.

In May of 1996, Sun posted a warning about "malicious applets" on its www.sun.com site. When launched, the malicious applets would consume your computer's resources in a downright rude and inconvenient way, frequently causing your browser to freeze, crash, and burn (just kidding about that last one). When evil applets are run, they take over the threads of execution that other applets are using. This seizure can have the following fun effects:

* Make your computer crash
* Make your computer hang
* Try to take control of your workstations

- ✳ Make your browser bark like a dog and then exit
- ✳ Irritate you with a big obnoxious bear that won't go away
- ✳ Forge e-mail
- ✳ Take over your workstation by generating big windows, lots of noise, and wasteful calculations
- ✳ Try to get your user name and/or password
- ✳ Kill all other applets while defending themselves against ThreadDeath

 If you're a sucker for pain, you'll enjoy the links to bad applets that can be found here:

`http://www.math.gatech.edu/~mladue/HostileApplets.html`

Here's where Sun keeps its FAQ on applet security:

`http://java.sun.com/java.sun.com/sfaq/index.html`

HOW EVIL APPLETS FUNCTION

Malicious applets don't gain their way into Java through a breach in the language security, but rather through its implementation. There *are* security holes in the non-Java areas of the network that applications can negatively exploit, but they don't indicate a weakness in Java itself.

Evil applets unravel their mischief by interfering with the threads of another applet's execution. This is a bug in the way that the security is checked — applets shouldn't be able to access threads other than their own, but these do. Hostile applets can sneak in disguised as an MPEG decompressor, and although the "denial of service" attack that they cause isn't horribly serious, it's definitely an inconvenience (and conducive to Java-paranoia!).

Sun and the browser manufacturers are confident that this problem can be addressed by the next round of savvy browsers that comes out. In addition, the implementation of end-to-end security will make the Net a less anonymous place, and one that's not as easy to clandestinely exploit.

WEB PATH **For more information on malicious applets, visit the following URL, where Mark LaDue's excellent paper on hostile applets can be read:**

`http://www.math.gatech.edu/~mladue/HostileArticle.html`

Simple

Simplicity was one of the main design goals behind Java. Its creators wanted it to look familiar, and therefore, more approachable, so they made it look a lot like C++. Programmers who are familiar with C++, as well C, Objective C, Ada, Eiffel, Pascal, Modula-3, and related languages should have a relatively short learning curve (a few weeks). It's simpler than those languages because it eliminates those elements it doesn't need (like header files, unions, structures, operator overloading, implicit type conversion, and multidimensional arrays). Java is also simple because it contains a fairly small number of language constructs. This simplicity makes it easier to learn, and it's therefore primed to replace C++ as the preeminent programming language.

Other elements that make Java simple are its automatic garbage collection, its automatic handling of referencing and dereferencing objects, and elimination of those buggy pointers from C/C++.

The ubiquitous HelloWorld program demonstrates Java's simplicity:

```
class HelloWorld {
    static public void main(String args[]) {
        System.out.println("Hello world!");
    }
}
```

High performance

In fact, it's more accurate to say that Java has the *potential* to become a high-performance language. Most Java applications can't really challenge the speed of C because the code is interpreted, not compiled, and there are many runtime checking operations. However, just-in-time (JIT) compilation is closing the gap. JIT compilation is much faster than execution in the interpretive environment, because it runs the pure language version of the original Java program, converted to bytecodes and then to machine language. The JIT compiler begins as soon as a bytecode program is executed. Without actually executing the bytecodes, it reads all of them in and translates them into the language of its host machine. Just-in-time compilation is now standard on the major development systems and Web browsers for the Windows 95/NT platform.

Comparing Java and C/C++

Languages such as Pascal, C, and C++ have brought a great deal of general functionality to programming, but Java's stellar abilities leave these languages looking incomplete and difficult. The features that Java possesses, such as its architecture independence, pure object-orientation, and internetworking, are more complete than the features of any of its predecessors. Much of Java's terminology comes from C++, and Java borrows its syntax as well.

Java is definitely easier to learn and use than C/C++, and has greater built-in functionality. As Java becomes more and more used in the programming world, C++ will probably slip from use, since Java can do practically anything C++ can, and Java's code can be reused. At this time, Java's main drawback is the fact that it's primarily interpreted, so C++'s performance is still superior.

However, with the development of just-in-time compilers, this performance gap will close.

The following subsections detail some ways in which Java differs from C/C++.

Pointers

Pointers contain the addresses of variables and have been responsible for many of the bugs in C++, since they make it much easier to trash memory. The complex pointer arithmetic that programmers use for dynamic data construction with C++ manifests lots of complex bugs, which can be a huge waste of time to track down.

Desiring a perfect language, Java's creators avoided bugginess by eliminating the weak pointer. Its function has been replaced by reference, by which Java passes all objects and arrays. Java's lack of pointers doesn't restrict implementation of complex data structures — it actually makes them easier to implement because they're more reliable when carried out with objects and arrays of objects.

Functions

Java lacks functions, but Java classes and methods can perform any C or C++ task that employs a function. The functions which a C programmer would expect to find in the standard library are implemented as *static* methods of various classes. For instance, trigonometric functions are available as static methods of the Math class. As static methods, you don't have to create a Math object to use them.

Multiple inheritance

Although multiple inheritance is a powerful way to derive a class from multiple parent classes, its complicated essence has also made it a source of many problems in C++; therefore, Java's developers decided to leave it out. Java's interfaces, which are similar to Objective C protocols, cover all the ground that multiple inheritance did. Although they don't provide any direct support for multiple inheritance, the functionality they implement is similar.

Goto statements

Goto statements were another component of C++ that was eliminated from Java for the sake of simplification. By removing goto, Java doesn't have to concern itself with rules that concerned goto, such as its effects from being placed in the middle of a sentence. Java's multilevel break and continue provides for most of the occurrences where C++ uses goto statements .

Unions and structures

C++ has three types of complex data types: structures, unions, and classes. Java adopted only the final type of this troika. Java classes eliminate the existence of unions and structures, and force you to use classes wherever you previously would have used unions and structures. All you have to do with Java is declare a class with the appropriate static (class) or instance variables. This results in a greater consistency, and doesn't diminish Java's power, since classes have no problem imitating unions and structures.

Strings

Java implements strings as the first-class objects, String and StringBuffer. This differs from C and C++ that lack built-in support for text strings. To represent strings, C and C++ programmers usually resort to using null-terminated arrays of characters. Java's strings function much more consistently and predictably, and because they perform runtime checking, they're much less plagued with error.

Operator overloading

Programmers can no longer overload the standard arithmetic operators in Java. Although operator overloading is an important feature in C++, Java creates parallel functionality through class implementation. The benefits of convenience that operator overloading brings to C++ are balanced by the simplicity that is produced by Java's elimination of it.

Typedefs, defines, or preprocessor

Because Java source code is simple, it doesn't require #define and related capabilities, a preprocessor, or typedef. Because these features have been removed, so has the need for a header file. Java derives definitions of other classes and their methods from its language source files. Because Java drops a great deal of the context that you're required to read in C and C++, it's much more easily and quickly manipulated. Everything about a class must be contained in a single file, in contrast to C and C++, where essential class information may be scattered in header files and multiple code files.

Automatic coercion

Unlike C and C++, Java doesn't permit automatic coercion, which refers to an implicit casting of data types. Although in C++ you can assign a value to a variable that can result in a loss of data, in Java, coercing data elements of one type into a less-precise data type requires you to use a cast. This explicit action results in greater accuracy and protection.

Command-line arguments

The Java run-time system permits passing of command-line arguments. The syntax is similar to C, but the program's name is not in the argument list, because its name is the same as its class.

TABLE 1-1   The Differences Between Java and C++ at a Glance

Java Has...	C++ Has...
Single inheritance	A preprocessor
Garbage collection	Operator overloading
Native multithreading	Header files
	Pointers
	Multiple inheritance

 TIP   For experienced C++ programmers, Java's new level of object-orientation may require some, but not too much, mental retooling. Learning the Java code will be a familiar task, but thinking in a wholly object-oriented manner may require some shifts in the way you perceive design.

 WEB PATH   This site further examines the intimate relationship between C++ and Java:

`http://www.neca.com/~vmis/cjava.html`

Other Features of the Java Language

There are a number of features in Java that deserve some detailed discussion; those elements follow.

Data types

Everything in Java is an object — except for the simple (or primitive) data types that are discussed here (if necessary, even these data types can be encapsulated within objects). There are four groups of simple data types: numeric, character, Boolean, and floating-point.

NUMERIC DATA TYPES

Numeric (or integer) data types are used to represent signed integer numbers. Here are the four integer types, followed by the size they take up in memory:

* byte (8 bits)
* short (16 bits)
* int (32 bits)
* long (64 bits)

CHARACTER DATA TYPES

The character data type can be employed to store single (and only single) Unicode characters. The *char* data type stored as a 16-bit unsigned integer, since the Unicode character set consists of 16-bit values. Type *char* variables are created like this:

```
char firstInitial, lastInitial
```

BOOLEAN DATA TYPES

Values with the states of *true* or *false* are stored in the Boolean data type. True and false are the only legal Boolean values in Java, so you can't interchange integers and Booleans like you can in C++ or C. Declare a Boolean value with this type declaration:

```
boolean gameOver;
```

FLOATING-POINT DATA TYPES

Use floating-point data types to represent numbers that contain fractional parts. The two floating-point types are *float* and *double*. Use the float type for reserving a 32-bit single-precision number and the double for a 64-bit double-precision number. In addition to the simple types, Java also has composite data types, which are based on simple types, and which include arrays, strings, classes, and interfaces.

ARITHMETIC AND RELATIONAL OPERATORS

All of the usual operators from C and C++ apply with the arithmetic and relational operators. The >>> operator was added to indicate an unsigned right shift, since Java doesn't have unsigned data types. In addition, Java employs the + operator for string concatenation.

ARRAYS

Java language arrays are first-class language objects, unlike those you'll find in C and C++. Java defines an array as a real object with a runtime representation. It's possible to declare and allocate arrays of any type, and arrays of arrays can be allocated if you want to obtain multidimensional arrays.

STRINGS

Unlike in C, strings in Java are real language objects. Java sports two kinds of string objects: the String class is used for read-only (immutable) objects, while the StringBuffer class is used for string objects that you want to modify.

Even though strings are Java language objects, the Java compiler parallels C's in providing the syntactic convenience that is enjoyed with C-style strings — the compiler recognizes that a string of characters inside double quotes is intended to be instantiated as a String object. This means that the declaration:

```
String hello = "Hello world!";
```

will instantiate a behind-the-scenes instantiation of a String class's object, initializing it with a character string containing the Unicode character representation of "Hello world!"

Garbage collection and memory management

The explicit memory management that C and C++ use can be an unwanted source of crashes, bugs, memory leaks, rotten performance, and other undesirables. Java's insightful developers therefore took out C-style pointers, pointer arithmetic, *malloc*, and *free*, and removed the memory management load from the programmer. By doing so, they made Java programming easier, removed classes of bugs, and improved Java's general performance.

The Java runtime system automatically collects all of its garbage. There's a new operator to allocate memory for objects, but there isn't any explicit free function. Once you have allocated an object, the runtime system keeps track of its status and automatically reclaims memory it is no longer useing. This process efficiently frees memory for future use. Here's an example from Sun's online Java language programmer's guide that shows what happens with automatic garbage collection:

```
class ReverseString {
    public static String reverseIt(String source) {
        int i, len = source.length();
        StringBuffer dest = new StringBuffer(len);
        // the scope of the "dest" object is this method only
        for (i = (len - 1); i >= 0; i--) {
            dest.appendChar(source.charAt(i));
        }
```

```
        return dest.toString();
    }   // at this point the "dest" object has no references and will
}       // be garbage collected when the system gets around to it
```

Java's background garbage collector

Smalltalk and Lisp programmers figured out long ago that it was very valuable to be able to ignore memory deallocation. The Java garbage collector is the first widespread application that thoroughly puts these programmers' ideas of automation to good use. Java runs a series of advanced techniques that make its garbage collection extremely efficient and clean. It's a smart collector — its run-time system takes advantage of inactive periods and runs the garbage collector in a low priority thread during the times that no other threads are competing for CPU cycles. This innovative use of a thread attests to Java's synergy — and the benefits of its excellent multithreading capacities.

Investigating the Java Environment

The Java environment is composed of a group of tools:

* The language that you use to create the code for your applications
* The architecture that you need to run the applications you've created
* The tools that build, compile, and run those applications

These tools work in tandem to carry out your Java programs. The Java jive goes something like this: After you've lovingly created a Java program, it has to run through the compiler to become information that the computer can understand. The compiler converts the Java code into its intermediate bytecode, all the while keeping a careful eye out for security problems.

After your bytecode is generated, it is executed one of two ways: by an interpreter or by a just-in-time compiler. When bytecodes are interpreted, their code is read and then executed. The interpreter itself is a program, so running the interpreter to read your bytecode means that you're running a program to run your program.

Running a program to run another program is a little on the indirect side, though, and it hurts Java's speed. Just-in-time compiling reads a program's byte-codes and then translates them into the machine's language. This is obviously a faster and more direct process; look for JIT compiling as the preferred way of executing Java.

The Java Developer's Kit (JDK)

Sun released the JDK as the official Java development package, so it's a very useful Java resource. The JDK gives you the basic tools and information that you need to use Java, and backs them up with good support. As you create your own Java Toolkit, keep the JDK in mind, because even if you're selecting third-party tools, the JDK is a model of what you need to develop professional-caliber Java applications. The following details what the 1.0.2 release of the JDK contains:

* Java Applet Upgrade Utility
* Java Applet Viewer
* Java Debugger API and Prototype Debugger
* Java Compiler
* Java Interpreter

 WEB PATH The JDKs for the SPARC/Solaris, new x86/Solaris, Microsoft Windows NT/95, and MacOS are available at his site:

`http://java.sun.com/java.sun.com/devcorner.html`

The full source for the JDKs is available at:

`http://java.sun.com/java.sun.com/source.html`

When Java was released, many developers were disappointed by its lack of tools and applications. Nobody was offering a GUI (graphical user interface), and Java development environments were still uncharted waters. That's beginning to change, though — an increasing number of companies, including Sun, Borland, Symantec, Microsoft, Metrowerks, Rogue Wave and SGI have all been involved in creating development environments.

Java APIs

Many of the actions that Java programs perform (especially the more high-end, exciting ones) are accomplished by invoking an API method. The APIs are included in Java's prebuilt packages, and include creating sockets, playing audio, drawing graphics, outputting files, and other fascinating tasks. This structure might sound familiar if you've programmed in Microsoft Windows, although its API procedures are kept in DLL (Dynamic Link Library) files. All of Java's APIs are implemented as classes and interfaces that are contained in packages. API documentation is generated by *javadoc*. Here are the Java APIs:

* *applet* — This package provides the applet-specific behavior used to imbue Web pages with sound and animation.

- *awt (abstract windows toolkit)* — This package contains graphical user interface tools such as frames, scroll bars, buttons, and so on. If you've used the Microsoft Windows APIs, the awt package will be familiar.
- *awt.image* — This subpackage of the awt contains classes that crop and filter bitmap images.
- *awt.peer* — Another awt subpackage, awt.peer contains the awt components' native implementation classes (Windows 95, Macintosh, and so on.). You don't have to deal directly with this API.
- *io* — This input/output package provides you with facile network and file access.
- *lang* — The lang package contains Java's core: its classes and interfaces. It covers math functions and thread creation, as well as operations on primitive data types and strings.
- *net* — The net package enables you to connect networked computers and perform network operations such as URLs and sockets.
- *util* — The util package gives you utilities such as stacks, random numbers, hash tables, and vectors.

WEB PATH **A Java API overview is available here:**
`http://java.sun.com/products/apiOverview.html`

Browsing with Java

At the time of writing, three browsers were available for use with Java: HotJava, Netscape Navigator, and Internet Explorer. By the time you read this, odds are that the browser selections have dramatically increased.

With both IE and Navigator running Java, the real question now is whether developers are going to support Netscape's LiveConnect or Microsoft's ActiveX architecture, or whether both can be supported. The better-supported of the two may well become the standard.

The following provides some coverage on what the original three Java browsers could do.

HotJava

HotJava, developed by Sun, was the first Java browser. Its original version quickly became outdated, and for a period of time, it couldn't run newly developed applets. However, Sun redeveloped and re-released it in May 1996. HotJava likes to run with JavaOS, which is the lightweight OS that JavaSoft designed for consumer devices and network computers.

Because HotJava has such close ties to Sun and a vested interest in maintaining Sun's powerful position, it includes several benefits that Netscape Navigator and Internet Explorer don't. For example, it has excellent extensibility — it's highly distributed, and doesn't truly support any Internet protocols or object types. Browsers normally have their components hardwired to the executable browser application, which results in fewer options for extensibility.

HotJava runs on Solaris 2.4, 2.5, Windows 95, Windows NT, Solaris for Intel and MacOS. HotJava *doesn't* run on SunOS 4.x, Windows 3.1, or Windows 3.11.

WEB PATH

HotJava is downloadable at:

```
http://java.sun.com/java.sun.com/HotJava/CurrentRelease/
installation.html
```

The HotJava Browser's features are viewable at:

```
http://java.sun.com/java.sun.com/HotJava/UsersGuide/users.html
```

Features that were newly incorporated into HotJava 1.0 include: enhanced HTML support, better hotlists, keyboard controls, HTTP password authentication, external viewer mapping, master volume control, disk caching, and lazy loading for images and applets.

Netscape Navigator

Netscape was one of Java's earliest, most important supporters. Netscape's first Javafied browser was Navigator 2.0, which had some security problems with JavaScript that were amended in Navigator 2.02. Netscape was responsible for introducing thousands of Web users to the beauty of Java, since most surfers were using Netscape Navigator when applets hit the wires.

Netscape didn't stop at mere support of Java — it adapted its LiveScript language and renamed it JavaScript, an object-based scripting language with Java-like syntax (more information about JavaScript follows shortly).

Internet Explorer

After a bit of hyped speculation, Microsoft eventually got around to licensing Java, and incorporated it into its 3.0 version of the Internet Explorer browser for Windows 95 and an earlier version (v1.5) for NT Workstation. It was actually missing from the initial Explorer 3.0 beta release, but was made available as an add-on at Microsoft's FTP site (thereby demonstrating how well Java works on the fly) and then incorporated into Explorer's second beta release. Explorer's quality level of Java incorporation is on a par with Netscape Navigator's, and it beat Netscape out in using a just-in-time compiler, which greatly increases the speed of Java applications. Netscape added a JIT compiler licensed from Borland for its Navigator 3.0 release, in August 1996.

What You Can Do with Java Today: Applets, Beans, and Chips

The following sections detail some more of the current Java pieces, including applets, beans, and chips.

Java applets

You can think of Java *applets* as miniprograms that unleash animation, moving text, moving figures, and other exciting moving things into your Web pages. Applets aren't applications; rather, they are Java classes that are loaded and run by an applet viewer or a Web browser. By using applets, you can whisk your Web pages away from the boring, placid world of static text and graphics and into the realm of fantastic action. Because an applet loads on to the user's computer, its performance isn't affected by modem speed or bandwidth constraints.

Applets can be served by any HTTP server, and they don't require any special software. A server handles Java applets just as it would a regular image, text, or sound file. The special stuff that goes down with applets has to do with the client side of a Java-enabled browser, which is responsible for interpreting the files.

For the sake of security, there are some things that applets just can't do (remember those evil applets that threaten Java security?). Most of these restrictions are designed to prevent applets from violating system security or the integrity of the data; hackers aren't able to exploit Java's ability to move code between systems for devious reasons. Here are some of the things that applets are restricted from doing:

* Load libraries of defined native methods
* Read every system property
* Create network connections to hosts from which they didn't originate

When a file isn't on the client's access-control list, an applet cannot

* Read, write, or rename files on the host where they're running
* Check for the existence of the file
* Check the file's type or size
* Check the timestamp showing the file's last modification
* Create a directory on the client file system
* List the files in this file (like a directory)

WRITING APPLETS

To add applets to a Web page, you use the <APPLET> tag. An applet's width, height, and parameters are described by this tag. When a Web browser encounters an applet, it downloads the accompanying code and executes it. If you're using a non-Java-enabled browser, the applet tag will simply be ignored. Here's an example of how the applet tag is described:

```
<APPLET STANDARD-ATTRIBUTES>
APPLET-PARAMETERS
ALTERNATE CONTENT
</APPLET>
```

If you wanted to add an applet to your home page, for example , you'd copy it into the home page's directory, edit the page, and then add the <APPLET> tag wherever you want the applet to pop up. If you wanted Sun's Java mascot, Duke, to appear on your home page, it could be written like this:

- `<TITLE>Evita's Home Page<TITLE>`
- `<H1>:Let the rainbow tour begin!<H1>`
- `Welcome to my home page`
- `<P>`
- `<APPLET CODE=IMAGELOOPITEM WIDTH=80 HEIGHT=90>`
- `<PARAM NAME=NIMGS VALUE=10>`
- `<PARAM NAME=IMG VALUE=DUKE>`
- `<PARAM NAME=PAUSE VALUE=1000>`
- `</APPLET>`

WEB
PATH Sun has a helpful Java tutorial page, which includes information on writing Java applets:

`http://java.sun.com:80/tutorial/index.html`

APPLET ATTRIBUTES

Applets require the following attributes:

* *code* — the name of the file that contains the applet's main class, code is usually a filename that ends in **.class**.
* *height* — specifies the applet's initial height, in pixels.
* *width* — specifies the applet's initial width, in pixels.

These attributes are optional for applets:

* *align* — explains the applet's alignment, which in turn affects the applet's placement on the page.
* *alt* — specifies alternate text that text-only browsers can display.

* *codebase* — refers to the applet's base URL in which its code is located. The display document's URL is the default when this attribute isn't specified.
* *hspace* — specifies the horizontal space surrounding the applet, is used only when the *align* attribute is set to *left* or *right*.
* *name* — refers to the applet's symbolic name.
* *vspace* — used only when the *align* attribute is set to *left* or *right*. It's the vertical space that surrounds the applet.

SOME SWEET APPLETS

WEB PATH **To see some of the tastiest applets on the Web, investigate the essential Gamelan site:**

```
http://www.gamelan.com/
```

Here's an applet-laden page:

```
http://www.applets.com/cgi-bin-applets/
```

Sun's applet page lives here:

```
http://java.sun.com/java.sun.com/applets/applets.html
```

The Applet Arcade contains some juicy applets:

```
http://members.aol.com/shadows125/arcade.htm
```

Java development environments

Most of the development supercompanies have introduced Java development environments. This is an area that's in hot flux, so it's probably best to follow the Internet's golden path to find out what's going down at the moment. An overview of some of the most important early development environments follows, along with the URLs where they can be downloaded.

SYMANTEC CAFE

Symantec Cafe is the first Java development environment for Windows. Although Cafe is based on C++, it is designed completely for Java. Cafe comes with a copy of the JDK, which it strives to supersede and debug. Here are some of Cafe's juiced-up components:

* A class editor for object-oriented navigating and class method editing
* A hierarchy editor for viewing and editing the Java class relationships
* A help file that contains the Java API methods for easy lookup from within the source editor

* Drag-and-drop editing (through its visual design tool)
* AppExpress, a visual tool that you can use to create a default Java applet or application
* An output window where you can see the results of your compilation (and any error messages it might receive)
* A Java source code parser that provides real-time object editor updates without compiling
* A Java run-time Virtual Machine and a bytecode compiler that work significantly faster than the JDK's

 WEB PATH **Take a look at what the Symantec environment has to offer at**

`http://cafe.symantec.com/cafe/overview.html`

Symantec also offers a just-in-time compiler, which seriously speeds up your Java applications. You can peruse it at

`http://cafe.symantec.com/jit/overview.html`

COSMO FROM SGI

Cosmo (see Figure 1-1) is a developing environment that offers an impressive array of software products for creating and viewing interactive multimedia, as well as tools for you to develop your own interactive applications. Cosmo is composed of four elements:

* Cosmo Create
* Cosmo Code
* Cosmo Player
* Cosmo MediaBase

 WEB PATH **All of the software elements support HTML, Moving Worlds VRML 2.0, and Java. The Cosmo software suite was created to enable applications like online shopping, distance learning, entertainment, media collaboration, and computer-based training. Check out Cosmo at**

`http://www.sgi.com/Products/cosmo/`

Figure 1-1   A look at SGI Cosmo.

NATURAL INTELLIGENCE'S ROASTER

Roaster was the first Macintosh Java development environment. It's based on Natural Intelligence's QuickCode Pro script editor, and includes

* A debugger
* A class disassembler
* A complete integrated development environment
* A project manager
* A fortified compiler
* Support for Power Macintoshes

 You can peer into Roaster's rundown at
`http://www.natural.com/pages/products/roaster/`

A site of applets created with Roaster:
`http://www.natural.com/pages/products/roaster/createdlinks.html`

JAMBA

Jamba is an accessible, drag-and-drop authoring software tool that lets you create full-flavored Java applets and applications without using programming or scripting. Jamba has a WYSIWYG page-layout environment that lets you select "live" objects by dragging and dropping.

Jamba uses Netscape's LiveConnect standard to provide connections between Jamba and JavaScript, Netscape's scripting language for the Internet. Jamba's motto, "Pour on the Java: hold the programming," accurately encapsulates Jamba's target market. With the release of Jamba and other JavaScript-friendly tools, Java is becoming more and more accessible to the average Web user.

 WEB PATH   **You can look into Jamba at**

`http://www.aimtech.com/prodjafaqs.html:`

JAVA BEANS

Java Beans are a set of component APIs that are open and wholly written in Java. Java Beans exploit Java's object-oriented reusability by letting developers create Java applets and applications from reusable components. Using Java Beans makes it easy for developers to transfer components' functionality to other Java applications and applets (and non-Java, platform-dependent applications, too). The efficiency of reuse will obviously speed development, and Java's neutral architecture means that the components can be lifted from a multitude of courses.

The Java Beans set of APIs is being touted as simple and compact, and it has garnered the support of many industry leaders, including Borland, Netscape, Oracle, IBM, and Symantec.

Java Chips

In May of 1996, Sun announced that it had licensed four companies to manufacture the picoJava microprocessor, or "Java chip." The creation of these chips fully harnesses Java's power, by committing it in silicon.

These chips herald Java's return to one of its original goals (during the days when it was still called "Oak") — the control of personal communication devices. Java chips will eliminate the computer's need for a Java interpreter and thereby make Java's power even more impressive. These processors are intended to be affordably priced and therefore useful for introducing the general consumer to full-brewed Java. The new processors will run applications at blazing speeds, and Sun predicts that the microprocessor market they'll create will hit $15 billion by the year 2000.

Although these chips could have a very exciting impact on computer processors, the integration of these chips into communication devices, such as cellular phones, and technology like VCRs and microwaves is something to keep a sharp eye on. These chips will increase our ability to communicate with machines and increase their ability to communicate with each other: A cellular phone containing a Java chip would be able to contact your computer and give it commands, or you could use your Java-chip-equipped home computer to program your microwave or VCR. The new client/server telephones will allow you to execute an unprecedented array of new-wave tasks from your phone set, including accessing Internet services through your phone.

Sun's licensing of these chips demonstrates its marketing savvy: it's predicted that the average home will contain between 50 and 100 microprocessors (the average business person has over 10 microcontrollers today). By grabbing an early piece of the pie and making Java the killer app for this burgeoning wave of microprocessors, Sun will ensure that its investment into Java will pay off.

JAVA CHIPS LICENSEES

The initial companies manufacturing this chip are LG Semicon, Mitsubishi Electric America, Samsung, and NEC; Canada's Northern Telecom and Xerox also anticipate chip production during 1997. With their licenses, these companies will be able to create devices that employ the chips in a multitude of fashions, including cellular phones, office and residential phones, beepers, home appliances, and cheap networked computers. The licensees will have broad access to the Java technology and will incorporate the chip in their respective products, which have worldwide distribution.

THE JAVA CHIPS FAMILY

The Java Chips family is composed of three tiers: the picoJava core, the microJava processor, and the UltraJava processor. It's the picoJava core that's responsible for executing the Java instruction set. With this chip, the Java instruction set no longer needs to be interpreted, which means that it saves money, memory, and performance quality. The picoJava core was designed to be wildly affordable, targeting sub-$25 Java-optimized processors for printers, cellular phones, and other consumer devices.

MicroJava is the second tier of the family. Founded on picoJava's core, its products add additional memory, communication functions, application-specific I/O, and control functions. MicroJava's processors will range in price from $25 to $100, and are targeted at consumer devices such as games, as well as network-based telcom carrier equipment and controllers.

With the fastest Java processors on the market, UltraJava is the high end of the microprocessor spectrum. Its target audience is 3D graphics and multimedia specialists through its advanced graphics circuits and next-generation enhancements of Sun's Visual Instruction Set.

HotJava

HotJava is a set of Java class libraries created by JavaSoft, a Sun company that develops and markets Java technology. The word originally referred to the first Java browser, one that was written in Java, but has since been extended to encompass both the set of libraries and the browser.

Developers can use HotJava to build dynamic, customized, network-aware applications and user environments. Its framework lets you develop highly customizable environments that are extensible and Internet-aware. The redesigned HotJava package was released for early access in May 1996, with a final version expected for release at the end of 1996. The updated HotJava includes HotJava class libraries as well as the HotJava Browser, for which source licenses may be purchased. The browser's also available free for non-commercial use.

JavaSoft anticipates that future editions of HotJava will feature WYSIWYG HTML editing, news reading and mail features, and a greater number of building blocks to create dynamic applications. By updating HotJava, Sun is definitely trying to maintain power over Java's status — JavaSoft was specifically designed to create tools, applications, and systems platforms that further ensconce Java as an Internet (and intranet) standard.

Java and VRML

With the release of Moving Worlds (SGI's proposal that was accepted for the VRML 2.0 language proposal), the relationship between Java and VRML assumes an entirely new significance. VRML's second release is a great deal more sophisticated and capable than the original version — it fully incorporates 3D sound, interactivity, behaviors, and the capacity for multiuser interaction. It's this last element that Java will act as the cream in the coffee — with the aid of Java, VRML 2.0's multi-user interaction can work in real time, and therefore take cyberspace communication into virgin territory.

The Moving Worlds proposal, which was the overwhelming favorite from the VRML 2.0 candidates, overtly incorporated support for Java as a scripting language. To many, VRML and Java are extremely complimentary: Mark Pesce, one of VRML's creators, points out that VRML is concerned with how things appear, while Java is concerned with how things behave. Pesce also predicts that the distinctions between VRML and Java will become hazy — and unimportant — at the user end.

 WEB PATH **For more insight into Pesce's thoughts on the union, investigate his home page:**

http://www.hyperreal.com/~mpesce

Java will be used with VRML for two important functions:

* As scripts that are loaded in-line to describe the interactions of objects in VRML worlds
* To describe extension nodes

LIQUID REALITY

Liquid Reality is the name of the first VRML tool kit written in Java. Created by Dimension X, Liquid Reality gives you everything you need to read and write in VRML and extend it with Java. It's a set of Java class libraries that lets you create viewers and tools for interactive VRML 2.0 worlds. It's possible to create a customized VRML 2.0 browser in under ten lines of code with Liquid Reality! The Liquid Reality toolkit can be extended by using Java, so you can create nodes that are tailored to your wants and desires.

In the VRML helix-world (see Figure 1-2) created with Liquid Reality, VRML 2.0's new capabilities shine through: the helix spins around the perimeter, while the red trusses and blue rings rotate around the center sphere. You can hear a (stereophonic) "whooshing" sound as the trusses go by, and the helix emits bizarre alienesque noises when it flies overhead.

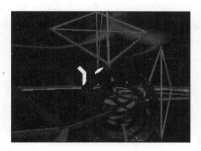

Figure 1-2 A helix created with Liquid Reality.

Multimedia and Java

Although Java's magnificent multimedia capacities were rather slow to emerge (although not to be recognized), that fact is changing. Because Java brings the ability to download data prior to execution, to alter patterns based on user input, and to control timing, its vast potential in the multimedia arena is one of the most logical and exciting places for Java implementation. Java's multimedia features include

* Basic digital audio support
* A media tracker that helps keep up with distributed media content
* Excellent graphics support, including support for creation of primitives and bitmapped images

✳ A multithreaded environment, which greatly ameliorates multimedia animation and timing

Java comes armed with a full arsenal of tools for creating killer graphics. Companies are busy creating slick, impressive Java development tools — but bare Java proffers a rich set of drawing primitives as part of its graphics class. This class includes methods that allow you to draw shapes such as circles and rectangles, as well as lines.

In creating multimedia applications, with or without Java, the question of bandwidth limitations must always be considered. Bandwidth is defined as the amount of information that you can send over a network connection; the greater the bandwidth, the more information can be sent. Since what users see is dependent on their bandwidth limitations, creating content with bandwidth conservation in mind is important.

Java helps to conserve bandwidth by delivering all the code that's necessary to run multimedia content to the user's machine. By doing so, it unclogs the increasingly twisted bottleneck of Web traffic.

JavaScript

JavaScript is an open, easily learned scripting language that was created by Sun and Netscape to be used with Netscape Navigator 2.0. Designed to unite the charged superpower of HTML and Java, JavaScript (originally called LiveScript) was designed to compliment HTML and Java and to seamlessly integrate with both.

Developing applets lies largely in the realm of professional programmers, but creating HTML pages with JavaScript can be fearlessly undertaken by mere mortals. By adding JavaScript to a Web page, you can control the interaction and behavior of your page. Since JavaScript delegates simple tasks to the browser, it keeps the action at the local level and thereby reduces network traffic. The bonus involved in this setup is that your response times are quicker.

JavaScript mimics much of Java's syntax, but it's an interpreted, not compiled, language (Java, on the other hand, must be compiled before it runs). When your browser downloads HTML text, the JavaScript application code comes along with it, and is downloaded with the HTML as text into the browser. The browser then executes the code, which can contain simple applications.

AUTHORING WITH JAVASCRIPT

If you're trying to learn JavaScript (or Java, for that matter), viewing the source is an excellent place to begin. Here's a simple example of a JavaScript:

```
<HTML>
<HEAD>
<TITLE>My First JavaScript Page</TITLE>
<SCRIPT LANGUAGE="Javascript">
```

```
<!—
document.write("This text appears before the body
 of the HTML page.<P>");
// —>

</SCRIPT>
</HEAD>
<BODY>
<H3> Hoyden's first Java Web Page </H3>
</BODY>
</HTML>
```

The tags that alert the browser that this file contains JavaScript code are

```
<SCRIPT>...</SCRIPT>
```

You can insert JavaScript code between these two tags for the browser to recognize, and run.

Since, at the time of writing, JavaScript lacks a debugger, its programs give you error messages when they spot mistakes (which are common). Practice is the key to effectively debugging JavaScript programs. The error messages will seem common after a while, and you'll be able to figure out where the bugs are burrowing.

Although some privacy problems plagued JavaScript when used in conjunction with Netscape Navigator 2.0, the release of 2.01 addressed these problems. JavaScript cannot be used to invoke Java applets, and for that reason, the privacy problems reported with JavaScript don't exist in Java applets.

 WEB PATH

Here's an important JavaScript Web site:

```
http://www.c2.org/~andreww/javascript/
```

The FAQ (Frequently Asked Questions) for JavaScript resides at

```
http://www.his.com/~smithers/freq/beta/jsfaq.html
```

Netscape offers a good collection of JavaScript resources here:

```
http://home.netscape.com/comprod/products/navigator/version_2.0/
script/script_info/index.html
```

DIFFERENCES BETWEEN JAVA AND JAVASCRIPT

Because JavaScript separately interprets each line and Java applets have immediately executable code, JavaScripts often run less quickly than Java applets. JavaScript lets you define objects but not object classes, and it lacks many of Java's complex object-oriented features. Although JavaScript is also missing the object inheritance that is such a benefit in Java, it's not a highly significant omission for most users, because JavaScript creates generally shorter, simpler scripts.

Unlike Java, JavaScript was specifically designed for interaction with HTML. Unlike an applet, a JavaScript can change an HTML page's text; JavaScript lets input from one HTML page influence another. For this reason, it's especially suitable for use with forms, which it handles quickly and efficiently. Here's a quick breakdown of some of the basic differences between Java and JavaScript:

JAVA

* Applets distinct from HTML
* Compiled on server before it's executed on client
* Applets consist of object classes with inheritance
* Its variable data types must be declared due to its strong typing
* Its static binding means that its object references must exist at compile time

JAVASCRIPT

* Its dynamic binding means that its object references are checked at run time
* It's not compiled, but interpreted by the client
* JavaScript code is both integrated into and embedded in HTML, unlike Java
* Its loose typing means that its variable data types aren't declared
* It doesn't have classes or offer complete object-orientation, although its code does use built-in objects

LIVING UP TO THE HYPE: JAVA CRITICISM

This Web page evaluates the hype that often shrouds Java, and contains interesting links that examine some of Java's problems:

http://www.neca.com/~vmis/java.html

Java surf spots

If you just can't get enough Java, try these sites for a great concentration of Java resources.

The Java Metalist is a wealth of useful Java information:

http://www.euroyellowpages.com/exhibitn/javahome.html

This commendable Java site contains Java history:

http://www.euroyellowpages.com/exhibitn/javahome.html

This page offers useful links and information:

http://www.neca.com/~vmis/cjava.html

The JavaWorld online magazine is available here:

http://www.javaworld.com/

This page sports lots of useful Java resources:

http://www.digitalfocus.com/faq/

Identify Java bugs here:

http://java.sun.com/JDK-1.0/knownbugs.html

The Java Widgets page is

http://www.c2.org/~andreww/javascript/widgets.html

An applet-laden page:

http://www.applets.com/cgi-bin-applets/

Apple Flavored Java, a page for Macheads:

http://www.seas.upenn.edu/~mcrae/projects/macjava/

Java user group information is available at

http://java.sun.com/java.sun.com/aboutJava/usrgrp.html

Here's where to find Sun's list of Java FAQs:

http://java.sun.com/java.sun.com/faqIndex.html

This URL leads to the Java Message Board, where people ask questions about the language and exchange information:

http://porthos.phoenixat.com/~warreng/WWWBoard

Cafe Au Lait is a wonderful Java resource:

http://sunsite.unc.edu/javafaq/

Where No Language Has Gone Before: Java's Heady Future

As the Web becomes increasingly clogged, Java's strength at exploiting the power of local applications will become even more valuable, since it will reduce Internet traffic jams. The local control that accompanies Java is extremely useful as well.

Look for future Java development in these areas:

* Animation
* Automatic audio cues that tell you when a link is activated or a link is activated (Microsoft has already endowed its Internet Explorer with an HTML tag to perform this function)
* Interaction between browser software and non-net software — this will allow you to link remote databases with local documents
* Local browser agents
* A new generation of technical support — Java brings the possibility of real-time technical support for your real-time problems
* Networked real-time games. Java will allow game applications to be local — the only function the network will perform in this situation will be broadcasting player position changes, and so forth.

One of the exciting things about Java is that it hasn't hit its potential. There are lots of clever applets on the Web, but Java could definitely be put to much more profound use than what's been accomplished to date. Whether Java will actually ameliorate the Web's content fundamentally hinges on the vision that its developers and users bring to it.

The increasing number of Java development kits foreshadows the Java explosion that will hit as it becomes (almost) as easy to use as HTML, thanks to JavaScript and cushy authoring tools. There's definitely lots of Java history to be made — developers have yet to truly unleash Java's full power, the consumer electronics industry has yet to explore Java's full potential in their technologies, and everyone knows that writers haven't fully exhausted the lexicon of Java puns!

Summary

In this chapter, we've given you a look at what the Java language is about, what it can do, and what it will do. It's uncertain how soon Java will encounter serious competitors — Microsoft's ultra-tabled Blackbird/Internet Studio will be released someday, and some of the original UNIX developers are toiling on a Java rival at AT&T's Bell Labs. Whether it's through Java, or through another language, one fact is clear: Java has broken boundaries, both in cyberspace and in the world of programming that won't be tempting to mend.

## CHAPTER TWO

JAVA SYNTAX AND SEMANTICS

2

IN THIS CHAPTER YOU LEARN THESE KEY SKILLS

I n this chapter, we provide an overview of Java's formal syntactic structure. Java is a carefully designed language; it is intended to break new ground as a programming language. It's a great deal purer and more accurate than its predecessors. In fact, Java was specifically developed as a response to programming problems in C++ and other similar languages. For the sake of familiarity, Java also employs C syntax wherever possible, since so many programmers are comfortable using it. This chapter will be easier to process if you've had some experience with C or C++, but if you haven't, don't despair! Most programmers find Java easier to learn than C or C++ anyway.

Understanding Syntax

A language's syntax is the spelling and grammatical rules that govern it. A computer language syntax gives programmers a system of notation to communicate information to the programming language processor. The syntax of programming languages must be very precise; if a grammatical rule is violated, it results in a syntax error.

The fact that Java was in development for years means that its designers spent many moons pondering its syntax, and toiled to extract other language's most desirable elements for use in Java. Java's syntax clearly mirrors some of C and C++'s most beloved features, and its direct, clear implementation mimics C/C++. Although Java's set of object concepts differs from that of C++, Java's is simpler, and therefore, easier to learn.

One thing Java's developers didn't want to import from C/C++, though, were those nasty bugs. Shipping C code has an average of one bug per 55 lines of code. Since about half of those bugs came from memory allocation and deallocation, Java is chock full of features that guard against such fallible elements. Some of Java's characteristics that distinguish it from C and C++ (and make it significantly less buggy) are as follows:

* Its small size, which enables easy fluency
* Its strong typing
* Its lack of undefined or architecture-dependent constructs
* Its concurrence
* Its lack of unsafe constructs
* Its ease of reading and writing
* Its object-orientation, which permits facile reuse
* Its character arrays are instances of the *String* object
* Its garbage collection removes worries of memory leaks and dangling pointers

Grasping Java syntax

There's generally a great deal of syntactical variation between computer languages. Language designers often create a language's syntax according to their personal preferences, choosing structures that make sense to the pathways in which their brains function. As creative and revealing as this approach may be, it can also result in a (sometimes frustrating) lack of uniformity among programming languages.

Java was developed with this uniformity issue in mind, which is one reason why its syntax contains many similarities to C, C++, and Objective C. For example, *for* loops have the same syntax in all four languages. Java borrows heavily from C++ — almost every syntax is the same between the two — so Java is highly familiar to programmers who are accustomed to using C++. Java's design is recognized as being superior to C++'s, though, and it's easier to learn.

Understanding semantics

Although a language's syntax deals with the rules determining its structure and spelling, semantics address the language's *meaning*. Even if a programming language's syntax is in perfect shape, unless its commands make sense and have meaning for the program, the language's semantic rules are violated. So keep in mind that even if your commands are syntactically perfect, unless they make sense in the context of the program, they're meaningless.

Being object-oriented

One of the reasons that the Java language is such a big deal is because of its supreme object-orientation. The essence of object-oriented design puts the onus of design on the objects (the data), and on the interfaces to these objects. Rather than focusing on the tools that you use to present the data, Java's object-orientation makes you much more concerned about the objects themselves.

Java's object-orientation is clearly inspired by C++, and takes extensions from Objective C for more dynamic method resolution. Unlike a dynamic language, Java compels you to make explicit choices as you're writing. You don't have to make these choices without assistance — it's always possible to write method invocations, and the compiler's always ready to tell you what you've done wrong. Java's interface brings lots of flexibility, and it also frees you from worrying about method invocation errors.

To become the supreme object-oriented language, Java added more restrictions, complexity, and classes to the foundations of C/C++. Although programming in Java entails more responsibility at the programming end, a much safer set of functions and classes have emerged from its carefully crafted structure.

Figuring Out How Java Syntax Functions

The following subsections describe how the Java language works.

Tokens

When you've submitted a Java program to the Java compiler, the compiler then parses the text and extracts individual *tokens*. These tokens are the smallest elements of the Java program that have any meaning for the compiler. These tokens compose a *token set*, which can be dissected into five categories:

* identifiers
* keywords
* literals
* operators
* separators

When the Java compiler tokenizes the source file, it removes any comments or white spaces that it encounters. The lean and mean tokens are then compiled into Java bytecode that can be run from within an interpreted Java environment, on any type of machine.

Comments

Learning how to create valid Java comments is a good introduction to the Java syntax. When you include text as a comment, your compiler will ignore it; so, although the compiler won't appreciate your well-crafted comments, other people will. The comments that you ensconce inside your code are extremely useful for people down the line who are trying to understand what you've written, and good comments will greatly clarify your code.

THE THREE COMMENT TYPES

These are all examples of valid Java comments:

```
// You can use this kind of Java comment for a single line
/* Or you can use this C++-inherited comment for several lines */
/** Or if you want to create external documentation, you can put
   this specialized type of comment immediately in front of any
   declaration */
```

Java's developers want you to fully express yourself through your comments, and for that reason, you've got three different types to choose from. You'll find familiar C and C++ syntax throughout the Java language, and Java's comment syntax is an example of how Java built on its forefathers; the first two ways of specifying comments in Java come from C and C++. In the first type, you begin with two slashes. Once the compiler runs across the double slash, it will ignore the rest of the line. Here's that syntax:

```
// text, which may not span more than one line
```

The second type of comment tells the compiler that a comment has begun through the appearance of a slash-asterisk. After encountering the slash-asterisk, the compiler will ignore everything until it reaches the closing asterisk-slash. This type of comment, unlike the first slash-slash example, can cover several lines:

```
/* text */
```

The third format is a specialized Java comment that builds on the slash-asterisk type. Its additional asterisk at the beginning sets off the javadoc program, which extracts all comments written in this format and creates external documentation with them. It can come immediately before a declaration:

```
/** text */
```

The *javadoc* processor can extract these comments into HTML documentation, so this type of comment (sometimes termed *doc comments*) may contain HTML markup tags for code usage examples. However, doc comments shouldn't have HTML structural tags like <HR> or <H1>. There's also a collection of special tags that can be used with doc comments to give your documentation additional formatting. All of these tags commence with the at sign (@). These unique *javadoc* tags have to be the first thing on the doc comment lines, and if more than one tag of the same type is used, they must be on subsequent lines. Here are the special doc comment tags:

* @author *text*   This tag rubs your ego by giving you an "Author:" entry before the specified text. You can only use it in front of a class definition.

* @exception *full-classname description*   This tag gives the documentation a "Throws:" entry, which contains the exception's specified class name and its description. Only use this tag in front of a method definition.

* @param *parameter-name description*   This tag adds the specified parameter, along with its specified description, to the current method's "Parameters:" section. The description can carry onto the next line if it's too long for a single line. Only use this tag before a method definition.

* @return *description*   This tag adds a "Returns:" section to the documentation that contains a specified description. It only works in front of a method definition.

* @see *classname*   Use this tag before classes, variables, or methods to add a "See Also:" entry to the documentation. Adding this entry provides a hyperlink to the specified class.

* @see *full-classname*   Use this tag before classes, variables, or methods to add a "See Also:" entry to the documentation. Adding this entry provides a hyperlink to the specified class.

* @see *full-classname#method-name*   Use this tag before classes, variables, or methods to add a "See Also:" entry to the documentation. Adding this entry provides a hyperlink to the specified method of the specified class.

* @version *text*   This tag handily adds a "Version:" entry that contains the specified text to the documentation. You can only use it before a class definition.

Scope

In Java, the idea of scope is very important when you're working with blocks of code. Scope refers to how blocks (defined as sections of a program) affect variable lifetimes. When a variable is declared in a program, it automatically has a scope associated with it, so the variable is only used in the designated part of the program.

Scope becomes really important when you're nesting blocks of code within other blocks. Here's an example of variables that are nested within different scopes:

```
Class AdiosWorld {
  public static void main (String args[]) {
    int c, d;
    System.out.println("adios, World!");
    for (c = 0; c < 10; c++) {
      int e;
      System.out.println("Adios!");
    }
  }
}
```

In this example, the scope is also responsible for determining how long variables are going to live, because when program execution leaves the variable scope, they're destroyed. The integer *e* is allocated in this instance when Java enters the *for* loop block. When the program exits the *for* loop block, the *e* variable is no longer accessible. All of the variables in the program scope are set free and destroyed as the program execution leaves *main*.

Separation

The semicolon is used in Java, as in C, to indicate a statement's end. A statement consists of symbols (like numbers and characters), arranged into a sequence that describes a complete, specific operation. Semicolons are the one and only thing that can tell the compiler that a statement has finished — blank spaces (or blank pages), new lines, and indentations all lack the power to do so. Here's how statements are used:

```
this is statement1; this is statement2;
this is statement3
```

Identifiers

Identifiers are Java tokens that represent names. You can assign these names to methods, classes, and variables, thereby enabling the compiler to identify them. Using identifiers also helps programmers recognize meaning in the code.

It's possible to be fairly creative with the names that you give your identifiers, although there are only three ways to start a Java identifier:

1. With a letter (a-z, A-Z)

2. With an underscore (_)

3. With a dollar sign ($)

Characters that follow the initial character may also contain digits (0-9).

Identifiers are also case-sensitive, and all keywords (a list is coming up shortly) naturally must be avoided.

These are examples of valid Java identifiers:

```
AdiosWorld
identify_me
inherentlysignificant
```

And these are invalid Java identifiers:

```
Adios World
identify_me!
switch
```

The first example is invalid because of the space, the second because it contains an illegal exclamation point, and the third because it is a keyword.

Taking in a Few Stylistic Considerations

In addition to paying attention to the restrictions of naming Java identifiers, there are also a few stylistic considerations that, when followed, make Java more consistent and easier to understand. For example, it's accepted that multiple-word identifiers are named in lowercase except for the beginning letter of words in the middle of the name. That means that kissMe is correct Java style, while KISSME, KissMe, and kissme are not.

It's also a good idea to avoid the dollar sign and underscore characters at the beginning of your code, because many C libraries use that convention. When imported, it can clash with your Java code. The underscore character is best used to separate words where a space would normally exist.

Literals

There are five literal types in Java: Boolean, character, floating-point, integer, and string.

BOOLEAN LITERALS

There are two obvious literal values for Boolean values: true and false. Any time you have the need to represent a state or condition that has two possible values, you'll use a Boolean literal. Because Boolean literals are used in almost every kind of Java control structure, they're almost as ubiquitous as integer literals. It's not possible to coerce these values into *String* literal types, because they're not strings.

If you're coming from C to Java, you'll appreciate Boolean literals, because they don't exist in C, and you have to represent true and false with 1 and 0.

CHARACTER LITERALS

Character literals can either be a single character or a group of characters that represent a single character. Characters are represented as unsigned 16-bit integers. These literals, members of the Unicode character set, are of type *char*. Just like in C/C++, special characters (such as unprintable characters and control characters) are indicated by a backslash (\) followed by the character code.

You can use these escape sequences in Java to represent special character values (see Table 2-1). It's permissible for these escape sequences to appear in any Java *char* or *String* literal.

TABLE 2-1   This table presents the handy Character Escape Sequences.

Escape Sequence	Character Value
\b	Backspace
\f	Form feed
\n	New line
\r	Carriage return
\t	Horizontal tab
\"	Double quote
\'	Single quote
\\	Backslash
\xxx	Octal number xxx, with xxx being between 000 and 0377.
\uxxxx	Unicode character, with xxxx being between one and four hexidecimal digits.

FLOATING-POINT LITERALS

Floating-point literals are used to represent numbers that contain decimal parts (like 8.936). You can also employ them for scientific notation.

Java floating-point literals are constructed of these components:

* a base-10 integer
* a decimal point
* a fraction (actually a series of base-10 integers)
* an exponent (an uppercase or lowercase "E" that's followed by a signed base-10 integer)
* a character-literal type designator

There are two ways to represent floating-point literals: type *float*, which is used for single-precision floating-point literals, and type *double*, which represent double-precision floating-point literals. Double is the default storage, and should always be used when you're dealing with critical calculations. If you know that you won't need the full 64-bits, you can conserve by using the *float* type, which has a 32-bit value and is indicated by adding an *f* or *F* to the end of a number (like 8.936F).

INTEGER LITERALS

Integer literals are the primary literals in Java programming. Their three formats correspond to the base of the number system that the literal uses:

1. Decimal (base 10) literals are ordinary numbers that don't have any special notation.

2. Hexadecimal numbers (base 16) have a leading 0x or 0X and are similar to C/C++.

3. Octal (base 8) numbers have a leading 0 in front of the digits.

This is the integer literal for the number 12 in decimal:

```
12
```

Here it is in hexadecimal:

```
0xC
```

And here it is in octal:

```
014
```

The default storing type for integer literals is *int*, which has a signed 32-bit value. It's also possible to force large numbers to be stored in the *long* 64-bit value by appending an *l* or *L* to the end of the number (as in *64l*).

STRING LITERALS

String literals are series of zero or more characters that always appear within a pair of double quotation marks. They represent multiple characters, and, unlike the other literals, have their own class: the String class. The way Java represents the string literal is very different from the way it's done in C++. C++ regards the object as an array of characters, while Java implements it as an object of type String. The fact that Java implements strings as objects isn't too crucial from a programming perspective, but it does attest to Java's object-oriented nature. This fragment demonstrates how a new instance of the class String can be created:

```
String name = "Nefarious" ;
```

Learning How to Convert Java

It's probable that at some point in your love affair with Java programming, you'll have to convert data from one type to another. The process of converting from one data type to another is known as casting. It's necessary to go through the casting process when a function returns a type different than the type that's needed for you to perform an operation. Here's the syntax that's used for casting:

```
(classname) variable
```

Operators

If you're accustomed to using C/C++'s operators, you shouldn't have a problem dealing with Java's. Operators specify what kind of computation or evaluation should be performed on a data object (or objects). Java's operators can be function return types, literals, or variables. All of the operators that can be found in most popular programming languages turn up in Java. In addition, Java throws in a few of its own operators. When operators have the same precedence level, they're usually evaluated from left to right (see Table 2-2).

It's possible to override operator precedence with the explicit use of parentheses. For example:

```
t = (u + w) * x
```

TABLE 2-2 This is a master list of Java's built-in arithmetic and Boolean operators.

Precedence Level	Operator	Operand Type	Operation Description
1	++	arithmetic	increment by 1 (or 1.0)
1	– –	arithmetic	decrement by 1 (or 1.0)
1	+	arithmetic	unary plus
1	-	arithmetic	unary minus
1	~	integral	unary bitwise complement
1	!	boolean	unary logical complement
2	*	arithmetic	multiplication
2	/	arithmetic	division
2	%	arithmetic	modulus
3	+	arithmetic	addition
3	-	arithmetic	subtraction
4	<<	integral	left shift
4	>>	integral	right shift (keep sign)
4	>>>	integral	right shift (zero fill)
5	<	arithmetic	less than
5	>	arithmetic	greater than
5	<=	arithmetic	less than/equal
5	>=	arithmetic	greater than/equal
5	instanceof	object, type	tests class membership
6	==	primitive	equals(identical values)
6	!=	primitive	is not equal to
6	==	object	equals (same object)
6	!=	object	unequal (diff.object)
7	&	integral	bitwise AND
7	&	boolean	boolean AND

(*continued*)

TABLE 2-2   This is a master list of Java's built-in arithmetic and Boolean operators. *(continued)*

Precedence Level	Operator	Operand Type	Operation Description
8	^	integral	bitwise XOR
8	^	boolean	boolean XOR
9	|	integral	bitwise OR
9	|	boolean	boolean OR
10	&&	boolean	boolean AND
11	||	boolean	boolean OR
12	?:	boolean	conditional (ternary)
	any, any		operator
13	=	variable, any	assignment
13	op=	binary	op assignment

JAVA OPERATORS VERSUS C OPERATORS

Java and C operators are rather similar; however, there are a few important differences:

* Java lacks C's comma operator. Java compensates for this loss by simulating this operator in the *for loop* initialization's limited context and increment expressions.

* If the object on the left-hand side is an instance of the class, or if it implements the interface on the right-hand side, the *instanceof* operator returns *true*. Otherwise, it returns *false*, or if the left-hand side is null.

* When you apply the + operator to *String* values, it concatenates them. When + only has one *String* operator, the other one is converted to a string. Conversion is automatically accomplished for primitive types, and for nonprimitive types, the *toString* method is called.

* The >> operator always performs a signed right shift, because all integral types are signed in Java. This action fills in high bits with the operand's sign bit. The >>> operator does an unsigned right shift, which fills in high bits of the shifted value with zero bits.

* AND and OR operations on integral operands are performed by the & and | operators, which also perform AND and OR operators on Boolean operands. Although || and && also perform logical AND and OR on Boolean operands, if the result of the operation is fully determined by the left-hand operand, they don't evaluate the right-hand operand.

OPERATIONS ON INTEGERS

Standard operations (such as addition, multiplication, subtraction, and division) all work smoothly on integers. The expression's result will always be *int*, unless one or more of the expression's variables/values are defined as *long*.

Just as in C/C++, the −− and ++ operators perform an increment or decrement by one, respectively; the effect of each depends on its placement in the expression.

OPERATIONS ON BOOLEANS

All Boolean bit operators, Boolean negation, and bitwise operators are legal operations on Boolean values. Even if the operands surrounding the operator are of a different type, if the relation involves >, =, and so on, it sill produces a Boolean result. The Boolean forms (|| and &&) will short-circuit the evaluation; otherwise, the two types of ANDs and ORs perform exactly alike.

OPERATIONS ON FLOATING POINTS

As with integers, standard operations work without problems with floating points. You can't use bitwise operations with floating-point values, although it's possible to perform a cast of the value to *int* before you try to apply the operator.

Expressions

After you've created variables, you can apply variables and literals with them to form *expressions*. You can think of an expression as a programmatic equation that legally combines values, variables, and operators. More formally, an expression can be defined as a sequence of one or more data objects and zero or more operators that produce a result. Java's expression syntax is a lot like C's. Here is a valid Java expression:

```
a = b / 7
```

a and *b* are the variables in this expression, while = and / are the operators. Like most expressions, it was described from left to right, the same direction that the compiler uses to process the expression.

In Java, unlike in C and C++, you generally can't use the comma operator to create compound expressions. It is legal, however, to use the comma operator in the continuation and initialization section of for loops.

Types

Data types are one of the core concepts in programming languages. They're used to define the storage methods you can use to represent information, as well as indicate how the information should be interpreted. Since a variable's data type determines how the compiler interprets the memory's contents, data types are crucially connected to the storage of variables in memory. To create a variable in memory, you have to declare it by notating the variable's type. It's also required that you give the variable a unique identifier to differentiate it from other variables. This is the syntax of the Java declaration statement:

```
Type Identifier [, Identifier];
```

When the compiler encounters this declaration statement, it knows that it has to set memory aside for a variable of type *Type* that has the name *Identifier*. As indicated in the optional bracketed *Identifier*, you can create multiple declarations of the same type, as long as they're separated by commas. The declaration statement closes with a semicolon, as do all Java statements.

Every variable or expression in Java is represented as a type, meaning that it has a defined type attribute. It's through types that a variable or expression's legal range of values is provided, using a defined type attribute. Because the types are so clearly defined, their errors can be detected early on during a program's compilation (this is a source of celebration for programmers all over the globe!).

Java programs are a great deal more portable than those written in C/C++, because all of Java's simple types are defined the same way in all implementations of the language, regardless of the platform.

By using the intrinsic system *Class* type, and the interfaces and classes based upon it, Java also gives programmers the option of creating fresh user-defined types.

Here are the simple (or atomic) types that Java supports:

BOOLEAN (small b) AND BOOLEAN (large B)

 Java has (small b) boolean variables defined as a primitive type and the (large B) Boolean class which will be discussed in Chapter 3. A boolean variable assumes the value true or false. Unlike C/C++, it's not possible to convert a Java boolean to or from a numeric type by casting, since it's a distinct data type. No conversion is allowed between booleans and other simple types, and the boolean keyword is required. These are examples of boolean variable declarations:

```
boolean status = false
boolean found;
```

There are lots of familiar operators that don't work with boolean data types. Here's an example of a compiler error:

```
a = true + false;        //Error!
```

INTEGER

Because Java is designed to be machine-independent, its representation for the *integer* type is somewhat unique. Since the bytecodes aren't reliant upon a machine, there's no need to impose a storage model. Rather, the *integer* type determines what the values' range and set of legal operations are, meaning that it indicates what the range of legal values that an integer can store (see Table 2-3).

TABLE 2-3 Here are Java's four integer types.

Name	Bits/Width	Legal Range of Values
byte	8-bit signed quantity	-127 to 128
short	16-bit signed quantity	-32767 to 32768
int	32-bit signed character	-2147483647 to 2147483648
long	64-bit signed quantity	~-9.223e18 to ~9.223e18

By dividing the integer types into four categories, the integers have standard definitions, which is imperative for Java's cross-platform usage. The various integer sizes correspond to different needs for speed and memory usage. The byte representation is very efficient in terms of memory and is the fastest (or usually the fastest) at calculating and processing, regardless of the computer architecture. When casting byte variables to other integer types, watch out for sign propagation.

FLOATING-POINT

The *float* keyword is used to designate a 32-bit, single-precision floating-point type. When both operands of a binary operation are type *float*, they result in a type *float*.

The *double* keyword is used for a 64-bit, double-precision floating-point type. An operation results in a type *double* if one of the operands is type *double*. This is an example of a floating-point variable declaration:

```
float volume ;
```

TIP Theoretically, floating points are not capable of holding perfect integers. A *float* variable of 1 is actually stored as 1.0, and trails zeros up to the level of precision. Because performing floating-point math can be messy for a computer, you're better off using just an integer if that's all you need.

CHARACTER

There's a definite difference between Java character types and Java strings of characters. The Java character type holds single character values (which are not strings) and is declared as *char*. A char can be cast to the integer types, but is considered unsigned.

Exploring the Relationship: Java and Unicode

Java incorporates the Unicode character set, which is based on the Unicode Worldwide Character Standard. According to the Unicode Consortium, the Unicode standard "is a character coding system that was designed to support the interchange, processing, and display of the written texts of the diverse languages of the modern world. In addition, it supports classical and historical texts of many written languages."

At this point, the Unicode standard contains 34,168 distinct coded characters that are derived from 24 supported scripts. The main written languages of all continents are represented in these characters. Java *char* and *String* types use the canonical form of Unicode encoding, which means that each character occupies two bytes. The Unicode characters \u0020 to \u007E are the equivalents of the ASCII and Latin-1 (ISO8859) characters 0x20 through 0x7E. Unicode characters \u00A0 to \u00FF match the ISO8859-1 characters 0xA0 to 0xff.

Because the canonical two bytes per character encoding is a good way to manipulate character data, it's the internal representation that you'll find used throughout Java. The 16-bit canonical form isn't really a very efficient way to store Unicode text, since the majority of text that Java programs use is 8-bit, and because many computer systems only support 8-bit characters. Support for Unicode display fonts and printing is very limited in present Java but is expected to improve.

Alternate encoding termed "transformation formats" have been developed in response to this storing issue. The methods *DataInputStream.readUTF ()* and *dataOutputStream.writeUTF()* provide Java with a simple support for UTF-8 encoding.

Examining Java's Keywords

In Java, there is a set of identifiers that can only be used in a Java-specific manner. These special identifiers are called keywords, reserved words, or Boolean literal values. Table 2-4 is a list of all the keywords:

TABLE 2-4 These are Java's reserved words.

abstract	else	int	static
boolean	extends	interface	super
break	false	long	switch
byte	final	native	synchronized
byvalue	finally	new	this
case	float	null	throw
cast	for	operator	throws
catch	future	outer	transient
char	generic	package	true
class	goto	private	try
const	if	protected	var
continue	implements	public	void
default	import	rest	volatile
do	inner	return	while
double	instanceof	short	

TIP   Not all of the keywords are currently in use: although *byvalues, cast, const, future, generic, goto, inner, operator, outer, rest,* and *var* are all off limits for nonkeyword use, they're currently not being used for Java.

Reserved method names

In addition to reserved keywords, Java also has reserved method names of the *Object* class (see Table 2-5). They're not formally reserved (as the keywords are), but they shouldn't be used as method names, since the methods are inherited by every class. The only time that you'd want to use these method names is when you're trying to intentionally override an *Object* method.

TABLE 2-5 These are the reserved method names.

Clone	getClass	notifyAll	equals	hashCode	toString
finalize	notify	wait			

Storing Variables Efficiently: Arrays

By constructing an array, you can store many like-typed variables together and then access them through a single *array variable* name. Arrays are efficient and useful because of their power to employ an integer expression from the index. An operation on a Java array returns the value of an element of the array. Here's the basic syntax for the operation:

```
array-variable [expression]
```

Arrays are regarded as first-class language objects by Java, and Java's language array is a real object with a runtime representation. Arrays are extremely helpful for processing large piles of data. Java's syntax and support for arrays is a lot like C's. In Java, you can't allocate arrays on the stack — they have to be dynamically allocated instead. Array variable names are standard identifiers that you augment with an index value. The index value gives you the option to specify location in the possible range of values you'd like to access.

All arrays in Java are declared with square brackets ([]), which can be placed either after the variable type or after the identifier. The size of all arrays must be explicitly indicated with the new operator or by imbuing it with a list of items upon creation. Here's a fragment showing how a *new* instance of the *Array* class is created for integer types that are 20 elements long:

```
int elements[] = new int[20]
```

It's because Java doesn't have pointers that you are required to specifically set the size of an array. In pointer languages like C/C++, you can just point wherever you like in an array and make new items. Although this may be convenient, it's also the source of lots of unreliable C code, since it can lead to the trashing of memory (and unleash the infamous "delayed crash" syndrome, which may allow a memory access violation to lurk for hours or days before it appears). By eliminating the pointer arithmetic, Java eliminates the bounds-checking problems that plague C/C++ and ensures that its array checking will lend itself to the creation of more reliable and robust code.

Here are some more examples taken from arrays:

```
int elements[] = new int[70] [88]
int x[] = new int [30];        //time to declare the arrays
```

Although arrays greater than one dimension aren't viable in Java, you can allocate arrays of arrays to obtain multidimensional arrays. It's necessary that you provide at least one dimension; you can wait until later in your coding process to allocate other dimensions. To declare an array of Object, you'd write it like this:

```
Object myArray[];
```

When this code is encountered, it's recognized as an uninitialized array of Object that doesn't have any storage yet. When you get around to determining how much storage it needs, it would gain an integer that would determine how many objects its array would contain, like this:

```
myArray = new Object[30];
```

The omnialert Java keeps a careful eye on its security by checking to make sure that the indices of all array accesses are within the range of the array. If the index happens to be outside the array's boundary, an *ArrayIndexOutofBoundsException* is generated and the program will terminate. These are examples of out-of-bounds subscripts that would cause runtime exceptions:

```
a[20] = 1;        //will raise ArrayIndexOutofBoundsException
a[-6] = 7423      //will raise ArrayIndexOutofBoundsException
```

Pulling Java's Strings

Unlike C, Java strings are objects, not arrays of characters. Java string objects are instances of the String class, and the + operator concatenates two String objects. Two kinds of String objects actually exist: the String class, which is for read-only objects that can't be altered, and the StringBuffer class, which is for mutable string objects. Although the two kinds of String can be easily interconverted, the rule of thumb is to use just the String whenever you can, since it's more time efficient. Here are examples of legal Java *String* object declarations:

```
String myname = new String("Harold Menken");
String myname = "Harold Menken";
```

The second way is faster, since it's shorter, although the first way is the conventional format.

The Java language compiler is so smart that it understands that Strings are a special syntactic feature. It's therefore accommodating when it encounters a string of characters that are enclosed in double quotes, and knows that it's supposed to be instantiated as a String object. To derive the number of characters from a string, String objects supply a length accessor method.

Keep it Flowing: Java's Control-Flow Statements

Control statements are used within Java source code to express logical flow. Most of Java's control-flow statements parallel the ones you'll find in C or C++. Java's *while* and *do-while* loops are constructed just like C's:

```
while (boolean) {

    /* ... */
}
```

```
do {
    /* ... */
} while (boolean);
```

In Java, you can also declare a variable in the initialization section:

```
for (expression; booleanExpression; expression) {
    /* ... */
{
```

Java's scope of declared variables only encompasses the body of the *for* loop. You could declare a variable in the *for* loop like this:

```
for (int I = 0; I < 20; I++) {
    /* ... */
{
```

Switch

Java and C have an identical *switch* statement syntax:

```
switch (expression) {
  case Constant!:
  /* ... */
  break;
  case Constant2:
  /* ... */
  break;
  default:
  /* ... */
  break;
}
```

Break and continue

Java's two control-flow statements are *break* and *continue*, and they take an optional label. If you use the label, the computation will proceed with the labeled statement. However, if the label isn't there, the statements have the same meaning that they do in C. The *break* statements are endowed with a unique meaning in the *switch* construct, and for that reason, they're ideal to use when you're putting a *switch* statement inside a *for* loop. If you add a label to the *break* statement, you can break out of a loop's *switch* statement. Here's an example:

```
loopStart:
for (int j=0; j<20;j++) {
  /* break goes here */
  switch (j) {
    case 4:
    break;
    default:
    if ((j%2) == 0)
        break loopStart; // goes to the loop
    break;
  }
}
```

Learning the Remaining Pieces

The following subsections explore some other portions of Java syntax, including: classes and interfaces, methods, fields, and exceptions.

Classes and interfaces

Java has a specific syntax for defining the classes and interfaces used as templates for creation of new object instances. Unlike C++, the definition of a class or interface must be complete within a single file. Furthermore, a public class or interface must be defined in a file whose name exactly matches the class or interface name.

```
[public] interface interfaceName
  [extends        Interface1. Interface2, …] {
  /* listing of static fields or methods */
}
```

Here's the syntax for *ClassModifiers*:

```
ClassModifiers class className [extends superClass]
                    [implements interfaces] {
    /* listing of fields or methods */
  {
```

You can use a combination of the following keywords for your `ClassModifiers`:

* **abstract** A class is abstract if it contains at least one method declared as abstract.

* **<empty>** This class is accessible within the current class package when an access specifier like *public* isn't given.

* **final** Final classes cannot be subclassed.

* **public** Public classes can be used by code that's outside the class package. The file has to be named `<ClassName>.java`, and only a single public class is permitted per file.

Methods

Java's syntax for defining a method is a lot like what you would use to define a function in C:

```
MethodModifiers ReturnType Name(argType1, arg1, …) {
    /* body of the method */
  }
```

All of these keywords can be used as `MethodModifiers`:

* **<blank>** This is accessible by methods in classes sharing the same package.

* **abstract** This defines a method by parameters and return type but does not provide an implementation. Subclasses must provide the code.

* **final** It's impossible to override this method.

* **native** A stub written in another language (like C) implements this method.

* **private** This is accessible only to other methods in this class.

* **protected** This is accessible only by a subclass.

* **public** This is accessible by any method.

* **static** Invoked with the `<Class>.method`, this method is shared by all instances of this class.

* **synchronized** This method locks the object upon entry, then unlocks it upon exit. If a Thread encounters an object that's already locked, it waits until the lock is released before it begins executing.

Fields

The syntax you use to define a variable declaration or structure field in C is like Java's syntax for defining a field, as this code demonstrates:

```
FieldModifiers Type FieldName;
```

The following keywords can be used as `FieldModifiers`:

* **<blank>** Accessible by methods in classes sharing the same package.
* **private** Accessible only to other methods in this class.
* **protected** Accessible only by a subclass.
* **public** Accessible by any method.
* **final** Must be initialized when declared and can not be changed.
* **static** Only one variable which is shared by an entire class exists.
* **transient** This keyword exists to support future implementation of persistent objects. A transient field would not be saved to permanent storage.
* **volatile** Tells the compiler and the Java Virtual Machine that this variable may be changed by multiple Threads so certain optimizations must be avoided.

Exceptions

Java's exception mechanism also doubles as an all-around error-handling mechanism. The two components of the exception mechanism are setting up an exception handler and signaling an exception.

A method uses the `try-catch` clause to set up an exception handler. A `try` block and a `catch` block are the components of the `try-catch` clause; the `try` block is the code that's executed when no exception occurs, and the `catch` block is used when an exception is raised. It's possible that more than one `catch` blocks exists, in which case, the `catch` that is closest to the thrown exception's class is used. This syntax demonstrates the `try-catch` clause:

```
try {
  /* try block */
} catch (ExceptionType e1) {
  /* catch statement 1* /
}catch (ExceptionType e2) {
  /* catch statement 2 */
}
```

TIP There's another clause that can be used in combination with *a try block* — the *finally* clause. This is an optional clause whose statements are executed regardless of whether the code terminates normally. By using the *finally* clause in this way, you can assure that the *file.close()* statement will be executed even if an exception were raised.

```
File file;
try {
  file = new File("someFile");

  file.write.("foo");
  file.write("bar");
} catch (IoException e) {
  /* the file couldn't be opened or maybe one of the writes
  failed. */
  return; // but the finally clause gets executed before
} finally {
  file.close();
}
```

Summary

Now that we've explained the crucial elements of the Java syntax, you have the foundation to be able to efficiently and effectively deconstruct and create code. In the next chapter, we delve into the intricacies of Java's base classes and objects.

## CHAPTER THREE

JAVA BASE CLASSES AND OBJECTS

IN THIS CHAPTER YOU LEARN THESE KEY SKILLS

I n the previous chapter, we covered the Java language syntax and structure. To complete the description of the language, we must study the basic library of predefined classes provided with Java. Many of the classes can be found in similar form in other object-oriented languages, but Java has many unique classes reflecting its emphasis on networking and the Internet Web. If you are impatient to get started coding your own Java, skip to the next chapter, but keep this chapter in mind for reference.

As discussed in Chapter 2, the Java standard library is organized in packages for management purposes. Here is a quick description of the packages and their contents.

* *java.applet* Classes used to provide functions for Web browsers.
* *java.awt* The Abstract Windowing Toolkit, these are classes for providing graphic user interface (GUI) functions in a hardware-independent manner.
* *java.awt.image* Image processing functions.

* *java.awt.peer* The classes connecting AWT objects to the underlying hardware. It is unlikely that you will ever need to work with these classes.

* *java.io* Input and output functions for network connections and files.

* *java.lang* Basic objects used by all programs.

* *java.net* Management of network connections.

* *java.util* Useful classes that didn't fit in anywhere else.

However, the package organization is not suited to the organization of an introduction to Java, and there are many classes that you don't need to know about at this stage, so this chapter discusses the classes in a sequence which we believe will be most useful.

NOTE We will limit the discussion to those methods which are most likely to be used at an introductory level. For an exhaustive discussion of all Java standard classes, consult the Sun Microsystems documentation. This is available in HTML form, either downloadable or browsable on the Net from the following URL:

`http://www.javasoft.com/doc/language.html`

Starting at the Base: Object and Thread

All classes in the Java language are ultimately derived from the Object class; therefore, any class you create can use the Object methods. However, it is difficult to understand the significance of some of these methods without also discussing threads, so the following discussion will bounce back and forth between thread and object.

Thread — what happens next?

When we say a Java program is running, there is at least one thread which is doing something. Since Java is a multitasking language, there may be more than one thread, but there is always at least one. On most hardware, threads are based on the implementation of multitasking by the underlying operating system, but in some cases, such as the Solaris operating system or Windows 3.1, the implementers of the Java Virtual Machine have had to create their own thread mechanisms.

What your program does next depends on a thread executing a method in an object. A thread gets a chance to do something when the underlying operating system decides to let it run. This decision can be based on a variety of considerations, such as the priority of the thread and the competing processes which the operating system is managing. As a programmer, you have no direct control over this decision, but you can influence it. There are many pitfalls for the unwary in multithreaded programs, such as programs that "deadlock" when two threads contend for the same object, or bizarre results when two threads modify the same object, but Java provides concepts to help you avoid these pitfalls. Important protections are built into the Object class.

Objects and threads

Objects have a basic mechanism called a `monitor` which can be used to control access to variables and methods by threads. Methods which are declared as `synchronized` force threads to pay attention to the state of the monitor of an object. For instance, take what happens when a thread starts the following routine:

```
public synchronized void depositBucks( float money){
  balance = balance + money ;
 ....
}
```

The monitor mechanism prevents any other thread from modifying the object while this method is being executed. If another thread also tried to call depositBucks, it would be deactivated and placed in a waiting queue. After the first thread left the depositBucks method, a waiting thread would be able to execute. As you can imagine, this synchronization method imposes some overhead, so it should be used in a discriminatory manner.

Many multithreaded applications require that threads cooperate in their treatment of an object. For instance, one thread may update the status of an object in a simulation as it evolves over time, while another refreshes the screen display whenever the system decides to repaint a window. The mechanism for this cooperation is built into the Object class `wait` and `notify` methods which are declared as follows:

* **public final void wait()** The thread halts until notified.
* **public final void wait(long millisec)** The thread halts until notified or time in milliseconds runs out.
* **public final void wait(long millisecs, int nanosec)** A high resolution time-out; the present version of Java actually does not have this close time resolution so this must be regarded as a potential future development.
* **public final void notify()** One waiting thread gets a chance to run.
* **public final void notifyAll()** All waiting threads get a chance to run.

It is important to realize that the thread which is blocked, waiting for access to an object, may be the system thread which handles key-press events and repaint requests. Permanently blocking this thread is one of the most common causes of Java programs "locking up" and becoming unresponsive.

Object methods

In addition to the thread-related methods just described, the Object class includes the following methods, several of which are frequently overridden by more specific methods in derived classes:

* **public boolean equals(Object obj)** Returns true if this object is equal in value to obj — each subclass which contains other objects should provide its own version of equals.
* **public final Class getClass()** Returns a Class object which is a run-time representation of the class of the current object.
* **public int hashCode()** The purpose of a hashcode is to provide a (usually) unique number for storing objects in hashtables. Hashtables are discussed later in this chapter.
* **public String toString()** Returns a string description of the object — very handy for debugging.
* **protected Object clone()** Returns a new Object which is a copy of the current one — derived classes must be declared as implementing Cloneable for this to work.
* **protected void finalize()** This method is called when an object is about to be discarded to give the programmer a chance to properly dispose of system resources other than memory. This is a "do nothing" method for Object and most classes.

Thread methods

The following sections explore the various Thread methods in detail.

CREATING THREADS

If you have a class derived from the Thread class, you would create a thread with:

```
myThread = new myThreadClass();
```

Your derived myThreadClass must have a run() method defined. When myThread.start() is called, the new thread will start executing the run() method. When the run() method returns or when myThread.stop() is called, the thread stops and can not be restarted. The Thread object still exists but is considered "dead."

Alternately, a thread may be created and attached to an object which implements the Runnable interface. Runnable classes are expected to have a run() method which the new thread will start executing when it is started. Threads are attached to Runnable objects by passing "this" to the Thread constructor. Here is an example of a Runnable class in which the constructor creates and starts an attached thread.

```
public class Example implements Runnable {
  Thread myThread ;
  String msg = "Hello World" ;

  Example() {  // class constructor
   myThread = new Thread( this );
   myThread.start();
  }

  public void run(){
    System.out.println("Msg is >" + msg );
  }

  public static void main( String args[] ){
    Example ME = new Example();
  }
}
```

THREAD PRIORITY

In a program with multiple threads competing for execution time, the programmer can try to ensure that the most important threads get the most execution time by setting priorities. There are three constants defined in the Thread class, MAX_PRIORITY, MIN_PRIORITY, and NORM_PRIORITY. Because the implementation of threads depends on the underlying operating system, the exact behavior of threads may vary from system to system and you may have to do some experimentation. For instance, if multiple threads have the same priority, you cannot rely on the operating system to give them equal execution time. The priority related methods are:

```
public final int getPriority();
public final void setPriority( int newP );
```

THREAD CONTROL

The following are some of the most useful methods for thread control. Programmers should be aware that causing a thread to sleep or be suspended while it is executing a synchronized method will prevent access by other threads to that object because of the monitor mechanism. The current Netscape browser issues a warning when a thread is suspended due to this concern.

* **public final boolean isAlive()** Returns false if the thread has not been started or is dead.
* **public static void sleep(long millisecs)** The thread stops executing until at least the specified number of milliseconds has expired.

- ✳ **public final void suspend()** The thread stops executing and enters a suspended state until resume is called.
- ✳ **public final void resume()** A suspended thread is allowed to resume execution.
- ✳ **public static void yield()** Lets the operating system run any other pending thread. Useful to prevent one thread from hogging all the CPU time.

Grasping Standard Language Objects

We now proceed to the classes commonly used for text and number manipulation. There are some surprises here for programmers coming from non-OO languages, so pay attention.

Wrappers

To get reasonable speed, Java does not treat integer, floating point, character, and boolean variables as objects, but as "primitive" data types. This avoids excessive overhead caused by the creation and destruction of objects when performing simple arithmetic, but leaves the problem of how to use these variables in many handy collection classes such as vectors and stacks. In Java, as in many OO languages, this is handled by creating "wrapper" classes for each of the simple variable types. These wrapper classes are named like the simple variables but start with an upper-case letter; thus, Boolean is the class wrapper for boolean variables. These wrapper classes also solve the language designer's problem of where to put various utility functions.

THE BOOLEAN CLASS

In addition to providing for Objects representing boolean values, the Boolean class has static methods which can understand "true" or "false" in input strings. Here are some of the more useful methods in the Boolean class:

CONSTRUCTORS FOR BOOLEAN OBJECTS

- ✳ **public Boolean(boolean value)** Constructs a Boolean object from a (small b) boolean variable.
- ✳ **public Boolean(String str)** Constructs a Boolean object from a String. Any String other than "true" (ignoring case) creates a False.
- ✳ **public static boolean getBoolean(String str)** Returns a (small b) boolean by parsing the string just like the constructor above.
- ✳ **public String toString()** Returns either "true" or "false" Strings.

THE INTEGER CLASS

Here is where you will find all the handy methods for converting integers to and from Strings.

CONSTRUCTORS FOR INTEGER OBJECTS

* **public Integer(int value)** Construct an Integer from a (small i) int.
* **public Integer(String str)** Construct an Integer from a String, assuming decimal digits.

CLASS METHODS IN THE INTEGER CLASS

* **public static int parseInt(String str)** Returns an int by parsing the string, assuming decimal digits.
* **public static int parseInt(String str, int radix)** Converts the string using specified base. For instance, Integer.parseInt("FF", 16) returns 255.
* **public static String toString(int i)** Returns the string form of an int, assuming base ten.
* **public static String toString(int i, int radix)** Returns the string form of an int using specified base.

TIP Any Integer method converting from a String can throw a NumberFormatException if the expected format is not found. To control the conversion process, you must use try and catch statements as in the following example. By printing the exception description, you can usually determine what went wrong, as in the following example:

```
try {
Integer myInt = new Integer( instring ) ;
}
catch( NumberFormatException ex ) { System.out.println( ex );
}
```

INSTANCE METHODS FOR INTEGER OBJECTS

* **public double doubleValue()** Returns the value of the Integer object as a double variable.
* **public float floatValue()** Returns the value of the Integer object as a float variable.
* **public int intValue()** Returns the value of the Integer object as an int variable.
* **public long longValue()** Returns the value of the Integer object as a long variable.

THE LONG CLASS

As you would expect, the Long Class, which provides a wrapper for long (64-bit) integer variables has constructors and methods similar to those for the Integer class. There are no surprises here, so let's move to the next wrapper class.

THE CHARACTER CLASS

The Character Class provides a wrapper for the primitive data type char. Recall from Chapter 2 that char has 16 bits and is designed to handle the Unicode character set, although support for Unicode is presently sparse in Java. Various class methods provide for testing and converting individual char variables.

CONSTRUCTOR FOR CHARACTER OBJECTS

* **public Character(char cval)** Construct a Character object from a char variable.

CLASS METHODS IN THE CHARACTER CLASS

* **public static int digit(char ch, int base)** Returns int corresponding to this character in this base. Returns minus1 for values of ch which are not digits in this base.
* **public static char forDigit(int digit, int base)** Returns char corresponding to this digit in this base. Returns zero for values of digit which are illegal in this base.
* **public static boolean isDigit(char ch)** Returns true if ch is a base-ten digit.
* **public static boolean isLowerCase(char ch)** Returns true if ch is a lower-case character.
* **public static boolean isUpperCase(char ch)** Returns true if ch is an upper-case character.
* **public static boolean isSpace(char ch)** Returns true if ch is a "white space" in ISO-Latin-1 character set.
* **public static char toLowerCase(char ch)** Returns ch converted to lower case or the original ch if not upper case.
* **public static char toUpperCase(char ch)** Returns ch converted to upper case or the original ch if not lower case.

INSTANCE METHODS FOR CHARACTER OBJECTS

* **public char charValue()** Returns a char variable with this value.
* **public String toString()** Returns a String with this single character.

THE FLOAT CLASS

In addition to the expected constructors and conversion classes, the Float class contains some constants and methods related to the limitations of representing floating point numbers in the IEEE standard 32-bit representation.

CONSTANTS IN THE FLOAT CLASS

* **public final static float MAX_VALUE** The largest possible float number.
* **public final static float MIN_VALUE** The smallest representable float.
* **public final static float NEGATIVE_INFINITY** Special representation for a negative number too large to represent correctly.
* **public final static float NaN** This stands for "Not A Number."
* **public final static float POSITIVE_INFINITY** Special representation for a positive number too large to represent correctly.

CONSTRUCTORS FOR FLOAT OBJECTS

* **public Float(float fval)** Creates a Float wrapper for fval.
* **public Float(double dval)** Creates a Float wrapper for a double — this may cause loss of accuracy.
* **public Float(String str)** Creates a Float wrapper object by parsing the string. May throw a NumberFormatException.

As with the Integer class, Float also has methods to return int, long, float, and double variable values, and a toString method.

THE DOUBLE CLASS

As you would expect, the Double Class, which provides a wrapper for long (64-bit) floating point variables has constructors and methods similar to those for the Float class. There are no surprises here, so let's move to a short discussion of how to use the wrapper classes and the pitfalls awaiting the unwary programmer.

USING WRAPPER-CLASS OBJECTS

The most important thing to remember about wrapper objects is that they are immutable once created. For instance, assuming you had an Integer object "myInt," there is no way you could increment the value in your Integer object in a statement like the following, even if the compiler would accept it:

```
myInt = myInt + 1 ;
```

Furthermore, a wrapper object passed into a method and modified will not be modified on return from the method. For instance, although the following will compile without error, the new Integer myInt is local to the method and is discarded on return from the method, so the original myInt is unchanged.

```
void AddOne( Integer myInt ){
 myInt = new Integer( myInt.intValue() + 1 );
}
```

The main reason you are likely to want to use a wrapper class object such as Integer instead of a plain int is so you can make use of useful Java classes such as Hashtable, Stack, and Vector that only work with Objects. For instance, if you were creating a calculator applet, you could use a Stack of operands to hold intermediate results as Double objects.

String and StringBuffer classes

String objects contain strings of (16-bit) characters and are immutable once created. A programmer using C might consider a String to be a "wrapper" for an array of char. Because String objects are immutable, you can't (for instance) replace every 'a' in a String with 'A'. You should use the StringBuffer class if you need to modify individual characters. The Java compiler uses a temporary StringBuffer object to perform the concatenation of String objects in the following simple example code.

```
String addFilename(String path, String filename ){
    String tmp = path + "/" + filename + ".txt" ;
    return tmp ;
}
```

STRING AND STRINGBUFFER CONSTRUCTORS

Since String and StringBuffer are so intimately connected, we will consider them together.

STRING CONSTRUCTORS

* **public String()** Constructs an empty string.
* **public String(String str)** Constructs a copy of str. Note that str might be a string literal — a string in double quote marks.
* **public String(char[] chars)** Constructs a String from an array of char.
* **public String(char[] chars, int offset, int count)** A String is constructed from the char array starting at char[offset] and continuing for a total of count characters. This constructor will throw an exception if the array boundaries are exceeded.

* **public String(byte[] ascii, int hibyte)** The array of (8-bit) bytes is turned into a String with the high byte of each (16-bit) character set to hibyte. Generally hibyte will be zero.
* **public String(byte[] ascii, int hibyte, int offset, int count)** As above except that the String will start with ascii[offset] and continue for a total of count characters. This constructor will throw an exception if the array bounds are exceeded.
* **public String(StringBuffer buf)** Constructs a String from a StringBuffer.

STRING INSTANCE METHODS THAT CREATE NEW STRINGS

Note that in all of these methods, the original String is unchanged.

* **public String concat(String str)** Creates a new String composed of this String plus str.
* **public String replace(char oldch, char newch)** Creates a new String in which all occurrences of oldch are replaced with newch.
* **public String substring(int startndx)** Creates a new String with characters from startndx to the end. If startndx is equal to or greater than the length of the String, an exception is generated.
* **public String substring(int startndx, int endndx)** Creates a new String with characters from startndx up to (but not including) endndx.

Here are some examples of using these methods.

```
String strA = "123456789" ;
String strB = "ABCDEFGHI" ;
String tmp = strA.concat( strB ) ;  / result "123456789ABCDEFGHI"
String tmp =  strA.replace( '3', 'X' ) ;  / result "12X456789" /
String tmp = strB.substring( 4 ) ;  // result "EFGHI"
String tmp = strB.substring( 1,3 ) ;  // result "BC"
```

STRINGBUFFER CONSTRUCTORS

* **public StringBuffer()** Creates an empty StringBuffer.
* **public StringBuffer(int length)** Creates a StringBuffer with initial capacity length but no characters.
* **public StringBuffer(String str)** Creates a StringBuffer with initial contents from str.

MODIFYING STRINGBUFFERS

STRINGBUFFER APPEND METHODS

Note that the following methods return the StringBuffer object itself, not new StringBuffer. This allows the Java compiler to take the concatenation example:

```
String tmp = path + "/" + filename;
```

and turn it into:

```
String tmp = new StringBuffer( path ).append("/").append( filename ).toString()
;
```

This stringing together of method calls with dots may look a little strange, but it is perfectly legal. Going from left to right, each method is applied to the result of the previous! What happens is:

1. A new StringBuffer is created with the "path" characters. The result is a StringBuffer.

2. The "/" string is added to the buffer. The result is a StringBuffer.

3. The "filename" string is added to the buffer. The result is a StringBuffer.

4. The StringBuffer toString method creates a new String which is assigned to the tmp variable.

5. The StringBuffer is discarded.

Here are the declarations of two of the StringBuffer append methods. Similar append methods are available for adding the string representation of char arrays, boolean, char, int, long, float, and double variables.

 TIP The append methods always ensure that the unused buffer area is large enough before adding new characters.

* **public synchronized StringBuffer append(Object obj)** Add the string representation of an arbitrary object to the buffer. The representation is obtained from the toString method of the Object.

* **public synchronized StringBuffer append(String str)** Add the characters from str to the StringBuffer.

CREATING A STRING FROM A STRINGBUFFER

* **public String toString()** Creates a new String object whose contents are the characters in the StringBuffer. Note that for efficiency, the characters are initially shared with the StringBuffer. A special mechanism creates a new copy for the StringBuffer if it is modified again. This mechanism is provided because most uses of StringBuffer are

as temporary objects for string concatenation.

STRINGBUFFER MODIFICATION METHODS

The following are some of the methods available for modifying a StringBuffer by inserting characters. There are similar methods for inserting the string representation of int, long, float, double, and boolean variables.

TIP As with the append methods, the StringBuffer returned is the working StringBuffer, not a new one.

* **public synchronized StringBuffer insert(int offset, Object obj)**
  Inserts the string representation of obj into the buffer at offset. Note that offset must be within or at the end of the existing characters in the buffer or an exception is generated.
* **public synchronized StringBuffer insert(int offset, String str)**
  Inserts the characters from str at offset.
* **public synchronized void setCharAt(int index, char ch)**
  Replaces the char at index with ch.

MISCELLANEOUS STRINGBUFFER METHODS

* **public synchronized char charAt(int index)** Returns the char at this position.
* **public synchronized void getChars(int bstart, int bend, char[]dest, int destoffset)** Copies chars from buffer from bstart to bend into the char array dest starting at destoffset.
* **public int length()** Returns the number of chars in buffer.
* **public int capacity()** Returns the total capacity of the buffer.
* **public synchronized void ensureCapacity(int cap)** Forces the StringBuffer to provide space for at least this many chars.
* **public synchronized void setLength(int newlen)** Trims back the characters in the buffer to this new length. If newlen is larger than the actual length, an exception is generated.

The Date class

The Date class, which is in the java.util package, lets you perform a variety of manipulations of dates and times. Internally, the date is a long integer equal to the number of milliseconds since midnight, January 1st, 1970, but the allowed range of dates is much smaller than this internal representation would indicate. Because Date needs to work with the underlying operating system representation of dates, it is limited to years between 1970 and 2037 on Windows systems.

DATE CONSTRUCTORS

* **public Date()** Constructs a Date with current operating system values of date and time.

* **public Date(int yr, int mo, int dy)** Date will be constructural with this year, month, and day and a time of 00:00:00 (midnight). NOTE: The year must be specified as years since 1900, months with Jan = 0, and days from 1 to 31.

* **public Date(int yr, int mo, int dy, int hr, int min, int sec)** As above, but with the time specified. Hours range: 0 to 23, minutes: 0 to 59, seconds: 0 to 59.

DATE MODIFICATION METHODS

* **public void setDate(int dom)** Changes the day of the month, range 1 to 31.

* **public void setMonth(int mm)** Changes the month, range 0 to 11.

* **public void setYear(int yy)** Changes the year, range 70 to 137.

* **public void setHours(int hr)** Changes the hour, range 0 to 23.

* **public void setMinutes(int min)** Changes the minutes, range 0 to 59.

* **public void setSeconds(int sec)** Changes the seconds, range 0 to 59.

* **public void setTime(long millisec)** Sets the Date using milliseconds since midnight GMT, January 1, 1970.

DATE OUTPUT METHODS

There are "get" methods for Date, Month, Year, Hours, Seconds, and Time analogous to the set methods just given. In addition, we have the following:

* **public int getDay()** Returns day of the week, with Sunday = 0.

* **public String toGMTString()** Returns a String formatted in the Internet GMT convention.

* **public String toLocaleString()** Returns a String formatted according to locale conventions as provided by the operating system.

* **public String toString()** Returns a String formatted using the UNIX ctime convention.

DATE COMPARISON METHODS

* **public boolean after(Date when)** Returns true if when is after current Date object.

- **public boolean before(Date when)** Returns true if when is before current Date object.
- **public boolean equals(Object obj)** Returns true if obj is a Date with identical value.

Exploring the Abstract Windowing Toolkit

The purpose of the AWT classes is to provide graphical user interface objects which can be used on any graphics hardware while preserving the programmer's interface design. This is a difficult design problem, and the AWT, as it presently stands, is not a perfect solution. We discuss the AWT classes in five groups, the GUI components which appear on the screen, Events which the operating system sends to components, the LayoutManagers which arrange the components, Graphics tools, and Image manipulation.

GUI components on the screen

All of the graphical user interface components such as buttons, labels, and text fields are derived from the abstract class Component. The Component class defines many methods used by various interface classes but because it is `abstract`, you never create a Component object as such. The Component class gives to derived classes variables and methods controlling size, color, fonts, and event handling. Here is a summary of the classes derived from Component:

- **Button** A labeled button in the operating system style.
- **Canvas** A general display class useful for display of images or drawing on directly.
- **Checkbox** A labeled checkbox in the operating system style.
- **Choice** An option menu in the "drop down" style.
- **Container** A container can hold other components and arrange them using LayoutManager objects. There are two types, Panels and Windows, with Windows having Dialog and Frame subclasses.
  - **Panel** A container which does not create a separate window, but lives inside another window.
  - **Window** A container displayed as a separate window.
    - **Dialog** A dialog box-type window which may be `modal`.
    - **Frame** A top-level application window. Frames can have menus, titles, icons, custom cursors, and close boxes.

* **Label** A passive component which displays label text in controllable style.
* **List** A scrollable list of strings that allows for selection of one or more items using a mouse or keyboard.
* **Scrollbar** A scroll bar which responds to the mouse and sends events to the enclosing container.
* **TextComponent** The parent of TextArea and TextField — never used directly.
  * **TextArea** A multiline text display based on the underlying operating system. TextAreas can be made editable if desired.
  * **TextField** A single line editable text field typically used for user input.

COMPONENT VARIABLES AND METHODS

The following sections explain the various component variables and methods.

INSTANCE VARIABLES

* **ComponentPeer peer** Peers are the "native" operating system equivalents of Components which directly take over the many functions. If a component has a peer, a reference to it is stored here.
* **Container parent** The Container object holding this Component — may be null for top-level Components.
* **int x, y** The x and y positions of the upper-left corner of the Component in the container's coordinate system (in pixels).
* **int width, height** The width and height of the Component in pixels.
* **Color foreground, background** The Color objects used to fill the background and draw the foreground text in the Component.
* **Font font** The Font object used to draw text in the Component.
* **boolean visible** True when the Component is visible on the screen.
* **boolean enabled** True when the user can interact with the Component, such as a button or text field.
* **boolean valid** True when the Component has been laid out. Set false when the Component size has changed to force recalculation of the layout.

FREQUENTLY USED COMPONENT METHODS

* **public Dimension minimumSize()** Returns a Dimension object with the minimum height and width the Component needs. Whether it gets displayed at this size depends on the LayoutManager and the space available in the container.

* **public Dimension preferredSize()** Returns a Dimension object with the height and width the Component would like to have. Whether it gets displayed at this size depends on the LayoutManager and the space available in the container.

* **public synchronized void reshape(int x, int y, int width, int height)** Tries to reposition the Component within a container with a new size.

* **public void resize(int width, int height)** Tries to change the size of the Component.

* **public synchronized void show()** Show the Component on the screen. Usually called after the Component has been created and added to a Container.

* **public synchronized void setBackground(Color c)** Sets the color to be used when clearing the screen rectangle the Component occupies. For best results, set the background color before the component is shown.

* **public synchronized void setForeground(Color c)** Sets the color to be used when drawing text and graphics on the Component.

* **public synchronized void setFont(Font f)** Sets the font to be used when drawing text.

Events sent to Components

Every graphical user interface must have a method for communicating user actions to the program; in Java this is accomplished with Event objects. The Java Virtual Machine gets a message from the underlying operating system which it turns into an Event object. The Component that first receives the Event is determined by the position of the mouse for mouse events or the Component having the focus for keyboard Events. The system tries to find a method to handle the event by working through the hierarchy of component objects and classes, calling the handleEvent method of each. If handleEvent returns false, the system looks further up the hierarchy of containers to find a suitable handler.

EVENT OBJECTS

Each Event has the following instance variables that are set according to the type of Event. Not every variable is set for every event — for instance, mouse events will have x and y but not key set.

* **public Object target** The Component targeted by the event.
* **public long when** The time of the event in milliseconds.
* **public int id** One of the standard constants identifying the Event type.
* **public int x, y** The x and y coordinates of a mouse event.

* **public int key** The key pressed in a keyboard event.
* **public int modifiers** For key presses, this contains flags indicating that the Shift or Ctrl key is down. For mouse events, the flags indicate whether the right or center mouse button is down.
* **public int clickCount** For mouse-down events, this will have 1 for a single-click, 2 for a double-click.
* **public Object arg** Used to give extra information about the event target.
* **public Event evt** Used to point to the next event when putting events in a linked list.

EVENT TYPES

The Event class defines constants for the following event types. Programmers working with GUI operating systems, such as Windows, will recognize that this represents a great simplification from the vast number of events that could be defined.

* ACTION_EVENT Button clicks, Check box selection, and List double-click selections.
* GOT_FOCUS, LOST_FOCUS Generated as focus moves between components. Due to problems with the present AWT, these are not always generated by all components.
* KEY_ACTION, KEY_ACTION_RELEASE Generated by function keys.
* KEY_PRESS, KEY_RELEASE Generated by normal keys.
* LIST_SELECT, LIST_DESELECT Generated by mouse clicks in List components.
* MOUSE_DOWN, MOUSE_UP Generated by mouse button clicks.
* MOUSE_DRAG, MOUSE MOVE Mouse movement with and without a button down.
* MOUSE_ENTER, MOUSE_EXIT Generated when mouse moves into and out of a component.
* SCROLL_ABSOLUTE Generated by moving scroll bar with mouse.
* SCROLL_LINE_UP, SCROLL_LINE_DOWN, SCROLL_PAGE_UP, SCROLL_PAGE_DOWN Generated by clicking on various parts of a scroll bar.
* WINDOW_EXPOSE, WINDOW_ICONIFY, WINDOW_DEICONIFY, WINDOW_MOVED Generated by manipulating a window.
* WINDOW_DESTROY Generated when window is closed.

EXAMPLES OF EVENT PROGRAMMING

Let us suppose we have an Applet (Applet is derived from Panel, which is derived from Container, which is derived from Component) which has a Button, a Scroll bar, a List box and a Canvas displayed on it.

A mouse click on a Button object will be turned into an Event with id = ACTION_EVENT, target = the Button object, arg = the Button label string. Generating this event is handled by the operating system = specific code which turns the initial mouse down into an ACTION_EVENT. A programmer has two options to catch this Event in methods of his Applet derived class, as shown in the following code:

```
public boolean handleEvent(Event evt ){
    if( evt.id == Event.ACTION_EVENT ) {
        System.out.println("handleEvent Action " + evt );
        // return true here if event has been handled
    }
    return super.handleEvent( evt );
}

public boolean action( Event evt, Object what ){
    System.out.println("action method " + what );
    return true ;
}
```

The handleEvent method receives the Event first. If we handled the required response to the button push here, we could return "true" and the system would consider the event handled. This code shows the correct way to pass unhandled events to the superclass, in this case: Applet. Because Applet does not override the handleEvent method of Component, the Component class would end up with the Event. Component turns ACTION_EVENTs into calls to the action method — the Object in the call to action is the arg in the Event.

This complex chain of events is necessary to give every object that might be affected a chance to handle user input. The choice of whether to use handleEvent or action methods is largely a matter of style. The handleEvent method gets the Event first and thus is slightly faster, but it becomes an ungainly block of code if many different events are to be handled. If you don't use handleEvent, the Component class provides the following methods in addition to action:

```
public boolean keyDown( Event evt, int key);
public boolean keyUp( Event evt, int key );
public boolean gotFocus( Event evt, Object what );
public boolean lostFocus( Event evt, Object what );
public boolean mouseDown( Event evt, int x, int y );
public boolean mouseUp( Event evt, int x, int y );
```

```
public boolean mouseDrag( Event evt, int x, int y );
public boolean mouseMove( Event evt, int x, int y );
public boolean mouseEnter( Event evt, int x, int y );
public boolean mouseExit( Event evt, int x, int y );
```

PROBLEMS WITH gotFocus AND lostFocus

The gotFocus and lostFocus Events are not correctly generated for all Components in version 1.02 of the Java language on all hardware, so programmers should be cautious in using them.

PRECAUTIONS WITH MOUSE EVENTS

Note that the x and y mouse positions are relative to the upper-left corner of the component, which is receiving the Event — the position is adjusted as the event is passed up the chain of containers. Many components handle mouse events internally — in our previous example, only the Canvas would pass MOUSE_DOWN events to the Applet.

SOME STANDARD COMPONENTS

The following sections explain some standard Java components.

LABEL

A Label Object is used to put constant text on a display. Be sure to set the color and font before adding the label to the display if you want other than the default values.

* **public Label(String str)** Create a Label object with the string left justified.
* **public Label(String str, int align)** As above but with alignment specified Label.LEFT, Label.CENTER, or Label.RIGHT.

BUTTON

Button objects are drawn and managed by the underlying operating system. When a Button is clicked on, an ACTION_EVENT event is generated.

* **public Button(String label)** Generates a Button object with a centered label.

CHECKBOX AND CHECKBOXGROUP

Checkbox objects provide a handy way of setting parameters in an applet. Check boxes are managed partly by the underlying operating system and partly by Java routines. Java handles the CheckBoxGroup object which lets you set up groups of check boxes from which only one may be checked at one time (also known as "radio buttons"). Here are the constructors for Checkbox and CheckboxGroup:

* **public Checkbox()** Creates an unlabeled check box, defaults to unselected.

* **public Checkbox(String label)** Creates a check box with label to the right.

* **public Checkbox(String label, CheckboxGroup grp, boolean state)** Creates a check box as a member of a group, with specified initial selection state. If grp is a valid CheckboxGroup, the appearance of the check box will be as a "radio button."

* **public CheckboxGroup()** CheckboxGroup objects do not have labels or show up on the screen, they just provide a logical group.

The following methods allow the programmer to set or read the state of a Checkbox object:

* **public String getLabel()** Returns the label string.

* **public boolean getState()** Returns true if the check box is selected.

* **public void setLabel(String label)** Changes the label on the check box and redisplays it.

* **public void setState(boolean st)** Changes the selection state of the check box.

CheckboxGroup objects have two convenient methods:

* **public Checkbox getCurrent()** This CheckboxGroup method returns the currently selected Checkbox object.

* **public synchronized void setCurrent(Checkbox bx)** Ensures this Checkbox is the only one in the group selected.

LIST

The List object provides for display of a list of selectable strings. If the list has more strings than can be shown in the available space, a scroll bar is provided. Although methods are provided for removing and replacing strings, users have reported that these methods do not always work as expected on all operating systems with version 1.02 of Java. There are two constructors for List objects:

* **public List()** Creates a List object of unspecified size.

* **public List(int nrows, boolean multiflag)** Creates a List object that requests a size sufficient to show nrows of text.

Methods for adding Strings to lists follow. When a list item is selected or double-clicked, the Event which is generated has the String for the "arg" object, thus the programmer should keep copies of the strings being put in the list for the purpose of later determining which string has been selected.

* **public synchronized void addItem(String itm)** Adds this String to the list at the bottom.

* **public synchronized void addItem(String itm, int ndx)** The String takes the specified position in the list, with ndx = 0 the top position. If the ndx specified is larger than the current list size, the String is added at the bottom of the list.

* **public int countItems()** Returns the number of items in the list.

* **public String getItem(int ndx)** Returns the String at the specified index. This function is not protected against out-of-range values of ndx, so be sure ndx < countItems().

* **public synchronized void clear()** Removes all items from the list. Problems with this function have been reported by numerous users.

* **public synchronized void delItem(int position)** Removes the item at position. This function is not protected against out-of-range values of position, so be sure position < countItems().

The following methods provide for access to the selected item or items in a List object.

* **public synchronized int getSelectedIndex()** Returns the index of current selection or -1 if nothing has been selected.

* **public synchronized int[] getSelectedIndexes()** Returns an int array with an entry for each selected item. The array has length zero if none is selected.

* **public synchronized String getSelectedItem()** Returns the currently selected string or null if none has been selected.

* **public synchronized String[] getSelectedItems()** Returns an array of Strings.

* **public void makeVisible(int ndx)** Ensures that the specified Item is visible in the List object but does not change the selection status.

* **public synchronized void select(int ndx)** Sets the status of the specified item to selected.

Scrollbar

Scrollbar objects are implemented by the underlying operating system so the programmer's approach must be indirect. The Scrollbar class defines constants HORIZONTAL and VERTICAL to indicate orientation.

* **public Scrollbar(int oriented, int value, int visible, int min, int max)** Constructs a Scrollbar object set at the initial value, with the

specified minimum and maximum values. If the "visible" parameter is nonzero, the width of the Scrollbar "thumb" is adjusted to indicate approximately what fraction of the total area is currently visible. By default the "line increment" is 1 and the "page increment" is 10.

* **public void setLineIncrement(int n)** Sets the line increment. We have observed that Scrollbar objects behave more reliably if this method is called, rather than relying on the default behavior.

* **public void setPageIncrement(int p)** Sets the amount to scroll when the scroll bar is clicked above or below the "thumb."

* **public void setValue(int val)** Moves the scroll bar to this value. If the value is out of the specified maximum/minimum range, the scroll bar is moved to the limit.

* **public int getValue()** Gets the present setting.

Layout managers and containers

LayoutManager objects are attached to Containers and are responsible for arranging Components within the Container. Java provides LayoutManagers to make it possible for the programmer's graphical interface design to work on a variety of hardware platforms with different display resolutions and system fonts. You don't have to use a LayoutManager; many of the current crop of Java graphic layout programs position components by absolute pixel addresses, but a LayoutManager will give the most consistent appearance on a variety of hardware.

Programmers don't work with Container objects directly, but with one of the three derived classes: Panel, Frame, or Dialog. Containers maintain a list of Component objects they contain; this list controls the order in which objects are displayed. You add components to a container with one of the three following forms:

* **public synchronized Component add(Component c)** Adds the component at the end of the list.

* **public synchronized Component add(Component c, int pos)** Adds the component to the container's list at the specified position.

* **public synchronized Component add(String name, Component c)** Adds the component with an associated name which can be used to control a LayoutManager. Not all LayoutManagers pay attention to names.

If you are going to use a LayoutManager in a container, you should create it and add it before any components are added to the container. In general, you never need to call any LayoutManager instance functions, each is called as needed by the container that owns it.

STANDARD LIBRARY LAYOUTMANAGER CLASSES

The following sections explain some of the standard library LayoutManager classes.

FLOWLAYOUT

This is the default for Containers: components are added from left to right until the horizontal space is filled, and then they start on a new line. The constructors are:

* **FlowLayout()** Uses default left alignment
* **FlowLayout(int flag)** Where flag = FlowLayout.CENTER, FlowLayout.LEFT, or FlowLayout.RIGHT
* **FlowLayout(int flag, int xgap, int ygap)** In addition to the alignment flag, this constructor specifies the amount of space (in pixels) to be left between components in horizontal and vertical directions.

BORDERLAYOUT

This is typically used for positioning scroll bars, buttons, and labels around a central component. You specify where the component goes using string literal names "Center," "North," "East," "South," and "West." There are two constructors for BorderLayout objects.

* **BorderLayout()** Uses no space between components.
* **BorderLayout(int xgap, int ygap)** Specifies the space to be inserted between components.

CARDLAYOUT

Provides for switching between groups of components like a Windows "tabbed dialog." This is useful when the number of components which have to be displayed is too large for a single screen. Typically, the components added to a CardLayout would be Panels, each containing other components and having its own LayoutManager. The constructors are:

* **CardLayout()** Uses no space at the edges.
* **CardLayout(int xgap, int ygap)** Allows specified gap on all sides of the "cards."

To control which component is displayed next, add them with unique names and use the show method. You can also move through the "cards" with first, last, previous, and next — these are exceptions to the rule that LayoutManager methods are not called directly.

- **public void show(Container parent, String name)** Displays the named component.
- **public void first(Container parent)** Shows the first component added.
- **public void last(Container parent)** Shows the last component added.
- **public void next(Container parent)** Moves through the list in the order components were added.
- **public void previous(Container parent)** Moves backward through the list.

GRIDLAYOUT

Components in a GridLayout are arranged in uniform cells in rows and columns. If either the number of rows or number of columns is 0 in the constructor, the LayoutManager adjusts the actual number of rows or columns to fit the total number of components added. The constructors are:

- **GridLayout(int rows, int cols)** Creates a grid with no gaps between components.
- **GridLayout(int rows, int cols, int xgap, int ygap)** Creates a grid with specified gap between components.

GRIDBAGLAYOUT

Similar to the GridLayout but adjacent cells can be merged. Managing a GridBagLayout is very complex and uses an auxiliary class "GridBag Constraints." Programming a GridBagLayout is beyond the scope of this book.

Graphics in Java

Java provides a large number of classes related to graphic screen elements.

ENCAPSULATING GEOMETRY

The classes Point, Dimension, Insets, Polygon, and Rectangle all are simple classes which encapsulate some aspect of screen geometry. In Java geometry, the x dimension increases to the right and y increases down. The upper-left corner of any container is 0,0 to the components inside it.

POINT

A Point object has public int variables x and y — Points can be created and manipulated by the following methods:

- **public Point(int x, int y)** Creates a Point.

* **public void move(int x, int y)**   Changes the x and y values in a Point.

* **public void translate(int dx, int dy)**   Moves the point by adding the specified increments.

DIMENSION

A Dimension object has public int variables width and height. The chief use of the Dimension objects is for components to specify their preferred and minimum size requirements.

* **public Dimension(int width, int height)**   Creates a Dimension object.

INSETS

An Insets object has public int variables representing the inside margins on top, left, bottom, and right edges of a Container. These objects are used in LayoutManagers.

* **public Insets(int top, int left, int bottom, int right)**   Creates an Insets object.

POLYGON

A Polygon object encapsulates an array of points and is typically used in drawing custom shapes on the screen. The points can be specified at the time of construction or can be added using the addPoint method. For the purposes of the inside method, the last point is considered connected to the first.

* **public Polygon()**   Constructs an empty Polygon.

* **public Polygon(int[] xpoints, int[] ypoints, int npoints)** Constructs a polygon with arrays of x and y values.

* **public void addPoint(int x, int y)**   Adds a new point to the end of the internal list.

* **public Rectangle getBoundingBox()**   Returns a Rectangle which encloses all points in the Polygon.

* **public boolean inside(int x, int y)**   Returns true if the specified point would lie inside the Polygon.

RECTANGLE

A Rectangle object has int variables representing the position of the upper-left corner, the width and the height. Rectangles are used to represent graphical "clipping" areas and bounding boxes.

* **public Rectangle()** Creates a Rectangle with all variables zero.
* **public Rectangle(int x, int y, int width, int height)** Creates a Rectangle at the specified position with the specified size.
* **public Rectangle(int width, int height)** Creates a Rectangle at 0,0 with the specified width and height.
* **public Rectangle(Point p, Dimension d)** Creates a Rectangle with upper-left corner at p, width and height from d.
* **public Rectangle(Point p)** Creates a Rectangle with upper-left corner at p, zero width and height.
* **public Rectangle(Dimension d)** Creates a Rectangle at 0,0 with width and height from d.

Instance methods are available to move and alter the size of Rectangles and to perform several tests useful in graphic functions.

* **public void add(int x, int y)** Enlarges the Rectangle so it includes the original corners plus the new point. Similar "add" functions can add a Point object or a Rectangle object.
* **public void grow(int delx, int dely)** Expands the Rectangle in all directions — it ends up larger horizontally by 2× delx and vertically by 2× dely.
* **public void move(int x, int y)** Moves the upper-left corner to this position; width and height stay the same.
* **public void resize(int width, int height)** Changes the width and height while the upper-left corner stays put.
* **public void reshape(int x, int y, int width, int height)** Changes all the variables.
* **public void translate(int delx, int dely)** Moves the rectangle by adding to the x and y coordinates.
* **public boolean inside(int x, int y)** Returns true if the point is inside the Rectangle.
* **public boolean isEmpty( )** Returns true if this Rectangle has zero or negative width and height.
* **public boolean intersects(Rectangle r2)** Returns true if this Rectangle overlaps Rectangle r2 by at least one pixel.

* **public Rectangle intersection(Rectangle r2)** Creates a new Rectangle representing the area where two Rectangles overlap. Width and/or height will be zero or negative if the two do not overlap.

* **public Rectangle union(Rectangle r2)** Creates a new Rectangle which includes all the points of both this one and r2.

GRAPHICS OBJECTS

The class which connects the hardware-independent AWT functions to the underlying operating system on a particular computer is called Graphics. All screen display and off-screen drawing is done via a Graphics object. Java components draw themselves on the screen with a Graphics object supplied by the system when the system calls the update method.

* **public void update(Graphics g)** Using the Graphics object supplied, clears your area to the background color; then it calls paint().

* **public void paint(Graphics g)** Paints all your foreground items such as borders, text, and so on. This is the method normally overridden when creating a custom screen component.

CLIPPING

Graphics objects incorporate a "clipping" rectangle that they can paint inside. When the system calls a component's update method, the Graphics object clipping rectangle has been set to the area which the system thinks needs to be redrawn. This could be as large as the entire component or as small as a corner which has just been uncovered by movement of another window. You can reduce the size of the clipping rectangle by calling the graphics method:

* **public void clipRect(int x, int y, int width, int height)** Sets the clipping rectangle to the intersection of the old clipping rectangle and the specified rectangle.

It is important to note that the result of clipRect is always a smaller clipping rectangle, you cannot expand the clipping rectangle attached to a Graphics object. For this reason, programmers who want to work with clipping rectangles use one of the following methods to get a working copy of a Graphics object.

* **public Graphics create()** Clones the Graphics object.

* **public Graphics create(int x, int y, int width, int height)** Clones the object and adjusts the clipping rectangle as in clipRect.

COLORS

Graphics objects always draw in a certain color. In the standard Component update method, this color is set to the component's background color to clear the rectangle; then set to the foreground color to call paint. Java provides a few standard colors, plus methods for creating custom Color objects which we discuss later.

* **public void setColor(Color c)** Sets the working color.

GRAPHICS PRIMITIVES

The Java Graphics class provides many of the usual primitive operations which draw in the current Color. There is no provision for changing the line width in any of these methods. Here are some of the most commonly used methods.

* **public void drawLine(int x1, int y1, int x2, int y2)** Draws a single pixel wide line between two points.
* **public void drawOval(int x, int y, int width, int height)** Draws an oval within the specified bounding box. There is a similar fillOval method.
* **public void drawPolygon(int[] xpts, int[] ypts, int npoints)** Draws lines to connect the points in order, but does not connect the first and last points.
* **public void drawPolygon(Polygon p)** Same as above, but uses a Polygon object.
* **public void fillPolygon(int[] xpts, int[] ypts, int npoints)** Draws a filled polygon including a connection between the first and last points. There is a similar method with Polygon object input.
* **public void drawRect(int x, int y, int width, int height)** Draws the specified rectangle — there is a similar fillRect method.

DRAWING TEXT

A Graphics object always has an associated Font used for text-drawing functions. The basic text-drawing methods provide for using Strings, char arrays, or byte arrays as text sources. The x and y positions in these methods define the start of a *baseline* for the characters, *not* the upper-left corner as in the drawRect method. Characters with descenders will be partly below this baseline. The spacing of characters depends on the font selected. Java does not maintain an "insertion point" or handle "carriage return/linefeed," so it is completely up to the programmer to locate text on the screen. The FontMetrics class is provided to assist you but complex text displays will probably require some experimentation.

* **public void drawString(String str, int x, int y)** Draws the string on the baseline defined by x and y.
* **public void drawBytes(byte[] b, int offset, int length, int x, int y)** Draws characters from the byte array starting at offset.

* **public void drawChars(char[] c. int offset, int length, int x, int y)** Draws characters from the char array starting at offset.
* **public FontMetrics getFontMetrics()** Creates a FontMetrics object for the current font. The use of FontMetrics in positioning text is discussed later.

DRAWING IMAGES

One of the reasons for the popularity of Java applets on Web pages is the ease with which images can be incorporated in displays such as animation. The graphics methods for displaying images follow. The Image and ImageObserver classes are described later, so don't worry about the "status of the Image object."

* **public boolean drawImage(Image img, int x, int y, ImageObserver obs)** The Image is drawn with upper-left corner at the x,y point at its native resolution. The color which appears on the screen may not match the original, due to browser limitations. The boolean value returned is related to the status of the Image object; if the image was incomplete, false is returned.
* **public boolean drawImage(Image img, int x, int y, int width, int height, ImageObserver obs)** Same as above, except that the Image is expanded or contracted to fill the specified width and height.
* **public boolean drawImage(Image img, int x, int y, Color bkg, ImageObserver obs)** Same as above, except that if a pixel in the image is transparent, the bkg color is substituted.
* **public boolean drawImage(Image img, int x, int y, int width, int height, Color bkg, ImageObserver obs)** Same as above, except that if a pixel in the image is transparent, the bkg color is substituted.

MISCELLANEOUS GRAPHICS METHODS

Although Java has garbage collection methods which eventually dispose of unused memory objects, Graphics objects tie up operating system resources which may be in shorter supply than memory. Therefore, it is considered good practice to dispose of extra Graphics objects obtained by such methods as "create" or "getGraphics" when they are no longer needed. You should not dispose of the Graphics object passed to `update` or `paint` by the system.

* **public void dispose()** Discards system resources associated with this Graphics object.
* **public void copyArea(int x, int y, ine width, int height, int dx, int dy)** Copies a rectangular area of the screen. Note that dx and dy define a displacement, not a new origin point.

FONTS AND FONTMETRICS

All text displays in graphical Java programs are done with fonts described with Font objects. Fonts are requested from the Java "Toolkit" by name, style, and point size. At the present state of development, Java programmers cannot use the full range of fonts present on typical operating system. You should expect to find Helvetica, Times Roman, Courier, and Dialog, or something close to them. If you ask for a font which the system can't supply, you get a default font, probably Helvetica. Courier will probably be the only monospaced font available and will thus be the font of choice for tables.

> ✳ **public Font(String name, int style, int size)** Creates a new font object as close as possible to the requested font. Style is specified with constants in the Font class — Font.PLAIN, Font.BOLD, Font.ITALIC, or Font.BOLD + Font.ITALIC.

You can also get and set the current Font object associated with any object derived from Component or from a Graphics object. If you want buttons or labels displayed with a particular Font, you should set the Font before the object is first displayed.

THE IMAGE CLASS AND MEDIATRACKER

Image objects represent an image in a hardware-independent fashion. Images are not constructed directly, but they can be obtained by reading one of the supported graphic file types or by the createImage method in the Component class. Working with Image objects is complicated by Java's special adaptations to optimize the behavior of applets on Web pages. This can best be illustrated by the following code which might appear in an applet:

```
public class myApplet extends Applet {
Image Logo ;
init() {
   Logo = getImage( getCodeBase(), "logo.gif");
... // more initialization..
} ;

public void paint( Graphics g ){
  g.drawImage( Logo, 0, 0, this );
...
}
```

Contrary to what you might expect, when this code is executed, the browser does not immediately start downloading the gif file, instead, the Image object is constructed with the URL information and the program continues. No attempt is made to download the image until the Image is actually needed. This approach greatly speeds the initial display of the applet at the cost of some complexity.

When the first attempt to draw this Image is made, presumably in the `paint` method, Java recognizes that it is not yet in memory and will start a separate thread to load it. The drawImage routine will probably display a large blank area. As increasing chunks of the image become available, the system will call the paint routine, resulting in the familiar gradual appearance of the image. And how does the system know to call paint again, you may inquire? It is because of the ImageObserver interface that is implemented in Component and inherited by Applet. Recall that drawImage takes an ImageObserver as a parameter; that is why we use "this" in the previous call to drawImage. As the thread loading the Logo image completes a new chunk of image, it notifies the `imageUpdate` method in the Applet, which in turn calls `repaint`, requesting that the system call `paint`.

USING A MEDIATRACKER OBJECT

For situations in which the progressive display of an image is not desirable, Java provides a mechanism called MediaTracker to force immediate loading of an image. Here is what our code might look like with a MediaTracker object:

```
init() {
    MediaTracker MT = new MediaTracker( this ) ;
    Logo = getImage( getCodeBase(), "logo.gif");
    MT.addImage( Logo, 0 );
    MT.waitForID( 0 ) ;   // alternately MT.waitForAll() ;
    ...   // more initialization..
    } ;
```

This forces the thread executing init to wait until the image is fully loaded.

MEMORY IMAGES

Java provides for creating arbitrary images in memory which can be drawn to the screen just like loaded images. The following code illustrates creating an Image, getting a Graphics object to draw into it, and performing some graphic operations. This is the "double-buffering" technique used for smooth animation.

```
Image memImg ;
void makeImg(){
  memImg = createImage( 200, 100 );
  Graphic tg = memImg.getGraphics();
  tg.setColor( Color.black ) ;
  tg.fillRect( 0, 0, 200, 100 ) ;
  tg.setColor( Color.red ) ;
```

```
      tg.drawRect( 10, 10, 180, 80 );
      tg.drawString( "Hey!", 30, 60 );
      tg.dispose();
  }
  public void paint( Graphics g ){
      g.drawImage( memImg, 0, 0, this );
  }
```

GETTING IMAGE SIZE

Because the system may not have determined the final size of an Image being loaded, the following methods return –1 if the requested information is not available. In that case, the imageUpdate method of the object passed as ImageObserver is called when the height or width is known.

* **public int getHeight(ImageObserver obs)** Returns image height in pixels or minus 1.

* **public int getWidth(ImageObserver obs)** Returns image width in pixels or minus 1.

IMAGE MANIPULATION CLASSES

Java provides a number of image processing classes in the java.awt.image package; these classes allow programmers to manipulate images down to the individual pixels. Because the logic of connecting these classes together is beyond an introductory-level book, we give code examples you can copy without having to worry about ImageProducer and ImageConsumer interfaces.

CROPIMAGEFILTER

The CropImageFilter provides for the creation of a new Image from a specified area of an existing image. In the following example, Orig is an existing Image — we create a CropImageFilter that is attached to a FilteredImageSource and an existing Image object.

```
CropImageFilter crF = new CropImageFilter( x,y,width,height );
Image newI = createImage(new FilteredImageSource(Orig.getSource(),crFA));
```

It is frequently convenient to have a Java applet read a single GIF file image which consists of multiple small images, then dissect the large image into the constituent small ones using CropImageFilter objects. The time saved in reading only one image file over the Net more than compensates for the time required to cut the image up.

CONVERTING AN IMAGE TO AN ARRAY IN MEMORY

The PixelGrabber class can extract a rectangular array of pixels from an Image into an array of 32-bit integers. Each integer corresponds to a pixel and can be examined and modified, then the array can be turned back into an Image. Here is a code fragment showing the creation of an array large enough to hold an image, and extraction from "Orig" using a PixelGrabber. We assume the "Orig" Image has been completely loaded in memory.

```java
int w = Orig.getWidth( this ) ;
int h = Orig.getHeight( this ) ;
int npix = w * h ;
int pixels[] = new int[ npix ] ;
int offset = 0 ; // offset in array to start at
int scansz =  w ; // size of scanline to take - in this case all
PixelGrabber PG = new PixelGrabber( Orig, x, y, w, h, pixels,
   offset, scansz );
try{ PG.grabPixels();
} catch(InterruptedException ex){
}
```

MANIPULATING A PIXEL

Each int has color data for a single pixel, with 8 bits each for Red, Green, Blue and Alpha components. "Alpha Component?" you ask — this is where it gets interesting. The Alpha component represents the opacity of a pixel, a value of 255 being totally opaque and 0 totally transparent. When the screen drawing routines rendering an Image encounter a transparent pixel, they don't change the screen pixel. GIF images can be created with a transparent color, or we can selectively set pixels to totally or partially transparent in the integer array created from an Image. Continuing with the previous example, the following code illustrates taking a pixel apart into constituents, exchanging blue for green, and turning transparent all pixels with red greater than 10.

```java
int red, green, blue, alpha ;
for( int i = 0 ; i < npix ; i++ ) {

  alpha = pixel[ i ] & 0xFF000000 ; // mask off alpha value
  red     = ( pixel[ i ] & 0x00FF0000 ) > 16 ;  /* shift red
  intensity to low 8 bits*/
  green = ( pixel[ i ] & 0x0000FF00 ) >   8 ;
  blue    =      pixel[i] & 0x000000FF ;
  if( red > 10 ) {
    pixel[i] = pixel[i] & 0x00FFFFFF ;
  }
  else { // note blue now in green byte location
```

```
    pixel[i] = alpha + ( red << 16) + ( blue << 8 ) + green ;
  }
```

RGBIMAGEFILTER

The most common type of Image input to a Java program is a GIF format file.
This format provides 256 colors in an "IndexColorModel" — this means that an
8-bit integer is used as an index to select a color from a color table. The
RGBImageFilter provides for changing any color in the color table and can
manipulate the Alpha channel as well.

The following code (SubsFilter.java) illustrates the use of an RGBImageFilter
to substitute a custom color in an Image. In this example, we substitute a color
for pure blue.

TIP   **If we substituted transparent for blue, we would have part of the "blue
screen" movie special effects toolkit.**

```
import java.awt.image.*;
import java.awt.*;

public class SubsFilter extends RGBImageFilter{

  Color   subsC ; // this color is substituted

  public SubsFilter( Color c ) {
    canFilterIndexColorModel = true;
    subsC = c ;
  }

  // note - Alpha channel 0xFF = solid, 0 = transparent
  public int filterRGB (int x, int y, int rgb) {
    int alpha = rgb & 0xff000000 ;
    if( alpha == 0 ) {  // true if the transparent color of GIF
        return rgb ;
    }
    int red   = (rgb & 0xff0000) > 16;
    int green = (rgb &   0xff00) >  8;
    int blue  =  rgb &     0xff;
    if((red == 0 ) && ( green == 0 ) && (blue == 255) ){
        red   = subsC.getRed();
        green = subsC.getGreen();
        blue  = subsC.getBlue();
    }
    return (alpha | (red << 16) | (green <<  8) | blue);
  }
}
```

Here is a code fragment showing the use of this filter to substitute red for blue in the "OrigI" Image.

```
try {
SubsFilter gf = new SubsFilter( Color.red ) ;
Image NewI = createImage(new
   FilteredImageSource(OrigI.getSource(), gf));
} catch (InterruptedException ex ){}
```

CREATING AN IMAGE FROM AN ARRAY IN MEMORY

We extracted pixels from an Image to an array of int with PixelGrabber. To re-create an Image we use a MemoryImageSource object. Here is a code fragment using the variable names we used in the PixelGrabber example.

 TIP Because creating an Image from the int array is slow we use a MediaTracker to wait for the complete Image.

```
MediaTracker MT = new MediaTracker( this ) ;
MemoryImageSource MIS = new MemoryImageSource(w,h,pixels, 0, w);
Image newImg = createImage( MIS );
MT.addImage( newImg, 0 ) ;
try {  MT.waitForID( 0 );
}catch( InterruptedException ex){    }
```

THE APPLET CLASS

The Applet class, which resides in the java.awt.applet package, provides many handy routines for supporting typical Applet functions. If you are writing a Java applet, you'll create a class derived from Applet. Here is a quick summary of commonly used applet methods.

* **public URL getCodeBase()** Returns a URL object based on the location of the Applet class file.

* **public URL getDocumentBase()** Returns a URL object based on the location of the HTML document in which the Applet is embedded.

* **public AudioClip getAudioClip(URL url)** Creates an AudioClip object from a URL; returns null if there is a problem.

* **public AudioClip getAudioClip(URL url, String name)** Similar to the above but used when the URL refers to a document or applet code and the name is a filename of a file located with the document or code.

* **public Image getImage(URL url)** Creates an Image object from a URL; returns null if there is a problem.

- **public Image getImage(URL url, String name)**   Similar to the previous example but used when the URL refers to a document or applet code and name is the filename of a file located with the document or code.
- **public String getParameter(String name)**   Creates a String object from data passed in the HTML applet tag.

Organizing Those Java Objects

The standard Java library provides some basic classes for organizing objects. This library is not as extensive as older OO languages such as Smalltalk, but it's a good start. These classes are used extensively in the internals of Java.

Vector and stack

The Vector class provides for keeping track of a collection of objects when you don't know in advance how large the collection will be or the type of objects that will be in the collection. The Stack class extends Vector with typical stack functions. Internally, Vectors manage an array of type Object, creating a new array and copying existing data whenever the array must change size.

THE VECTOR CLASS

Vectors expand to hold the number of objects required, but this process can be made more efficient if you know roughly the size needed.

CONSTRUCTORS

- **public Vector()**   Constructs a Vector with default capacity of ten objects and a default increment strategy of doubling.
- **public Vector(int initial)**   Constructs a Vector with specified capacity and the default increment strategy of doubling.
- **public Vector(int initial, int increment)**   Constructs a Vector with capacity for "initial" objects which will be expanded in "increment" jumps. If "increment" is zero, the doubling strategy is followed.

CLASS METHODS

- **public final synchronized void addElement(Object obj)**   Adds the object at the end of the internal array.
- **public final synchronized void insertElementAt(Object obj, int ndx)**   The Object is inserted at this position, bumping all others at or above ndx up one.

* **public final synchronized int capacity()** Returns the current array size. Note that this is not the available space.

* **public final synchronized void ensureCapacity(int minCap)** Ensures that the Vector has at least this capacity by incrementing if necessary.

* **public final boolean isEmpty()** Returns true if there are no Objects stored.

* **public final int size()** Returns the number of Objects in the Vector.

* **public final boolean contains(Object obj)** Returns true if this object is in the Vector.

* **public final int indexOf(Object obj)** Returns the index of this object in the Vector or minus 1 if it is not found.

* **public final synchronized void copyInto(Object[] array)** Copies all the objects into a separate array. The programmer must ensure the array is large enough.

* **public final synchronized Object firstElement()** Returns the first Object in the vector. Note that the vector does not remove the Object.

* **public final synchronized Object elementAt(int ndx)** Returns the Object at this index. The programmer is responsible for ensuring the index is valid.

* **public final synchronized Object lastElement()** Returns the Object at the end of the vector.

* **public final synchronized Enumeration elements()** Creates an Enumeration object which can iterate over the entire set of objects.

* **public final synchronized boolean removeElement(Object obj)** Removes this Object from the Vector; returns false if the Object is not found.

* **public final synchronized void removeElementAt(int ndx)** Removes the Object at this position. The programmer is responsible for ensuring the index is valid.

* **public final synchronized void setSize(int newSize)** If newSize is less than the number of Objects in the Vector, the excess is discarded. If it is more, this acts like ensureCapacity.

* **public final synchronized void trimToSize()** Adjusts the internal array to the exact size needed.

* **public synchronized Object clone()** Creates a Vector which is a clone of the original — this is returned as an "Object" to fit the definition of the Cloneable interface but should be cast to a Vector.

TIP This does not copy the Objects in the Vector, only the references to the Objects.

THE STACK CLASS

This extends the Vector class to create a last-in-first-out stack of Objects with a capacity as large as needed. Since this is an extension of Vector, you can also use the Vector methods to look at or modify the Stack.

* **public Stack()** Creates a Stack with default size 10.
* **public Object peek()** Returns a reference to the top Object.
* **public Object pop()** Returns the top Object and removes the Object from the stack.
* **public Object push(Object obj)** Places the Object on the top of the stack.
* **public boolean empty()** Returns true if the Stack is empty.
* **public int search(Object obj)** Searches down from the top of the stack to find a reference to the Object. If found, the int is the relative position in the stack with 1 = top. If the Object is not found, it returns minus 1.

THE HASHTABLE CLASS

The purpose of this class is to store Objects with an associated key and efficiently locate an Object by a key. All Java objects have a "hashCode" method which returns an int which is likely (but not guaranteed to be) unique to that object. Hashtables make use of this hashCode method, plus some additional testing to ensure that an Object stored with a unique key will always be retrievable by that key. An example of Hashtable use in programming might be maintaining a list of employees names and addresses keyed by social security number.

Hashtables, like Vectors, expand as needed. To ensure efficient storage and retrieval, the table should always have a proportion of open slots. The target for this proportion is called the load factor.

HASHTABLE CONSTRUCTORS

* **public Hashtable()** Constructs a Hashtable with default size of 101 entries and a load factor of 0.75.
* **public Hashtable(int capacity)** Constructs a Hashtable with specified initial size and the default load factor.
* **public Hashtable(int capacity, float loadfactor)** Constructs a Hashtable with specified initial size and load factor.

* **public synchronized Object put(Object key, Object value)**
  Stores the value object under this key. Returns any Object which might have been stored under this key before or null if the key has not been used before.
* **public synchronized Object get(Object key)** Returns the Object stored under this key or null if there is none.
* **public synchronized boolean containsKey(Object key)** Returns true if this key is in use.
* **public synchronized boolean contains(Object value)** Uses an exhaustive examination of all stored Objects to return true if this Object is in the table.

THE ENUMERATION INTERFACE

The Enumeration interface defines the methods needed to iterate through a set of values from one of the collection classes such as Vector and Hashtable. Only two methods are needed:

* **public abstract boolean hasMoreElements()** Returns true if there are more elements.
* **public abstract Object nextElement()** Returns the next object — it is the programmer's responsibility to check for the existence of more elements before calling this method.

These methods are "abstract" — each class implementing the Enumeration interface must supply a version of these methods suitable to its content. You should not use the Enumeration methods if you are modifying the collection object at the same time.

Learning the Ins and Outs of Input and Output

The standard Java library contains a large number of I/O-related classes grouped in the java.io package and the java.net package. The number of separate methods is too large for an exhaustive listing, so the following is a quick survey.

The Stream classes

The basic concept of the stream classes is that of reading or writing a stream of bytes. These classes do not provide for skipping about in files or simultaneously reading and writing data to the same file. The following is a list of the InputStream classes and a short description of how they are used.

INPUTSTREAM-BASED CLASSES

The following sections examine the InputStream-based classes.

INPUTSTREAM

This is the superclass from which all input streams classes are derived. All input streams support the following methods:

* **public int available()** Returns the number of bytes which can be read immediately (without blocking).
* **public void close()** Closes the stream. Once closed, the object cannot be reused. Programmers should be sure to always close a stream to let the operating system recover possibly scarce resources.
* **public boolean markSupported()** Returns true if this stream supports "mark" and "reset" methods.
* **public synchronized void mark(int readlim)** Creates a single "bookmark" in the stream which can be returned to as long as you don't read more than readlim bytes. This is typically used to hold a place while you read ahead in a file to see what the content is. The programmer is responsible for staying within the readlim limits.
* **public synchronized void reset()** Resets the stream to the previously set mark.
* **public int read(byte[] buf)** Reads into a byte array and returns the number of bytes read.
* **public int read(byte[] buf, int off, int len)** Reads up to len bytes into the array starting at buf[offset]. Returns the number actually read.
* **public long skip(long nb)** Reads and discards nb bytes from the stream. This is not a very fast process.

FILEINPUTSTREAM

Supports reading local files as an InputStream. Constructors provide for opening a file based on file name, a File object, or a FileDescriptor object.

* **public FileInputStream(String name)** Attempts to open a file by name, throwing a FileNotFoundException if it fails.
* **public FileInputStream(File f)** Attempts to open a file using a File object, throwing a FileNotFoundException if it fails.

* **public FileInputStream(FileDescriptor fd)** Constructs a FileInputStream based on an existing FileDescriptor object for an open file.

PipedInputStream

 This class works with a PipedOutputStream to create a "pipe" — useful for communication of data between threads. We use these in Chapter 11.

ByteArrayInputStream

Use this class to gain access to a byte array in memory as if it were a file. Naturally, there is a ByteArrayOutputStream, too.

SequenceInputStream

This class provides a way of seamlessly combining data streams from more than one input stream. Any number of input streams can be specified in the constructor.

FilterInputStream

This class provides a base class from which streams that perform filtering functions can be defined. FilterInputStream objects are created with an open InputStream of some type as input.

BufferedInputStream

This highly useful class, derived from FilterInputStream, provides for buffering data so that many bytes can be read between actual disk or network access. This is particularly recommended for network connections.

* **public BufferedInputStream(InputStream ins)** A constructor based on an open InputStream, it uses the default buffer size of 2048 bytes.
* **public BufferedInputStream(InputStream ins, int bufsz)** Same as the preceding example, but with user-specified buffer size.

DataInputStream

The DataInputStream class, which is derived from FilterInputStream, implements methods used for reading the Java primitives such as int, long, and float variables from binary input streams. It also has the commonly used readLine method, which creates a String object by reading ASCII text until a carriage return, newline, or carriage return/newline pair is encountered.

✳ public FileInputStream(FileDescriptor fd) Constructs a FileInputStream based on an existing FileDescriptor object for an open file.

PipedInputStream

 This class works with a PipedOutputStream to create a "pipe" — useful for communication of data between threads. We use these in Chapter 11.

ByteArrayInputStream

Use this class to gain access to a byte array in memory as if it were a file. Naturally, there is a ByteArrayOutputStream, too.

SequenceInputStream

This class provides a way of seamlessly combining data streams from more than one input stream. Any number of input streams can be specified in the constructor.

FilterInputStream

This class provides a base class from which streams that perform filtering functions can be defined. FilterInputStream objects are created with an open InputStream of some type as input.

BufferedInputStream

This highly useful class, derived from FilterInputStream, provides for buffering data so that many bytes can be read between actual disk or network access. This is particularly recommended for network connections.

✳ public BufferedInputStream(InputStream ins) A constructor based on an open InputStream, it uses the default buffer size of 2048 bytes.

✳ public BufferedInputStream(InputStream ins, int bufsz) Same as the preceding example, but with user-specified buffer size.

DataInputStream

The DataInputStream class, which is derived from FilterInputStream, implements methods used for reading the Java primitives such as int, long, and float variables from binary input streams. It also has the commonly used readLine method, which creates a String object by reading ASCII text until a carriage return, newline, or carriage return/newline pair is encountered.

OutputStream

This is the superclass from which all output streams are derived. All OutputStreams implement the following methods:

 TIP Instead of returning error conditions, these classes throw Exceptions of the IOException type. Example code for dealing with IOExceptions is shown in Chapter 11.

* **public close()** Closes the stream. This should be the last action performed on a stream since it cannot be reopened once closed.
* **public flush()** Ensures that any buffered bytes are actually written.
* **public void write(int b)** Writes a single byte — the low-order byte of the int. Note that this and the following write routines block until the output is accomplished.
* **public write(byte[] buf)** Writes the entire contents of a byte array.
* **public write(byte[] buf, int offset, int len)** Writes len bytes starting with buf[offset].

FileOutputStream

Provides for writing a stream to a disk file specified by filename, a File object, or a FileDescriptor object. Typically, an opened FileOutputStream is used to create a DataOutputStream or PrintOutputStream for greater flexibility in writing data.

PipedOutputStream

 X-REF This class works with a PipedInputStream to create a "pipe" mechanism typically used for communication of data between threads. An example appears in Chapter 11.

ByteArrayOutputStream

Use this class to write to a byte array in memory as if it were a file.

FilterOutputStream

The base class used for output streams which perform filtering functions. FilterOutputStream objects are created from an opened OutputStream of some type.

BufferedOutputStream

This class is useful for buffering data, so that many bytes can be written between actual disk or network accesses. As with the BufferedInputStream you can specify buffer size or use the default.

* **public BufferedOutputStream(OutputStream outs)** Constructs a BufferedOutputStream based on the open OutputStream with buffer size of 2048 bytes.
* **public BufferedOutputStream(OutputStream outs, int sze)** Same as the previous example, but with specified buffer size.

DataOutputStream

The DataOutputStream class, which is derived from FilterOutputStream, has methods for writing Java primitives such as int, long, and float, as well as String. Note that output is in binary form using Java conventions for byte order.

PrintStream

This class adds formatting to output string representations of many Java primitives and Strings. The System.out object which Java always creates is a PrintStream. Note that the "println" routines terminate by sending a linefeed but that "print" methods do not. It is also important to note that these methods do not handle Unicode characters in strings — the high byte of characters in strings is discarded. Here are some of the PrintStream methods:

* **public void print(Object obj)** Outputs the string obtained by calling the object's "toString" method.
* **public synchronized void print(String s)** Outputs the string. Similar print methods exist for char arrays, single char, int, long, float, double, and boolean primitives.
* **public synchronized void println(String s)** Outputs the string with a following newline character. Similar print methods exist for Objects, Strings, char arrays, single char, int, long, float, double, and boolean primitives.

DISK FILE OPERATIONS

To provide a hardware-independent approach to disk file directory and file names, Java has the File class. File objects can be used to create input or output streams or RandomAccessFile objects.

File Object Constructors

Note that successful construction of a File object does not mean that the file or directory actually exists.

* **public File(String path)**   Constructs a File object than can be used to obtain a directory from this path.
* **public File(String path, String name)**   Constructs a File object specifying a path and file name.
* **public File(File dir, String name)**   Constructs a File object from a File that specifies a directory plus a file name.

FILE OBJECT METHODS

Here is a partial list of methods for File objects:

* **public boolean exists()**   Returns true if the file or directory exists.
* **public boolean isFile()**   Returns true if this File object describes a file.
* **public boolean isDirectory()**   Returns true if this File object describes a directory.
* **public boolean canRead()**   Returns true if the permissions for this file include read.
* **public boolean canWrite()**   Returns true if the permissions for this file include write.

FILEDESCRIPTOR

FileDescriptor objects encapsulate the operating-system-level handles of open files or sockets. They cannot be created directly but can be obtained from an open InputStream, OutputStream, or RandomAccessFile. The class has three static FileDescriptor objects which represent the standard System.in, System.out, and System.err streams.

RANDOMACCESSFILE

This class provides a large number of methods for reading and writing to local files. In contrast to the stream methods, RandomAccessFile objects can be positioned to read or write anywhere in a file. Methods are provided to read and write all of the Java primitive objects plus byte arrays and Strings. Instead of returning error conditions, these methods throw IOExceptions in case of errors.

NETWORK CONNECTIONS

As a network-oriented language, Java provides a wealth of classes and methods for dealing with network resources. These classes are in the java.net package. The use of many of these classes is beyond the scope of this introductory book, so we only discuss the URL class.

The URL class

A URL represents a Uniform Resource Locator as used by Web browsers to download data from the Net. You are most likely to be using URLs obtained from the Applet methods:

* **public URL getCodeBase()** The Applet method which returns a URL pointing to the Web server directory where the applet class file is stored.

* **public URL getDocumentBase()** The Applet method which returns a URL pointing to the Web server directory where the HTML file with the Applet tag is stored.

You can use these URLs to open any text or binary file stored in these directories as an InputStream and then use any of the InputStream classes to read the data.

THE SYSTEM CLASS

Every Java program has a System object which encapsulates many useful functions related to the operating system. The System object has three standard streams, in, out, and err. The out and err streams are of the PrintStream type so you can use code like:

```
System.err.println("debugging information goes here");
```

The other System methods you are likely to use are:

* **public long currentTimeMillis()** Returns the system time in milliseconds. This time is from the same clock that time-stamps Events, so you can determine the delay between two mouse clicks.

* **public void gc()** Starts a garbage collection cycle. It is frequently convenient to do this when you are sure the program will have some spare time.

* **public void exit(int status)** Used only with Java applications. The program exits and the status value is sent to the operating system as an error code.

BONUS

Miscellaneous goodies

The following section explores the random class.

Random Class

This class, which is in the java.util package, lets you create an object which is a random number generator. You can get a Random object which always generates the same sequence of pseudo-random numbers by specifying a seed value.

* **public Random()** Takes the seed for the generator from current system time.
* **public Random(long seed)** Creates a Random object with this seed.
* **public synchronized void setSeed(long seed)** Resets the object to start a new sequence.
* **public double nextDouble()** Returns a new random double variable.
* **public float nextFloat()** Returns a new random float variable.
* **public int nextInt()** Returns a new random integer.
* **public long nextLong()** Returns a new random long integer.
* **public synchronized double nextGaussian()** Generates doubles with a Gaussian distribution, having a mean of 0.0 and standard deviation of 1.0.

Mathematical functions — the Math class

You can't create a Math object, the class exists to provide the mathematical functions you would expect to find in any computer language, plus the commonly used floating point constants e and pi. Note that the floating point functions all use double variables for maximum accuracy. The following sections explain the various floating-point functions in detail.

TRIG FUNCTIONS

* **public static double acos(double d)** Returns the arc cosine of d, result 0.0 through pi for d in range – 1.0 to 1.0, Double.NaN (Not a Number) for values of d out of range.

* **public static double asin(double d)** Returns the arc sine of d in the range –pi/2 to pi/2 or Double.NaN.

* **public static double atan(double d)** Return the arc tangent of d in the range –pi/2 to pi/2 or Double.NaN.

* **public static double cos(double d)** Returns the cosine of the angle d (in radians).

* **public static double sin(double d)** Returns the sine of the angle d.

* **public static double tan(double d)** Returns the tangent of the angle d.

MISCELLANEOUS MATH

* **public static double abs(double d)** Returns absolute value of d. Similar "abs" methods return the absolute value for int, long and float variables.

* **public static double ceil(double d)** Returns the "ceiling" or smallest whole number greater than or equal to d.

* **public static double floor(double d)** Returns the "floor" or largest whole number less than or equal to d.

* **public static double log(double d)** Returns the natural logarithm (base e) of d.

* **public static double max(double a, double b)** Returns the larger of a or b. Similar "max" methods exist for int, long, and float variables.

* **public static double min(double a, double b)** Returns the smaller of a or b. Similar "min" methods exist for int, long and float variables.

* **public static double pow(double a, double b)** Returns a to the power of b.

* **public static synchronized double random()** Returns a random number between 0.0 and 1.0. There is also a random number generator class Random which we discuss later.

* **public static double rint(double d)** Rounds to the nearest whole number returning a double.

* **public static int round(float f)** Rounds a float to a 32-bit integer.

* **public static long round(double d)** Rounds a double to a long integer.

JAVA APPLETS AND APPLICATIONS

I n this part of the book, we build on the conceptual framework of Part 1 to discuss the structure and function of Java applets and applications. We begin with an overview of the process of writing a Java applet, including its runtime requirements, handling variables, constructors, and methods, and cover the basic structure of a Java applet and its core functions. We help you build a sample Java applet to prove the concept and to cement your understanding. Next, we embed an applet within an HTML document, cover the use of the various HTML tags and attributes from the perspective of formal syntax and semantics, and discuss recommended usage techniques. We also offer workarounds and wrappers to accommodate users whose browsers may not be Java-enabled; we show how to present equivalent information and when to change or upgrade your software. To conclude, we shift to the strategic reuse of existing Java code — extending applets to accommodate new classes or methods, adding support for more sophisticated data types and displays, proper design techniques and implementation approaches, and ways to test and debug your efforts — and then we help you put them to best use.

DJ: What was the impetus to develop your own code?

RF: Based on capabilities, especially for networking, the KC Multimedia Group began to move into development, because of its potential to add value to our own Internet offerings and Web sites. We developed our Java-based Guestbook application primarily as a way to offer (and charge for) a broad collection of Java-based applets, applications, and utilities. Today, we're serving up nearly 4,500 individual Java-related items, through a Java-based database interface, and helping our customers incorporate and use the many products that our site has to offer.

DJ: What's your primary business focus today?

RF: Today, the KC Multimedia Group is getting interested in broader, more general applications. Our JARS site (www.jars.com) is a collection of Web documents — basically a collection of hot new Java applets, with reviews and reactions from a panel of hand-picked industry experts that we call "judges" — that are generated on-the-fly by a document and code database. The site is created as it's viewed, by bringing up and presenting information from the database through a collection of Java applets and information. This structure lets us turn on a dime, and manage a constantly changing lineup of applets and related information.

DJ: What else is your company involved in?

RF: We run two other major Web sites, with related business activities: the JavaWorld site (www. javaworld.com), which gives us an opportunity to stay in touch with current developments in the Java trade, and to apply much of what we learn by following this market niche so closely. We also run an online Web software purchasing service, called WebWare Online (www.webwareonline. com), where members can purchase and obtain a wide variety of Web-related development, management, and maintenance tools, at special group discounts.

Under the hood, WebWare Online relies on a special Java-based application (also available in applet form), called the Guestbook which handles user registration, interaction, item selection, and purchase through a largely Java-based interface. The nice thing about our upcoming version of the Guestbook is that it is built as a Java application, and can be managed independently from any Web browser. We currently offer about 4, 500 licensed applets through the guestbook, and we're looking closely at the new version of the Java Developers Kit (JDK 1.1), and trying to figure out how to incorporate this new SDK into our ongoing development work.

WRITING
JAVA APPLETS

4

It's easy to turn your nice, respectable Web page into an eye-catching, multi-media experience by including a Java applet in an HTML file — just use the <APPLET> tag. On executing Java applets, Java-enabled browsers deliver your information as animation or "live" demos and don't require the installation or use of new helper applications or "plug-ins." Java lets you present your information dramatically without changes to the software or to the configuration information that servers use in handling Web services.

In this chapter, we show you how to design and code a simple Java applet. You'll learn about basic applet structure and how applets are created and saved. With that out of the way, we take you step by step through creating an example Java applet called DocFooter. This Java applet places a document footer at the end of any HTML document in which it is invoked. Before we start, however, you'll need to understand what's involved in using Java and making Java applets run.

Understanding What Makes Java Run

A Java applet is created as an ASCII text file with a .java extension, which indicates that the file contains Java source code. The .java file is compiled by javac, the Java source code compiler. Successful compilation results in a file with a .class extension — a binary file that contains Java bytecode. A .class file is not readable by the human eye, but you can access it with javap, the class disassembler.

Along with the Java applet we create in this chapter, DocFooter.java, we create a Java executable class called DocFooter.class. You will use specialized HTML statements (which we cover in detail later) to launch this applet from within an HTML document.

The following summarizes the relationship between a Java applet and its .class file:

* **DocFooter.java**   Java applet source code file
* **DocFooter.class**   bytecode compiled Java class
* **<APPLET CODE="DocFooter">**   HTML tag specification

Where applets are created and compiled is subject to strict requirements imposed by the Java run-time system. The Java compiler puts the compiled class binary in the same directory as the source code file. For our example, we assume the following directory structure:

* **/html**   contains ".html" documents
* **/html/images**   contains ".gif" image files
* **/html/audio**   contains ".au" audio files
* **/html/classes**   contains ".java" and ".class" files

In addition, you must set the CLASSPATH environment variable to guide the compiler to the standard class library. In the following examples, the "." tells Java to look first in the current directory. The first example is in UNIX syntax, the second in DOS syntax.

```
SET CLASSPATH =.:/html/classes:/java/lib/classes.zip
SET CLASSPATH =.;C:\html\classes;C:\java\lib\classes.zip
```

Examining Variables, Constructors, and Methods

A t this point, we need to introduce the variables, constructors, and methods in the java.applet.Applet base class and in the other classes which we will be using. In the next three sections, we cover major variables, constructors, and methods as we explore the Java Applet class. For an exhaustive list of methods, consult the HTML files in the /JAVA/DOCS/A directory installed by the Java Developers Kit (JDK).

Applet is descended from the Object class and, as the outline that follows shows, many of the variables and methods we need are defined in the Component, Container, and Panel classes. In line with the current thinking in object-oriented program design, the Applet class has no public variables, which prevents direct modification of variables and can lead to programming errors. There are a number of public `get` and `set` methods such as `getBackground()` and `setBackground()`.

Class inheritance

The following diagram shows where the Applet class sits in the overall hierarchy of Java classes.

```
java.lang.Object
   |
   +—java.awt.Component
          |
          +—java.awt.Container
                 |
                 +—java.awt.Panel
                        |
                        +—java.applet.Applet
```

Applet constructor

Applet() creates an instance of the Java Applet class that is called by the browser as the necessary first step in running any Java applet.

```
public Applet()
```

Applet instance methods

You can use these methods (from Applet and parent classes) in Applet-derived classes.

destroy() cleans up resources after killing an applet; it is called implicitly by the browser when an applet is exited.

```
protected void destroy()
```

getAudioClip(URL) gets an AudioClip object that contains audio data, given a URL object (URL is a class that represents a Web Uniform Resource Locator) that points to the location of an ".AU" (audio) file.

```
public AudioClip getAudioClip(URL url)
```

getBackground() is a Component method that gets the Color the system is using to paint the background of the applet.

```
public Color getBackground()
```

getCodeBase() gets a URL pointing to the applet's class file.

```
public URL getCodeBase()
```

getDocumentBase() gets a URL pointing to the HTML document in which the applet appears.

```
public URL getDocumentBase()
```

getForeground() gets the Color being used by the system to display text or draw in the applet.

```
public Color getForeground()
```

getImage(URL) gets an Image object from a URL.

```
public Image getImage(URL url)
```

getImage(URL, String) gets an Image object from the String fname (usually a GIF file) relative to the URL. (Note: This Image will initially have no image data, because Image data is not loaded until it's needed, to avoid slowing execution of the applet.)

```
public Image getImage(URL url, String fname)
```

requestFocus() is a Component method that requests that the browser give the focus to the applet.

```
public void requestFocus()
```

getFont() is a Component method that gets the font currently in use.

```
public Font getFont()
```

getFontMetrics(Font) is a Component method that returns an object of type FontMetrics, which describes ascenders, descenders, character widths, and other font characteristics.

```
public FontMetrics getFontMetrics(Font f)
```

getImage(URL, String) gets an image from the filename specified relative to the URL.

```
public Image getImage(String name)
```

getImage(URL) gets the image specified by the URL.

```
public Image getImage(URL url)
```

getParameter(String) gets the string associated with parameter pname from the parameter list in the <APPLET> HTML tag. It returns null if pname does not exist.

```
public String getParameter(String pname)
```

gotFocus(Event, Object) is a Component method that is called by the system when a component has received the input focus.

```
public boolean gotFocus(Event evt, Object what)
```

init() initializes the applet. It is called automatically by the browser program just after the applet is constructed.

```
protected void init()
```

isActive() signals if the applet is active in the current HTML document.

```
public boolean isActive()
```

keyDown(Event, int) is a Component method that is called by the system when a key is pressed.

```
public void keyDown(Event evt,int key)
```

lostFocus(Event, Object) is a Component method that is called by the browser when the focus has moved away from the applet.

```
public void lostFocus(Event evt, Object what)
```

mouseDown(Event, int, int) is called if a mouse button is depressed while the pointer is at (x,y) pixel of display relative to the upper-left corner of the applet (0,0). The (x,y) values are passed as parameters to this method. (All mouse routines are Component methods and should return true if they have handled the event and false otherwise.)

```
public boolean mouseDown(Event evt,int x, int y)
```

mouseDrag(Event, int, int) is called if the mouse pointer is moved while the mouse button is depressed at (x,y) pixel of display relative to the upper-left corner of the applet, (0,0). The most recent (x,y) values are passed as parameters to this method.

```
public boolean mouseDrag(Event evt,int x, int y)
```

mouseEnter(Event, int, int) is called when the mouse enters the applet, regardless of the state of the mouse button.

```
public boolean mouseEnter(Event evt, int x, int y)
```

mouseExit(Event, int, int) is called when the mouse exits the applet, regardless the state of the of mouse button.

```
public boolean mouseExit(Event evt, int x, int y)
```

mouseMove(Event, int, int) is called if the mouse pointer is moved with mouse button up to (x,y) pixel of display, relative to (0,0), the upper-left corner of the applet.

```
public boolean mouseMove(Event evt,int x, int y)
```

mouseUp(Event, int, int) is called if the mouse button is released while the pointer is at (x,y) pixel of display relative to (0,0), the upper-left corner of the applet.

```
public boolean mouseUp(Event evt,int x, int y)
```

paint(Graphics) is a Component method that is called by the system with a Graphics object suitable for painting the applet graphic components.

```
public void paint(Graphics g)
```

play(URL) plays an audio clip specified by a URL. If the URL cannot be found, nothing happens.

```
public void play(URL url)
```

play(URL, String) plays an audio clip specified by a filename relative to a URL.

```
public void play(URL url, String fname )
```

repaint() is a Component method that starts a sequence of events that results in repainting the applet's display.

```
public void repaint()
```

resize(int, int) requests that the browser resize the applet. At present, the Netscape browser does not honor the resize request; however, the applet viewer does.

```
public void resize(int width, int height)
```

setBackground(Color) is a Component method that sets the color the system will use to paint the background of the applet.

```
public void setBackground(Color c)
```

setFont(Font) is a Component method that sets the font to be used in future drawString operations.

```
public synchronized void setFont(Font f)
```

showStatus(String) displays status information as a string at the bottom of the browser display window.

```
public void showStatus(String msg)
```

start() is called by the browser when the applet's HTML page is visited. This routine is typically used to start threads for animation. (Note: The start routine may be called more than once if the browser "forward" and "back" functions are used to move between HTML pages.)

```
public void start( )
```

stop() is called by the browser when the applet's HTML page is no longer on the screen. This routine is typically used to stop the execution of animation threads.

```
protected void stop( )
```

update(Graphics) is the first routine called by the system when repainting an applet. The default routine clears the applet area to the background color before calling the paint routine (a Component method).

```
public void update(Graphics g)
```

Exploring Applet Structure

Now, let's take a look at the structure of a specific Java applet. As we said previously, Applet is a subclass of Panel, which is a subclass of Container, which is a subclass of Component, which is in turn a subclass of the basic system class, java.lang.Object.

Any applet is an extension or specialization of the base Applet class. Here's a specification for the basic structure of the DocFooter applet we create in this chapter:

```
import java.applet.Applet ; // Import the system base class Applet.

class DocFooter extends Applet {
   ... body of class ...
}
```

Notice that the class name (DocFooter) is the value of the <APPLET> tag's code attribute:

```
<APPLET code="DocFooter.class">
```

An applet contains five important methods that are invoked by the browser: init, start, paint, stop, and destroy. These methods are called implicitly by the browser; you do not have to call them directly. The parent (Applet) class methods will be used unless you override them with your own definition.

The five methods are specified in the following section:

```
import java.applet.Applet; /' Import the system base class Applet.

class DocFooter extends Applet {
   public void init() {
      ... body of method ...
   }
   public void start() {
      ... body of method ...
   }
   public void paint(Graphics g) {
      ... body of method ...
   }
   public void stop() {
      ... body of method ...
   }
   public void destroy() {
      ... body of method ...
   }
}
```

init()

The Applet class init() method is invoked after the applet has been loaded into memory by the Java run-time system. This method allows you to code tasks to initialize instance variables, resize the Applet, import or include any resources, and set text properties such as font and color for objects.

The following is a simple specification of the init() method:

```
protected void init () {
   resize(500,100);
   logo = getImage(getDocumentBase(),"images/logo.gif");
}
```

This code example requests the browser to resize the display area reserved for the applet to 500 by 100 pixels. Netscape's browser ignores this request and uses the WIDTH and HEIGHT parameters from the <APPLET> tag; the appletviewer will resize accordingly. The init() method also retrieves a GIF image from the file system. The example code instructs the run-time system to retrieve a file named "logo.gif" in the /IMAGES directory, specified relative to the current HTML document.

start()

The Applet class start() method is invoked by the browser every time the applet's HTML document is displayed. This provides a way for the applet to launch background threads on start-up; for example, playing a looped animation or an audio sound bite.

Here's a sample specification for start():

```
protected void start() {
    requestFocus();
}
```

This example gets the current window focus once the browser renders the applet's HTML document. If our applet had a field for user input, we could have requested that the browser set the focus to that field.

paint(Graphics g)

The paint method is called by the browser to display the applet whenever the applet display area is exposed by scrolling the Web page, or in response to a repaint() request.

stop()

The browser invokes the stop() method immediately after the applet's HTML document is no longer displayed. This method is used to terminate any executing threads spawned by or belonging to the applet and is always called prior to the execution of destroy() as part of the standard sequence for terminating an applet.

We provide a sample specification for this method in the following code:

```
protected void stop() {
    myAudio.stop() ; // Terminate an audio clip.
}
```

This example code terminates the audio clip once the applet's HTML document has been removed from the display window.

destroy()

The browser executes the destroy() method to remove the applet from memory, and completely terminates its execution. If the applet is still active, stop() is called before calling destroy(). The following is an example destroy() specification:

```
protected void destroy() {
    closedB(); /* Close an open database with an instance method. */
}
```

This example code calls an instance method (defined in the subclass) that closes any open database and commits any pending updates before terminating the applet's execution. The destroy() method allows applets to terminate gracefully, without leaving data in an uncertain state, and ensures that the applet's resources are released.

Creating Your First Java Applet

In this section, we guide you step by step through the creation of a simple Java applet, DocFooter.java. Before you start, you need to determine the problem to be solved and the system resources that are required.

DocFooter design

The DocFooter applet produces a dynamically created footer that can be appended to an HTML document. The HTML code <APPLET CODE= "DocFooter"> must be embedded within the HTML document to include this applet. You also need to provide values for the DocFooter apple's input variables, as follows:

```
<PARAM  NAME=email VALUE="name@address">
```

The DocFooter applet appends a byline to an HTML document. A footer should contain information about the HTML document, including the author's name, when the document was last updated, and who to contact if a user runs into a problem. Table 4-1 suggests information that would be useful in a document footer.

Our DocFooter applet creates a footer with the following information:

* Company logo
* Date last updated
* Date and time of this access (from user's system clock)
* Author's e-mail address
* Copyright notice

Now that we have identified the information DocFooter is to render, let's identify the system resources required to create an instance of a document footer.

The company logo in our example is a GIF image file. Its absolute path is /html/images/logo.gif; however, the applet locates it relative to the HTML document's URL. If you don't have a GIF file of your company logo, use one of those provided in the JDK /demo/animator/images/Duke directory of "Duke" — the Java mascot. Just copy the one you choose to the /html/images directory and rename it "logo.gif."

TABLE 4-1 Suggestions for Document Footer Information

Author's name organization	Author's phone number	Author's address	Author's e-mail
Author's postal address	Document owner's name	Document owner's e-mail address	Document owner's postal address
Legal disclaimer	Date of document's last update	Company logo	Copyright notice
Document's URL	Navigational links		

Figure 4-1 shows what the document footer looks like.

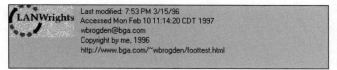

Figure 4-1 Information in the document footer produced by the DocFooter applet.

Step 1: Create DocFooter.java and insert import declarations

Change to the /html/classes directory and use your favorite text editor to create a file named "DocFooter.java." When you save it, be sure to save the file as plain ASCII text. Next, determine which system-level packages you need to complete the document footer, in addition to the java.lang package that provides basic language classes and is automatically included in all programs by the compiler. For the DocFooter applet, you need these system packages:

* **java.applet.Applet**   contains all Applet class variables, constructors, and methods
* **java.awt.***   to provide interfaces and classes for drawing in the applet
* **java.awt.image.***   for the Image class created to hold the GIF image
* **java.util.***   for the utility classes, to get the Date class
* **java.net.**   URL for the URL class

Start your Java source code with the following statements to let the compiler know which of the standard packages you will be using:

```
import java.applet.Applet ;
import java.awt.* ;
import java.awt.image.* ;
import java.net.URL ;
```

Step 2: Insert class declaration

Insert the DocFooter class declaration to indicate the superclass for your DocFooter class:

```
public class DocFooter extends Applet {

}
```

This asserts that your new subclass name, DocFooter, is derived from or specializes a general system class named Applet. This class declaration also specifies that the DocFooter class is a public class, which allows any other class to use it. Java expects one public class or interface in every source code file. This is a necessary step for each applet you write.

Step 3: Insert class variables

At this point, you declare some class instance variables and decide which will be public (visible to other classes), which will be protected (visible only to subclasses derived from the DocFooter class), and which will be private (visible only to instances of the DocFooter class).

These variable instance declarations are normally entered immediately after the class declaration, but as long as they are declared before they're used, they may be declared anywhere in the class definition. They must appear outside any methods defined for the class.

The following is the specification for your instance variables:

```
    // declaration of instance variables
private String date;       // date of last update of HTML page
private Date   today ;     // date of access
private String email;      // author's e-mail address
private String copyright;  // copyright blurb
private Image logo;        // GIF image of company logo
```

Step 4: Define init() method

You also need to code the set of initialization actions required when the applet is loaded into memory before being displayed. The init() method is called by the browser just after the applet object's creation.

The specification of the init() method for the DocFooter class is

```
/* method invoked by browser to initialize the applet */
public void init() {
  resize(500,100); /* 500 pixels wide & 100 pixels high display */
  logo = getImage(getDocumentBase(), "images/logo.gif");

  /* Get applet named parameters from <APPLET> tag area. */
  date = getParameter("LAST_UPDATED");
  email = getParameter("EMAIL");
  copyright = getParameter("COPY_RIGHT_NOTICE");
  today = new Date() ;
}
```

Four activities are completed during initialization of the applet in the init() method.

1. The system is requested to allocate a display area 500 pixels wide and 100 pixels high.

2. An Image object is created based on the GIF image file containing the company logo. The image will not be retrieved from the file system until it is needed. The path, /images/logo.gif, is relative to the /html directory, which is the document base, so the absolute path to this GIF image file is /html/images/logo.gif.

3. The named parameters from the <APPLET> tag are retrieved and stored as type String.

4. A Date object with today's date is created as the "today" variable.

Step 5: Define paint() method

In step 5, you code the paint() method for the DocFooter class. The browser calls this method the first time the applet is displayed if the applet area is reexposed by scrolling, or in response to a repaint() request. The system supplies a Graphics object suitable for the display hardware, as determined by the browser.

Here's the specification for the paint() method:

```
/* definition of the paint() method of the DocFooter class */
public void paint(Graphics g) {
```

```
      // Render the logo image in the canvas
      // for drawImage; x and y refer to upper-left corner of image.
   if( logo != null ) g.drawImage(logo,0,0, this);
   // Render string data into the canvas at specific spots, note
   // that for drawString, x and y refer to lower-left corner of
   // text.
   if(date != null)g.drawString("Last modified: " + date ,110,15);
   g.drawString( "Accessed " + today,110,30);
   if( email != null ) g.drawString( email, 110, 45 );
   if( copyright != null ) g.drawString(copyright,110,60);

      // Get the URL of the document with the embedded <APPLET> tag.
      // Note that an error in creating the URL will result in a
      //  MalformedURLException so the statements creating it are
      //  enclosed in a "try" "catch" structure.
      try {
        appletURL = new URL(getDocumentBase(),"");

         // Convert the URL to a String.
         String urlstring = appletURL.toExternalForm();

         // Render the URL string to the canvas.
         g.drawString(urlstring,110,75);
      } catch(Exception e) {
        System.err.println("Problem with URL");
      }
   }
```

This method defines how an applet is rendered in the HTML document that invokes it.

PUTTING IT ALL TOGETHER

Here's a listing of the complete DocFooter applet source code:

```java
import java.applet.Applet ; // Import Applet system package.
import java.awt.* ;         // Import all items of awt system package.
import java.awt.image.* ;
import java.util.Date ;  /* Import only the Date class from util
  package.*/
import java.net.URL ;

public class DocFooter extends Applet {

/* declaration of instance variables */
URL      appletURL ;
private String date;     // date of last update
private Date   today ;   // date of this access
private String email;      // author's e-mail address
private String copyright;    // copyright blurb
private Image logo; /* GIF image of company logo */
    /* Make sure your logo is no larger than 80x80 pixels;
       otherwise, you must adjust the canvas size. */

/* method invoked by Browser to initialize the applet */
public void init() {
  resize(500,100); /* 500 pixels wide & 100 pixels high  */
  logo = getImage(getDocumentBase(), "images/logo.gif");
    /* Retrieve GIF file from images, a subdirectory of the
       location of our HTML file. */

    // Get applet parameters from <APPLET> tag as String objects.
    // Note that these will be null if the parameter is not found,
    // so we check before painting.
  date = getParameter("LAST_UPDATED");
  email = getParameter("EMAIL");
  copyright = getParameter("COPY_RIGHT_NOTICE");
  today = new Date();  // Create Date object with today's date.
}

// definition of the paint() method of the DocFooter class
```

(continued)

PUTTING IT ALL TOGETHER (continued)

```
// The system calls paint with a Graphics object appropriate
// for the particular operating system and hardware.
public void paint(Graphics g) {

  // Render the logo image in the canvas
  // for drawImage; x and y refer to upper-left corner of image.
  if( logo != null ) g.drawImage(logo,0,0, this);

  // Render string data into the canvas at specific spots.
  // Note that for drawString, x and y refer to lower-left
  // corner of text.
  if( date != null ) g.drawString("Last modified: " + date
  ,110,15);
  g.drawString( "Accessed " + today,110,30);
  if( email != null ) g.drawString( email, 110, 45 );
  if( copyright != null ) g.drawString(copyright,110,60);

  // Get the URL of the document with the embedded <APPLET> tag.
  // Note that an error in creating the URL will result in a
  // MalformedURLException so the statements creating it are
  // enclosed in a "try" "catch" structure.
  try {
    appletURL = new URL(getDocumentBase(),"");

    // Convert the URL to a String.
    String urlstring = appletURL.toExternalForm();

    // Render the URL string to the canvas.
    g.drawString(urlstring,110,75);

  } catch(Exception e) {
    System.err.println("Problem with URL");
  }
 }
}
```

Step 6: Compiling DocFooter.java

At this point, it's time to compile the "DocFooter.java" file into the "DocFooter.class" binary file, which will be located in the /html/classes directory. A successful compilation using the Java compiler, javac creates this binary representation of the DocFooter class. To compile DocFooter.java, switch to the /html/classes directory and enter the following on the command line:

```
chevelle:/html/classes>javac DocFooter.java
```

We assume that you're working in a UNIX environment. (Note: chevelle:/html/classes> is your temporary UNIX prompt. A DOS prompt would be similar.)

If your system can't find javac, check your path environment variable and make sure it includes a path to the Java Developers Kit installation directory and its binaries. Java expects the spelling and case of the filename to exactly match the class DocFooter.

A successful compilation will create a file called "DocFooter.class" in the /html/classes directory. Therefore, the absolute filename for the bytecode is /html/classes/DocFooter.class. This is the binary executable invoked by the browser when an <APPLET> tag referencing the DocFooter class in an HTML document is executed.

If your compilation is unsuccessful, you will see a display of the errors detected in your Java code along with explanations. To correct the errors, edit your Java code file and ensure that it agrees exactly with the preceding code. Save the file and recompile. Repeat as needed until you're successful.

Step 7: Create example.html

You will need a document with HTML code including the <APPLET> tag to test the applet with a browser or the appletviewer. For testing purposes, create a file with the following text and save it as a plain ASCII text file named "example.html." (Adding applets to HTML documents is discussed in more detail in the next chapter.)

```
<HTML>
<HEAD>
<TITLE>DocFooter Example</TITLE></HEAD>
<BODY>
You will need a JAVA compatible browser such as Netscape 2.0 with
   Win NT or 95 to see this. <BR>
<HR>
<BR>

<APPLET codebase="classes" code="DocFooter.class"
   WIDTH = 500 HEIGHT = 100 >
```

```
<PARAM NAME=LAST_UPDATED        VALUE="11:03 AM 2/23/96" >
<PARAM NAME=EMAIL               VALUE="wbrogden@bga.com" >
<PARAM NAME=COPY_RIGHT_NOTICE   VALUE = "Copyright by me, 1996" >
This text is seen if browser can't do JAVA.
</APPLET><BR>

<HR>
</BODY>
</HTML>
```

Step 8: Running the applet

In a Java-compatible browser, open "/html/example.html" (using Open File from the File menu). Alternatively, use the appletviewer program that comes with the Java Developers Kit, switch to the /html/ directory and type:

```
appletviewer example.html
```

Summary

When you're writing an applet, the first thing you should do is decide which system packages to import. Next, define the methods that the browser calls for your applet. Not all of the standard methods — init(), start(), paint(), stop(), and destroy() — are required in every case; what you actually define depends on the problem. Init() and paint() are the most commonly defined methods when subclassing the Applet class.

Finally, compile your Java code into a binary file containing bytecode. The binary file is created by the javac compiler and has a ".class" extension. The file is executed by a Java-compatible browser after an HTML document with an embedded <APPLET> tag is loaded into a browser's display window.

Congratulations! You're a Java author! In the next chapter, we turn our attention to the HTML document side of the operation and discuss the details of the <APPLET> tag that is used to invoke Java applets.

THE JAVA DEVELOPMENT PROCESS

IN THIS CHAPTER YOU LEARN THESE KEY SKILLS

EXAMINE REQUIREMENTS ANALYSIS FOR THE PRACTICAL JAVA PROGRAMMER PAGE 137

EXPLORE DEVELOPMENT ENVIRONMENTS PAGE 141

LOCATE JAVA RESOURCES AND FILL UP YOUR TOOLKIT PAGE 146

DESIGN FOR DEBUGGING AND TESTING PAGE 147

GO FASTER, FASTER, FASTER WITH JAVA OPTIMIZATION PAGE 147

5

N ow that you have had a taste of Java programming with the DocFooter applet of Chapter 4, let's back off a bit and look at the Java development process as a whole. You may have already formed habits of program development with other languages, but Java introduces so many new elements that even experienced programmers should take a fresh look at the development process.

Examining Requirements Analysis for the Practical Java Programmer

W hen confronting that blank piece of paper (you do start your projects on paper first don't you?) it helps to locate your problem in the total spectrum of possible requirements. Here, we look at some aspects of that spectrum and how they influence our choices of Java program design elements. Here is an assortment of possible Java projects which we use for illustrative examples.

* *Sound System Configuration Problem.* Your company sells specialty sound system components all over the world by catalog, but because the variety of components is overwhelming, your customers need lots of hand-holding to be sure what they order is compatible. Customer support is eating up your profits and nobody wants to take the night shift that gets calls from the far east.

* *Expense Account/Trip Report Submission Problem.* Your boss wants you to come up with a program that will take expense account submissions from workers on the company network and file them in a standard format in a special accounting directory. This has to work with the Macs, WinTel PCs, and UNIX boxes.

* *Online Game Design.* Wow! You won the lottery and now you have time to indulge yourself in the programming project you always wanted, a multiplayer online game. A game of exploration and discovery that will be even better than "Civilization."

* *Make My Home Page Jazzy.* Your home page on the Web just looks too dowdy; maybe an evening's work with Java can spruce it up with dramatic effects.

Distribution medium: applet vs. application

The first choice we have to make is whether the project is best suited for an applet to be accessed by a Web browser, or an application to be distributed as a stand-alone program.

All file and networking techniques are available to applications, but applets are limited by typical browser security considerations. With current browsers, applets can't write files or read files from any source except that of the HTML page in which the applet is embedded. It looks like our proposed Expense Account Program would have to be an application if we want it to write to the network file system.

One advantage of an applet is the increasing distribution of Java aware-browsers; this is great for casual users because they don't have to download any special software to use your Online Game program. However, because of the limit on applets writing files, you would have to do some specialized programming to save the state of the game on your Web server so a user could recover from a lost connection.

 WEB PATH For a real example of a multiplayer Java game, see the "Solar Vengeance" Applet at the following URL:

http://www2.tcc.net/solven.htm

Amount of user input

Another major consideration is the amount and type of user input. Our Expense Account example might involve free-format text entry to explain the reason for the expense, selections from a controlled list of expense types, and entry of error-checked dates and amounts. We don't want to have a cramped data entry screen, so we would probably use the CardLayout layout manager to spread the input fields over several panels. Also called a "tabbed dialog," this input format will already be familiar to our users because it is increasingly used in commercial software. The rest of our user-interface design would flow logically from this decision.

On the other hand, the Jazz up the Home Page project with very little user input probably won't even require a layout manager and could use absolute positioning of components like the DocFooter applet of Chapter 4.

Graphic presentation of results

Some projects, such as our proposed online game of exploration, will be dominated by the requirement for graphic presentation of results. The need for a map display controlled by scroll bars forces us to choose a BorderLayout for the map display because this is the only layout manager that gives attractive behavior to Java Scrollbar objects. The rest of the program design must always consider how to keep the map display current.

 Custom graphics displays also imply that one or more of our main classes will be derived from the java.awt.Canvas class. An example of a class extending Canvas appears in Chapter 8.

A major design decision in a graphics-intensive program is the extent to which we employ importing graphic elements as images versus generating them with graphics "primitive" routines. Presently, Java only provides simple graphic operations, such as single-pixel-wide line drawing, whereas Java's image manipulation methods are more sophisticated. Thus, it is common for complex displays to be created by combining imported images rather than by drawing pixel by pixel.

To thread or not to thread?

Java's capacity for multithreaded programming is powerful and flexible, but it introduces considerable complexity, especially for programmers who are used to single-threaded procedural programming. The design decision to use multiple threads should not be taken lightly because of the danger of multiple threads modifying the same object at the same time. The following sections describe some of the situations in which multiple threads may be required.

ANIMATION

Applications which present a continuously changing sequence of images are easily created with a thread which calls `repaint()` and then sleeps for a controlled amount of time. If a large number of images has to be loaded, the thread can load and display an initial image, then continue to load the additional images.

NETWORK DATA ACCESS

Programs which must be updated continuously with information from the network while remaining responsive to user input can have a thread devoted to loading data. An example would be the online game which needs to get the most recent moves by other players while remaining responsive to user requests to scroll the map display. When the thread has downloaded a new set of game state data, it can notify the user interface to update the map.

TIMED RESPONSES

Another example where a thread could be used would be an interface where help messages should appear after the mouse cursor has rested on a component for a controlled amount of time. A thread would be started when the mouse entered the component and would watch for the expiration of the specified time to display the help message.

Is there a Base class hiding in there?

Some projects cry out for a design in which you create a base class which is extended by specialized derived classes resulting in an elegant hierarchy. The key design decision in the Sound System Configuration problem could be the creation of a base CatalogItem class, derived from the Java Object class which would encapsulate everything catalog items have in common, such as stock number, price, and source. This base could then be specialized to cover the factors which affect component compatibility, such as power requirements, plug type, and frequency response.

Your Web page applet could check the compatibility between components represented by the derived classes, then write out an order to e-mail using the common base class instance variables of catalog number and price.

However, you should not feel obligated to start every project with a new class hierarchy. Many Java projects only involve subclassing the standard Java library objects.

Is there an interface hiding in there?

If your attempt to design around a class hierarchy is not working out, consider the use of one or more interfaces. An interface specifies methods which a class must provide but does not require a particular class origin. In our example, the

Sound System Configuration problem, we might have Amplifier and Tuner classes derived from CatalogItem. These classes might have quite different internals, but if both implemented a SignalPlug interface, a simple compatibility testing method could determine if they could be connected. We demonstrate program design with interfaces further in Chapter 11.

Where can I borrow some code?

The Internet is rich with Java resources available for download, study, and reuse. In addition, the "demo" examples which come with the JDK illustrate many showy and useful applications. When undertaking the Jazz Up My Home Page project, a few minutes of surfing the Net or browsing the demos could turn up dozens of possibilities with source code available for free.

Throwaway objects

Many programmers coming to Java from C feel uncomfortable with creating and discarding objects. They tend to want to create objects and then keep them around as instance variables for the remainder of the life of the program. In designing your Java program, you should feel free to create and discard any temporary objects you need.

In fact, for objects that encapsulate system resources, it can be dangerous to try to keep them around. For instance, if you get a Graphics object by doing getGraphics on a component and try to keep it around, this may tie up a scarce system resource, or the Graphics object may become outdated and unusable as the underlying operating system shuffles resources around.

But will it be fast enough?

In the early stages of designing a Java project, don't worry too much about speed. Concentrate instead on clarity and ease of testing. If there are calculations which you know will be time consuming, try to encapsulate them in a class. That way, if you later find a more efficient algorithm, you only have to change one class, not the entire program.

You should also consider putting in class methods and variables which can be used to check the correctness of your program, but later can be removed to reduce the memory requirements and improve the speed.

Exploring Development Environments

For the first nine months or so after Sun unleashed Java on the programming world, the Java Developers Kit was the only possible development environment. Now, there are a number of commercial and shareware systems for a variety of hardware systems. These range from full-blown Integrated Development Environments (IDEs) to specialized Web page designers which make use of Java applets. In this section, we survey the advantages of different development environments for typical tasks such as editing, class browsing, and debugging during Java program development. Hopefully, this will give you an idea of what to look for when shopping around.

The Java Developers Kit

The great advantage of the JDK is that it is available for free downloading from Sun's Web site. Another attraction is that you can continue to use your favorite editor to create program files. Just be sure that files are saved as pure text with the ".java" extension. Unless your editor is very flexible, you won't get any syntax coloring or checking. The Java utilities don't care whether text lines end with a linefeed character or carriage return, but if your editor expects CR/LF, you will be surprised when you look at the Sun example code because it is linefeed only.

It is important to remember that, in Java, all the code for a Java class must be contained in a single file. You can define more than one class in a file, but only one class can be declared public, and the file name must match the public class name exactly. This can lead to rather large files so an editor with "bookmark" capability and multiple window capability can be handy.

INTEGRATED DEVELOPMENT ENVIRONMENTS (IDES)

Commercial IDEs always provide editors for Java source code. In general, these are based on the company's C++ IDE editor, with modifications for Java keyword highlighting and syntax checking. Typically, this editor is tied to the compiler error reporting mechanism to put your cursor on the line which has caused a compiler error.

 Although the typical editor is file oriented, some IDEs provide connections between a class browser and a special editing window so that you can select a method in the class browser and have an editing window pop up allowing you to edit that method directly. Figure 5-1 shows the "class editor" window in the Symantec Cafe IDE in action with code you will meet in Chapter 11. In the upper left pane of the window we have selected the TWGenFilter class which caused the editor to show the names of the methods in this class in the upper right pane. We selected the filterAndWrite method which caused the code for this method to appear in the bottom editing window.

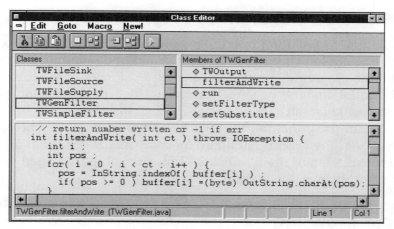

Figure 5-1 An example of an editor which understands Java source code structure and lets you select a method to edit without having to hunt for it in a file. This example is from Symantec Cafe IDE.

Screen building

The following sections examine the development and uses of screen building tools that are currently available for the Java environment. Included in this category are screen layout aids and visual programming tools. These types of utilities are extremely useful in a Java environment.

SCREEN LAYOUT AIDS

Because the JDK does not provide any support for screen design, layout aids were one of the first programmer's assistance utilities to become available; many of them were released as shareware by early Java enthusiasts. Layout aids understand Java AWT components such as buttons, labels, and list boxes, and allow you to place components where you want them. The aid can then write the necessary Java code to create and place the component objects, such as a dialog, within a container.

Some form of screen layout assistance is present in all commercial Java development environments. The biggest limitation of the early layout aids has been that they ignore Java's LayoutManager interface and position components on the screen by absolute pixel position.

As the publicity surrounding Java for enhancement of Web sites grew louder and louder, many Webmasters became interested in incorporating Java applets but were unable to take the time to learn Java programming. To answer this need, a tremendous number of Java-enabled Web page layout tools sprang up, both as shareware and commercial offerings. Some of these manipulate the input parameters to "stock" applets and some write Java code.

VISUAL PROGRAMMING TOOLS

The ultimate evolution of the screen layout aid is a visual programming tool that can not only layout the screen design but also gather enough information from the programmer about the expected behavior of the components to write substantial amounts of connecting code. This type of development tool was pioneered by Microsoft's Visual Basic.

Visual programming for Java development is rapidly becoming available due to the "Java Beans" standard for components. We can already see the start of an explosion of small software firms supplying specialized Java components for programmers to pick from.

Class browsing

The following sections detail how the Java Developers Kit (JDK) and Integrated Development Environments (IDEs) simplify the development and organization of Java programming.

THE JAVA DEVELOPERS KIT

In object-oriented programming, programmers must constantly refer to the variables and methods of both the standard class library and the custom classes being created. The Java language design team created a system of comment conventions which can produce class documentation directly in HTML form when Java source code is run through the javadoc utility. Since the entire Java class library was commented with this convention, there is a complete set of hypertext-linked HTML files which can be accessed with a Web browser. This huge set of documents can be accessed at the Sun Web site or downloaded in its entirety.

X-REF Refer back to the section in Chapter 4 entitled "Class inheritance" to view a portion of the "java.applet.Applet.html" file showing how the Applet class is derived from Panel which is derived from Container, and so on. Due to the links in the HTML document, when you are looking at this file with a browser you can click on any of the class ancestors of Applet to get the documentation for this class. The power of this technique, particularly when you are just learning Java, is fantastic.

Other portions of the file give the method prototypes for all methods in the Applet class. Every time another Java class is mentioned, it has a hypertext link to the documentation for that class. It beats leafing back and forth in a book trying to find a class definition, especially when you have not yet gotten used to the way Java is organized.

INTEGRATED DEVELOPMENT ENVIRONMENTS

Most IDEs have language help systems which give language information at about the level of the Sun HTML documents and make use of hypertext links.

You can also expect to find various views of the class hierarchy, both of the standard library and the classes you are constructing in your project. Figure 5-2 shows Symantec Cafe's "Hierarchy Editor" view of part of the project which is the subject of Chapter 11. This shows the relationship between three of the interfaces in the project and the classes which implement those interfaces. Clicking on one of these boxes will bring up a "class editor" so you can examine or edit classes. Once you get used to tools like this, you won't want to go back to a plain editor.

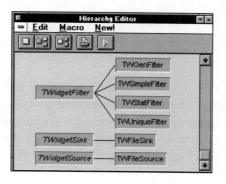

Figure 5-2 The Symantec Cafe "Hierarchy Editor" view of part of the project used in Chapter 11.

Compiling

X-REF The JDK provides two compilers — javac and javac_g — the first is the one for normal use, and the second inserts extra information used by the JDK debugger. Like all JDK utilities, these are run from the command line. Command-line compiler options are discussed in Chapter 9.

Commercial IDEs provide menu selections to set up options and run their compilers. In general, the compilers provided with IDEs are significantly faster than the JDK compiler. Furthermore, integration of compiler options with project management makes it easy to recompile all project code with a single mouse click.

Debugging

The JDK includes a command-line driven debugger (jdb.exe) with a syntax similar to UNIX debuggers. This program is generally considered difficult to use. Most programmers find that liberal use of System.out.println() statements is faster and simpler than using jdb.

Commercial IDEs, on the other hand, provide integrated debugger support using windows to set breakpoints, step through code, examine objects, and change variables. At least one IDE debugger provides for dynamic creation of new objects and direct calls of object methods with an expression evaluator. Since Java is inherently multithreaded, a debugger must provide for examining the state of threads.

Locating Java Resources — Filling Up Your Toolkit

The following sections explore how to locate Java resources. Included in this list is information from Sun, JavaSoft, Gamelan, Internet newsgroups, and CompuServe. Utilizing these resources will aid you in you quest for successful Java programming.

Sun and JavaSoft

When it became apparent that Java was going to be a big thing, Sun split responsibility for various aspects of Java into divisions. They all seem to be accessible through www.javasoft.com. The organization of that site changes frequently, so we can't tell you the exact URLs, just go and browse around. You can find white papers on the thinking behind Java's design, FAQ (frequently asked question) lists, draft specifications on proposed Java extensions, the latest JDK for downloading, and a wide variety of other goodies.

Gamelan

Designated the official directory for Java by JavaSoft, Gamelan has literally thousands of references to applications, applets and various resources all neatly categorized and searchable. Many of the authors of these applets and applications provide source code on request in the spirit of mutual assistance that has marked the Java community.

```
http://www.gamelan.com
```

Newsgroups

The original USENET comp.lang.java newsgroup became so active that it had to be divided into the following groups. Browsing through these groups, you can find URLs for example Java code, free downloads of Java toolkits, and references to other Java sources. If you don't have the time to follow them all, at least take a look at the programmer and announce newsgroups.

```
comp.lang.java.programmer
comp.lang.java.tech
comp.lang.java.setup
comp.lang.java.security
comp.lang.java.misc
comp.lang.java.api
```

```
comp.lang.java.announce
comp.lang.java.advocacy
```

CompuServe

If you have a CompuServe account, stop by the general Java forum (**GO JAVAUS**) or visit the Symantec Developers Tools (**GO SYMDEV**), Borland (**GO BDEVTO**), or Microsoft (**GO MSLANG**) for development-environment-related questions. You may also find information about the behavior of Java applets in your browser in the various forums devoted to browser vendors.

Designing for Debugging and Testing

U nless you are *very* good or *very* lucky, debugging and testing will be an integral part of the development of your applications. Refer to the Discovery Center for this chapter to find out how to design your Java code to simplify the testing and debugging processes (page *284*).

BONUS

Going Faster, Faster, Faster — Java Optimization

T he following sections outline a few areas to consider in optimizing your Java developments.

General considerations

There are fundamental reasons why Java will never be as fast as C code. For one thing, there is extra code involved in checking the type of objects and ensuring that array references are in bounds. Furthermore, each access of an object must go through a memory pointer. However, this should not discourage us, there is plenty of room for optimization in the typical Java program. Two Web sites which track current thinking in Java optimization are:

```
http://www.preemptive.com/lectures/Optimization.html
http://www.cs.cmu.edu/~jch/java/optimization.html
```

The CMU site also has timing tests on commercial Java compilers.

As always, the best optimization is a good algorithm, for example, finding out if a word is present in an array of strings will be much faster if the strings are stored in a hash table, as opposed to a one-at-a-time check of the entire array. Assuming you have picked the best algorithm for the job, postpone further optimization until you are sure the program is working correctly.

Many good practice recommendations from C are also good practice in Java; take for example the familiar example of removing invariant calculations from loops. Instead of:

```
for( int i = 0 ; i < myStr.length() ; i++ ){   /* length() is
  called for every iteration */
  sum += myStr.charAt(i) ;
}

/* the following code saves the extra calls to the length()
  method*/
int tmp = myStr.length() ;
for( int i = 0 ; i < tmp ; i++  ){
  sum += myStr.charAt(i) ;
}
```

Some optimizations depend on a detailed knowledge of Java internals. For instance, when you declare a two-dimensional array with the following declaration:

```
int t[][] = new int[ 20][40] ;
```

Java creates a one dimension array of 20 objects, each element of which is another array of 40 ints. Thus, getting the [i, j] element in the following code involves two object reference operations.

```
for( int i = 0 ; i < 20 ; i++ ){
  for( int j = 0 ; j < 40 ; j++ ) { sum = sum + t[i][j] ; }
}
```

By using a temporary array reference for each row array, we greatly reduce the number of operations. This is shown in the following code where we also use a simpler form of the summation statement which takes fewer operations and uses a decrementing counter which is slightly faster than incrementing.

```
int tmp[] ;
for( int i = 19 ; i >= 0 ; ){
  tmp = t[ i- ] ;
  for( int j = 39 ; j >= 0 ; ) { sum += tmp[ j-- ] ; }
}
```

The compiler -O option

The java compiler from the JDK recognizes the -O optimization switch. When this is specified, the compiler will try to "inline" methods which are declared as final, static, or private. This option also turns off the insertion of line number debugging information into the class files, thus reducing the size of the files and the downloading time.

Remove extra code used in testing

In our discussion of debugging, we made frequent use of local variables which could be checked or printed out. Don't forget to go back and simplify this code after you are sure it is working correctly. You could also remove any toString() methods to save space and reduce download time.

Adjust thread priority

Multithreaded applications can improve the speed of applications by making use of slack time: for instance, you could be carrying out computations while waiting for the user to decide on an option. However, this background thread should have a low priority to ensure rapid response when the user finally acts.

No sleeping on the job

The thread sleep method can be handy for controlling the timing of events, but is not necessarily the best approach when all you want is to give other threads the chance to run. If you have one thread performing a lengthy calculation, your application might appear to have died to a user who clicks a button with no result. Calling the thread yield method frequently in your calculation loop gives a chance for the other threads to respond. However, there is considerable overhead in calls to yield so there is no reason to do it more often than 10–20 times a second.

If your program is an animation or simulation which computes a new state of the system then calls repaint to show the new state, you can use the wait — notify approach instead of sleep to give the system time to paint the screen and catch up on other chores. Here is a sketch of the code required, assuming we have an applet implementing runnable.

```
public void run(){
    while( true ){
        calculateState() ;
        repaint();
        waitForIt();
    }
}

// wait must be called from a synchronized method
synchronized void waitForIt() {
    try{ wait(); } catch(InterruptedException e) {}
}

public void paint(Graphics g ){
    .... do all the painting here
    notifyAll();
}
```

Here is the sequence of events as performed by the system thread and applet thread.

```
Applet Thread                    System Thread
    call calculateState()                               \
    call repaint()
    call wait()
                        respond to repaint request
                        call simulation object paint method
                        paint screen with new state
                        call notifyAll()
    calculateState()
```

Watch out for multiple repaints

If your application involves tracking the course of a mouse and repainting the screen in response, you will encounter serious performance problems. This is due to the fact that mouse events can be generated much faster than the system paint can keep up with. The solution is to track the mouse position by catching all mouse move or drag events, but only to request a repaint when there is not one pending already.

Summary

I n this chapter, we examined the Java development process. As discussed, you may have already formed habits of program development with other languages, but Java introduces so many new elements that even experienced programmers must take a fresh look at the development process. After all that, let's move on to embedding an applet in an HTML document, the topic of our next chapter.

EMBEDDING AN APPLET IN AN HTML DOCUMENT

aving written a Java applet and created a new Java class, DocFooter, you now need to test the new applet. To do this, the applet must be embedded in an HTML document, where it is specified in the form of a new HTML element, the APPLET element and can be invoked by a Java-aware browser.

This chapter teaches you what you need to know about the APPLET element and how to control the Java applet's behavior using its attribute list. You'll also learn how each applet embedded in an HTML document is invoked by a Java-aware browser. We present simple examples of the APPLET element and show you how to specify the APPLET element you use in executing the DocFooter class.

Applying the APPLET Element

ny Java applet that has been compiled into bytecode can be added to an HTML document, using the new HTML APPLET element. The APPLET element adheres to the following general syntax:

Note: [ ] identifies optional parameters:

```
<APPLET
   [CODEBASE = codebaseURL]
   CODE = appletFile
   [ALT = alternateText]
   [NAME = appletInstanceName]
   WIDTH = pixels   HEIGHT = pixels
   [ALIGN = alignment]
   [VSPACE = pixels] [HSPACE = pixels]
>
   [<PARAM NAME = Attribute1 VALUE = value >]
   [<PARAM NAME = Attribute2 VALUE = value >]
      . . .
[alternateHTML]
</APPLET>
```

The optional <PARAM> tag lets you to specify applet-specific attributes that your applet can retrieve as Strings. These Strings can be used in an HTML document to customize the applet's behavior and supply their respective values like command-line variables. The code that follows provides the complete applet syntax with the HTML tags we used in our DocFooter example, as well as optional tags examples:

```
<APPLET codebase=classes code=DocFooter.class
   WIDTH=500 HEIGHT=100
   ALIGN=left
   ALT = "Turn your Java on"
   NAME = "Footer1"
   VSPACE=10 HSPACE=40
>
<PARAM name=LAST_UPDATED        value="11:03 AM 2/23/96" >
<PARAM name=EMAIL               value="wbrogden@bga.com" >
<PARAM name=COPY_RIGHT_NOTICE   value = "Copyright by me, 1996" >
You should get a JAVA capable browser.
</APPLET>
```

CODEBASE and CODE

CODEBASE, CODE, WIDTH, and HEIGHT are parameters specified by the first part of the APPLET tag. The browser uses these to locate the applet code and to reserve space in the HTML document display. Codebase directs the browser to look for code in the classes directory associated with the HTML document's URL. Code provides the name of the Java code file that is to be loaded. Any other class files used by the applet are loaded from the codebase directory as well. Codebase is an optional parameter; if it is not specified, the browser looks for class files in the HTML document's directory. It is important that the use of upper/lower case in both the class name and the filename are identical.

WIDTH and HEIGHT

WIDTH and HEIGHT are parameters that tell the browser to reserve space in the document display before the Java code is loaded ("x" pixels wide by "x" pixels high), similar to the way browsers deal with images, reserving space before the complete image is available. To place an invisible applet on a page, specify height and width of zero.

Current browsers ignore the Java language resize() method for applets. Although the applet viewer provided in the JDK responds to the resize() method, you'll have to specify width and height correctly in the APPLET tag for general Web browsers.

VSPACE and HSPACE

VSPACE and HSPACE are optional parameters for specifying the amount of space (in pixels) that surrounds the applet above and below (vspace) and on each side (hspace) of the applet area. You will find that the Netscape 2.0 browser appears to ignore these parameters.

ALIGN

ALIGN is another optional parameter and is used to designate where the browser is to place the applet area in relation to any other design elements. ALIGN can have possible values like those for the IMG tag: left, right, top, texttop, middle, absmiddle, baseline, bottom, and absbottom. The Netscape 2.0 browser does not support these parameters correctly, so try removing the ALIGN parameter if you don't get the results you want with your applet.

ALT

The alt parameter designates a string to be displayed if the browser understands the <APPLET> tag but does not have Java capability. Netscape 2.0 allows turning the Java interpreter on or off via a check box under Options on the Security Preferences menu. The alt parameter is a way to remind users to turn Java back on after turning it off to avoid wasting time on slow applets (as can often occur on Web pages).

NAME

Applets that coexist on a Web page communicate by means of the `name` parameter. The `AppletContext` method `getApplet(String name)` returns a reference to the named applet if it can be found on the page and then allows communication between applets. Unfortunately, the current generation of browsers does not seem to support this method.

PARAM

The `PARAM` tag is used in transferring text information to your applet code using the `getParameter( String param_name )` applet method. Since the parameter-matching code is not case sensitive and quote marks are parsed out, the following tags are equivalent:

```
<PARAM name=EMAIL
<param NAME=EMAIL
<param name="email"
```

It is wise to get into the habit of using quotes around the value string, because you must enclose any spaces in a value string to avoid fatal confusion in the browser.

For complex information, avoid creating a name/value pair for each item by using a string with values separated by commas or spaces, as in this example:

```
<PARAM name=fontVal value="TimesRoman 14 BOLD">
```

When your applet gets the `fontVal` string, a `StringTokenizer` can parse the string into its components. Farther along in this chapter, we present an applet that employs this technique.

Between the last <PARAM> tag and the </APPLET> tag, you can designate text and HTML code to be displayed if a browser can't recognize the <APPLET> tag. This is a good area for a message which directs users to a vanilla version of your Web page.

</APPLET>

The final element of an applet tag must be `</applet>` to tell the browser that the applet has ended. If your applet does not show up as expected on your Web page, this is the first thing you should check.

SIDE TRIP

PROGRAMMING WITH *PARAM*

If "getParameter()" does not find a named PARAM tag in your <APPLET ... </APPLET> text, it will return a null rather than an empty string. It is good idea to make sure your Java program takes this possibility into account — even if your HTML is always perfect, you might want to share the code someday. In our DocFooter class, we checked for a null String in the paint method. For more complex applets, it is best to provide for a default string using something like the following:

```
if((date = getParameter("LAST_UPDATED")) == null) date = "UNKNOWN";
```

Studying the Class Library

The browser's Java run-time system loads standard classes from a local class library. In Netscape 2.0, this file is:

```
...\program\java\classes\moz2_0.zip
```

In Netscape 3.0 the filename is "java_30."

For the browser to locate any class, only one file needs to be opened because all classes are kept in a zipped (but uncompressed) collection of files. (When you add files to a zip archive with no compression, choose "none" under the compression pull-down list.)

The Security Manager

A SecurityManager object controls the system resources an applet is permitted to access, and file access and network connections must be approved by the SecurityManager, which provides controlled access to system resources. For example, File class objects are prohibited from accessing the local hard disk by Netscape 2.0, but InputStream objects that are derived from the URL of a local HTML document are permitted access.

A browser's security manager is established at startup and cannot be replaced or modified. When writing your application, however, you can create your own SecurityManager.

Exploring Some HTML Examples

L et's look at two examples of APPLET syntax in real HTML documents. The first will let you use Java on your Web page without your having to do any Java coding, and the second illustrates how to pass complex parameters to your applet.

Applet code from somewhere else

If you want to liven up your Web page, but don't have time to set up the JDK or if your service provider can't support Java's long file names, just insert the following in your HTML document:

```
<applet codebase=http://java.sun.com/applets/applets/NervousText
code="NervousText.class" width=200 height=80>
<param name=text value="Lookit me Ma!">
</applet>
```

When someone using a Java-aware browser visits your site, their browser will fetch the NervousText.class code from Sun's Web site, feed it your text and create an animated page.

More complex parameters

In this example, the Java code is stored at your Web site, but we simplify matters by storing both the HTML document and class file in the same directory. A browser expects to find all of your custom class files in the same directory as the HTML document if the Applet tag does not include a CODEBASE parameter. In the following example, we create the Java class called Headline that basically displays a headline with a drop-shadow effect in this initial form, although it can be extended to include color cycling or animation.

STEP 1: CREATE OR MODIFY AN HTML DOCUMENT

If you already have a Web page, you can modify it to announce your arrival in the Java world, or you can start with the following simple HTML document entered with a text editor and saved in plain ASCII text as Test.html. Save the code in a convenient directory. (It is best to create a new subdirectory for each new project.)

```
<HTML>
<HEAD>
<TITLE> Test of the Headline Applet </TITLE>
</HEAD>
<BODY>
<APPLET  CODE="Headline.class" WIDTH=400 HEIGHT=80 >
<PARAM NAME=text VALUE="Announcing">
<PARAM NAME=font VALUE="Helvetica 60 BOLD">
</APPLET><br>
I am pleased to announce that I have joined the Web Revolution
    with JAVA!.<br>
</BODY>
</HTML>
```

STEP 2: INPUT THE JAVA CODE

Type in the following code using a text editor that saves plain ASCII text and save the code in the directory you used for the HTML document. You must save the file with the name Headline.java because the compiler expects the file name to match the class name. We have inserted many (commented out) System.out.println() debugging statements in this code as suggestions of the type of statements you might use if you get in trouble.

```
/* simple applet to demonstrate getting parameters from the HTML
 * named parameters */

import java.applet.Applet;
import java.awt.*;
import java.util.StringTokenizer ;

public class Headline extends Applet {
  String fontName ;
  int fontSize ;
```

```java
int fontStyle ;
String hText ;
Font myFont ;

/* Note: We don't need to define a constructor @md
 *  the default Applet constructor will be used */

// init is called automatically by the run-time system
//
public void init() {
  // System.out.println("Start init");
  setBackground( Color.white );
  hText = getParameter("text");
  if( hText == null ) hText = "Ooops" ;
  String tmp = getParameter("font") ;
  //
  // now create a StringTokenizer based on the value
  // string from the "font" parameter
  //
  StringTokenizer stk = new StringTokenizer( tmp );
  // the default StringTokenizer includes space as a delimiter
  //
  // set some defaults in case the full set of parameters is not
  //     there for some reason
  //
  String fontSizeStr = "32" ;
  String fontStyleStr = "BOLD" ;
  fontName = "Courier" ;
  //
  // note that in the following we expect tokens in a specific
  // order @md name, size, and style
  if( stk.hasMoreTokens() ) fontName = stk.nextToken();
  if( stk.hasMoreTokens() ) fontSizeStr = stk.nextToken();
  if( stk.hasMoreTokens() ) fontStyleStr = stk.nextToken();
  //
  // Construct a temporary Integer object from the parameter
  // string then use it to set the (small i) integer fontSize.
  // If the Integer class can not turn the string into an
  // integer, it will throw a NumberFormatException which
  // we must be prepared to catch. It may look clunky, but it
  // is a lot better than crashing due to an unknown cause.
  //
  try{
```

```
      Integer SZ = new Integer( fontSizeStr );
      fontSize = SZ.intValue() ;
   }catch( NumberFormatException e) {
     System.out.println("Bad font size in " +
             fontSizeStr + " use default" );
     fontSize = 32 ;
   }
   // The Font class defines three style constants, PLAIN, BOLD
  and
   //   ITALIC
   fontStyle = Font.PLAIN ;  // the default
   if( fontStyleStr.equals("BOLD") ) fontStyle = Font.BOLD ;
   if( fontStyleStr.equals("ITALIC") ) fontStyle = Font.ITALIC ;
   myFont = new Font( fontName, fontStyle, fontSize );
   //     If you want to check the font, uncomment the following
   // System.out.println("Font is " + myFont );
   //     Because the Font class implements the "toString()" method
   //     this statement can give very useful information.
 }


   // paint is called whenever the applet is exposed
public void paint( Graphics g) {
   int shift = 1 ;
   // if we didn't set the font, the default font would be used.
   g.setFont( myFont );
   g.setColor( Color.black );
   //
   // note that the x and y in drawString refer to the type
   // baseline which is on the lower left
   //
   g.drawString( hText, 5, fontSize + 4 + shift );
   g.setColor( Color.red );
   g.drawString( hText, 5 - shift , fontSize + 4  );
 }


 }  // end class Headline
```

STEP 3: COMPILE

Compile with the following command while in the `Headline.java` directory:

```
javac Headline.java
```

Windows 95 and Windows NT will run the compiler from an MSDOS window since the compiler is command-line oriented. You will miss any error reports when the window closes if you use the program manager Run command.

STEP 4: FIX COMPILER ERRORS

If you didn't get any errors, congratulations and go to Step 5 while the rest of us try to figure out what went wrong. The compiler's generally informative error messages include the line that caused the error with a pointer to where things seem to have gone wrong. If, for example, a slip of the finger resulted in a left parenthesis being typed where a left curly brace should be, we might see:

```
Headline.java:55: '{' expected.
 public void paint( Graphics g) (
                                 ^
Headline.java:67: Unbalanced parentheses.

 ^
Headline.java:67: '}' expected.

 ^
3 errors
```

There are three errors, but when you fix the first, the rest go away. Just FYI, any programmer's editor with C-oriented features, such as checking parentheses balance, is ideal for Java.

STEP 5: DEBUG

Now that it compiled, it's time to test with our HTML document. There should be two files in the current directory: `Headline.class` and `Test.html` (or your Web page with modifications). From a command line window, use the applet viewer:

```
appletviewer Test.html
```

The applet viewer creates a window for each applet on a page without showing any other HTML display. The initial size of the applet window will be the WIDTH and HEIGHT from the HTML code; however, the applet window will respond to a `resize()` call in your code. Any Java errors, `System.out.println()` or `System.err.println()` calls in your code will put messages out to the command-line window. Compiled Java code carries information about source code line numbers, making error reports very informative. Most programmers find that using `System.out.println()` statements extensively tells them all they need to know about what's going on in the program. The JDK command-line debugger is rather primitive at this time.

STEP 6: USE IT WITH A BROWSER

If everything worked using applet viewer, now try it with a Java-aware browser. At this point, most problems are related to formatting and positioning of the applet on the page. If there's a problem, you'll find detailed error messages on the "Java console" window. In Netscape, use the Options, Show Java Console menu item to see this window.

STEP 7: ON TO THE WEB

If you have a Web page, you no doubt have used a transfer program such as ftp to move class and HTML files from your system to the Web server. Be sure, however, that:

* 8-bit transfer is turned on.
* The class filenames don't get mangled. If the transfer protocol mangles the filename, there should be a rename command you can use to put it right.

STEP 8: TRY IT ON THE WEB

If the applet doesn't show when you access the page with your Web browser, check the "Java console" for error messages. Problems at this stage are usually related to a bad transfer of the class files to the server.

Summary

Congratulations! You have successfully gotten your first Java applet onto the Web. In this chapter, we covered how a Java-enabled browser works with your Java and HTML code. In the next chapter, we extend applets with dynamic behavior, graphics, and sound.

EXTENDING YOUR APPLETS

Because Java programming language is the new thoroughbred in the OO programming stable, it shares OO programming's extensibility: new functionality and features can be added to a Java class unobtrusively and with relative ease. The extensions won't adversely affect other parts of an application, and the scope of the changes are localized.

Extensibility lowers maintenance costs and brings new capabilities to market faster. With this kind of flexibility, we're expecting great things from Java. In this chapter, we show you how easy it is to extend an applet. We also investigate how to decide whether to extend the old or to start from scratch in extending your Java holdings.

Understanding Applet Analysis and Extension

OO programming languages have the virtue of allowing you to quickly adapt an existing class to meet new requirements, a virtue shared by Java. You can create a new class as an extension of an existing class.

Add a new method and — Shazam! — you have a new class with new functionality without having to reinvent the wheel.

New Java classes can be extensions of any individual existing class, a trait called single-class inheritance, to distinguish it from the multiple inheritance found in C++. (Multiple inheritance is typical in many C++ implementations and means creating a new class from more than one existing class — not surprisingly.) In addition, Java provides interfaces that give you the same advantages as multiple inheritance without the nasty overhead on your system.

With Java, the primary question becomes when to extend an existing applet versus when to write a new one. The answer to these questions usually emerges following an analysis of your existing library of classes.

In such an analysis, there are three primary areas of focus that can help you to derive the correct answer to the extend-or-create dilemma. The following analytical foci help you to determine how your existing classes and methods overlap your new needs:

* functionality
* data handling
* interfaces and user interaction

Analyzing each of these areas helps to determine the degree of overlap between existing and planned capabilities as well as to assess their differences. Bear in mind that some classes may possess a close match to the required functions, data handling, or interface interaction but may also possess extra, unneeded facets. The greater these differences, the more likely it is that a new piece of code is needed.

These three foci help you decide whether your class library possesses reusable aspects of function, data handling, and user interaction suitable for your new applet. By digging through each existing class, you can identify good candidates for a parent or superclass for your new class. Then, you can determine the similarities as well as the differences. If the differences outweigh the similarities, keep looking.

You may not find a class with more similarities than differences; if this happens, think hard about creating a new class from scratch. You'll extend the basic Java Object class, which automatically gets you a number of useful methods, so you won't have to create your new class completely from scratch. This is as close to scratch as Java gets.

This analytical process makes a strong argument for defining a complete and robust class library, which requires thorough design and attention to detail in that library throughout the library's entire life cycle. Note also that additional intellectual effort must be expended when creating public classes, methods, interfaces, and exceptions because of their broad availability (and, generally, their equally broad use).

If your design is properly implemented, the result should be a highly extensible class library. This permits more efficient and responsive programming efforts because extensible libraries have broadly applicable components, much as the tools in a toolbox can be used both to adjust an air conditioner and tune up an internal combustion engine.

Choosing Extension Versus Rewrite

After extensive class analysis, another alternative is to rewrite or modify an existing class to satisfy new requirements. This can be dangerous, because you run the risk of affecting existing applications that already rely on this class. You need to recompile all affected applications, so this adds to your maintenance burden. In other words, proceed down the rewrite path with extreme caution!

Extension can be defined as a method of specializing an existing class to create a new class. Such a new class inherits all the public and protected methods and variables of the more general superclass. You can think of extension of a class as specialization of that class, because you intend to change or add functionality. So, as you move down the class hierarchy, you specialize classes. As you move up the class hierarchy, you generalize classes.

The purpose of extension is to leverage the work and effort put into the existing class you intend to specialize, perhaps to solve a variation on a common problem or to play upon a common theme. The rule of thumb here is to shoot for more overlap rather than less, whether in the area of functionality, data handling, or interface interaction.

Rewriting is defined as substantially modifying classes, methods, constructors, or variables from an existing class. Rather than leveraging prior work, a rewrite is an extensive modification of existing code to alter its originally intended use. The rule of thumb here is to require more variation than similarity, whether for functionality, data handling, or interface interaction — or all three simultaneously.

It's also a good idea to evaluate your investment in existing classes, methods, and constructors before making sweeping changes to them: If your future plans outweigh the current implementations, it's probably okay to continue down this path. If they don't, you'll probably want to take a different approach, such as defining a new set of classes, methods, and so forth, and leaving the existing ones intact.

Extending the Headline Applet

In this section, we extend the Headline applet from the previous chapter with popular animation techniques. By using the Runnable interface methods, we give our applet a life of its own. As you may recall, Java uses the interface concept to add large chunks of functionality to classes without the complexity of C++ multiple inheritance.

Since we are extending Headline, we need a new class name and source code file. Start a new source code file to be named CHeadline.java in the same directory you used for Headline. The import statements are:

```
import java.applet.Applet;
import java.awt.*;
// Note! we don't have to import java.util.StringTokenizer
// because that functionality is built into the Headline class
// init method which we inherit from Headline.
```

Now add the CHeadline class definition showing that the class will be derived from Headline with the addition of the Runnable interface.

```
public class CHeadline extends Headline implements Runnable {
```

The extra variables we need for this extension are a Thread object and a Color object:

```
// variable added to track the most recent color used
Color light = Color.red ;
Thread myThread ;
```

The Runnable interface specification says that Runnable classes must have a run routine. A Thread attached to a Runnable object automatically executes the run() routine when it's started. The Applet class has a start() method that is executed by the browser when the applet is first shown on the display — this is an ideal place to create and attach our Thread and start it running. The Applet class also has a stop() method which is executed by the browser when the applet is no longer displayed — the ideal place to stop our thread and dispose of it. If we just left the thread running, it would continue to use part of the browser's execution time. The routines we have to add to support the Thread and implement Runnable (in skeleton form) are as follows:

```
public void start(){}
public void run(){}
public void stop(){}
```

We also want to rewrite the paint() method since we now have a Color variable in place of Headline's constant, but we are inheriting all of Headline's variables as well as init() method, which sets the text and font parameters.

Add the thread related methods as follows:

```
// the only function of start is to start a thread
public void start() {
  if( myThread == null ) {
    myThread = new Thread( this ) ;
    myThread.start();
  }
}

// myThread will call this run() method
public void run() {
  while( myThread != null ) {
    try {
    myThread.sleep( 200 ); // that's 200 milliseconds
      light = light.darker();
      repaint();
    myThread.sleep( 200 );
      light = light.brighter();
      repaint();
    } catch(InterruptedException e ) {}
  }
}

public void stop() {
  if( myThread != null ) {
    myThread.stop();
    myThread = null ;
  }
}
```

At this point, you might try compiling CHeadline.java. Change the CODE statement in your HTML <APPLET> tag to CODE="CHeadline.class" and run the appletviewer on the revised HTML — it looks the same as it did before (except possibly flashing visibly) because, although CHeadline is creating and running a thread which repaints frequently, it's still using Headline's paint() method, which has a hard-coded color! Add the following paint() method code:

```
// this version of paint overrides the paint in Headline.java
public void paint( Graphics g) {
  int shift = 1 ;
  g.setFont( myFont );
  g.setColor( Color.black );
  // note that the x and y in drawString refer to the type baseline
  //  which is on the lower left
```

```
    g.drawString( hText, 5, fontSize + 4 + shift );
    g.setColor( light );
    g.drawString( hText, 5 - shift , fontSize + 4  );
}
```

Now compile CHeadline.java and run the applet viewer. You have achieved a simple animation effect of cycling color, but it still has some annoying flashing. The flash is caused by the way the system handles repaint requests. A repaint call starts an independent sequence of events, when the system gets a chance, it creates a Graphics object and calls the applet's update method. By default, update clears the entire applet area to the background color and then calls paint. By adding the following code, we override the default update and call paint without clearing the background.

```
public void update( Graphics g) {paint( g ) ;}
```

When you compile CHeadline.java and test it, you should get the color cycling effect without flashing. The simple addition of a Thread and implementation of the Runnable interface has changed our static headline display into an active attention-getter.

The use of a thread to change an applet's attributes with time is one half of the techniques used in many animation applets. The other half is the use of off-screen drawing techniques to combine images before they are displayed, thus producing seamless animation.

Rewriting the Headline Applet

In the previous section, we extended the Headline class with CHeadline to add functionality, while building on the tested Headline code. Now, however, we are going to add some functions that require a total rewrite. This new applet, "GHeadline" will demonstrate techniques of off-screen graphic manipulation and show you how to make applets that blend in with your Web-page background.

If you don't already have a Web page with a background image, the following is a short test example using a .gif file of a bloodhound head. Note that the <APPLET> tag now specifies a new parameter with the name "bkg" which is set to the same file name as our HTML page BACKGROUND.

```
<HTML>
<HEAD>
<TITLE> Test of the Headline Applet </TITLE>
</HEAD>
<BODY BACKGROUND="Hound.gif">
<H1>Some text before the applet<br></H1>
<hr>
```

```
<APPLET  CODE="GHeadline.class"
    WIDTH=400 HEIGHT=100  >
<PARAM NAME=text VALUE="Announcing">
<PARAM NAME=font VALUE="Helvetica 60 BOLD">
<PARAM NAME=bkg  VALUE="Hound.gif">
</APPLET><br>
<H2>
The ME corporation announces a fabulous product!.<br>
</H2>
</BODY>
</HTML>
```

Now to create the new GHeadline class. Copy Headline.java to a new file GHeadline.java or start a new file. We use the following import statements:

```
import java.applet.Applet;
import java.awt.*;
import java.util.StringTokenizer ;
```

The class variables required include those from Headline and CHeadline and additional objects we will use to manipulate off-screen images. Here is the way the class declaration and class variable code should look:

```
public class GHeadline extends Applet implements Runnable {
  String fontName ;
  int fontSize ;
  int fontStyle ;
  String hText ;
  Font myFont ;
    // variable to track the most recent color used
  Color  light = Color.red ;

  Thread myThread ;

  Image bkgI = null ;
  int bkgWidth, bkgHeight ;
  Image memImg ;
```

The `init` routine, originally used in Headline to get parameters from the HTML applet tag, now has to get the additional "bkg" parameter which is the name of the background texture file being used on your Web page. Contrary to what you might expect, the `getImage()` routine does not immediately read the image from the specified file; instead, it sets up another process thread which can read the image when the image is needed. Java provides the `MediaTracker` class (in the java.awt package) which we use in the following code to wait until the image is actually loaded. When the image is available, we can get the height and width.

```
/* init is called automatically by the runtime system */
 public void init() {
    setBackground( Color.white );
    hText = getParameter("text");
    if( hText == null ) hText = "Ooops" ;
    String imgN = getParameter("bkg");
    if( imgN != null ) {
        bkgI = getImage( getDocumentBase(), imgN );
        // To force the image to be loaded immediately, we
        // have to use a MediaTracker.  Otherwise, we can't be sure
        // when the Image will be available.
      try {
        MediaTracker trkR = new MediaTracker( this );
        trkR.addImage( bkgI, 1 ) ;
        trkR.waitForID( 1 );
        // now that we have the image we can get its size
        bkgWidth = bkgI.getWidth( null );
        bkgHeight = bkgI.getHeight( null );
      } catch(Exception e){}
    }
    String tmp = getParameter("font") ;
    StringTokenizer stk = new StringTokenizer( tmp );
// the default StringTokenizer includes space as a delimiter
//
// set some defaults in case the full set of parameters is not
// there
    //
    String fontSizeStr = "32" ;
    String fontStyleStr = "BOLD" ;
    fontName = "Courier" ;
    //
    // note that in the following, we expect tokens in a specific
    //  order — name, size, style
    if( stk.hasMoreTokens() ) fontName = stk.nextToken();
    if( stk.hasMoreTokens() ) fontSizeStr = stk.nextToken();
    if( stk.hasMoreTokens() ) fontStyleStr = stk.nextToken();
    //
    // construct a temporary Integer object from the parameter
    // string then use it to set the (small i) integer fontSize
    try{
      Integer SZ = new Integer( fontSizeStr );
      fontSize = SZ.intValue() ;
    }catch( NumberFormatException e) {
      System.out.println("Bad font size in " + fontSizeStr + " use
```

```
        default" );
        fontSize = 32 ;
    }
    fontStyle = Font.PLAIN ;   // the default
    if( fontStyleStr.equals("BOLD") ) fontStyle = Font.BOLD ;
    if( fontStyleStr.equals("ITALIC") ) fontStyle = Font.ITALIC ;
    myFont = new Font( fontName, fontStyle, fontSize );
}
```

In addition to the thread creation and thread start functions we used before, we can also use the start routine to create the image space in memory. This space exactly matches the size of our applet.

```
// the only function of start is to start a thread
// and create the memory Image
public void start() {
    if( myThread == null ) {
        myThread = new Thread( this ) ;
        myThread.start();
    }
    if( memImg == null ) {
        memImg = createImage( size().width, size().height );
    }
}
```

The run routine, which is executed by myThread, remains the same from the CHeadline class. You might think that we could use this thread to compose the off-screen image, but this approach could lead to some strange results due to the fact that the thread executing run and the system thread executing paint behave independently and a paint might occur when run was only partly through with a rebuild of the off-screen image. Synchronization of multiple threads is provided for in Java but is beyond the scope of this book.

```
// myThread will call this run() method
public void run() {
    while( myThread != null ) {
    try {
        myThread.sleep( 200 );
            light = light.darker();
            repaint();
        myThread.sleep( 200 );
            light = light.brighter();
            repaint();
        } catch(InterruptedException e ) {}
    }
```

}

The stop and update routines are the same as we used before:

```
public void stop() {
  if( myThread != null ) {
    myThread.stop();
    myThread = null ;
  }
}

public void update( Graphics g) {
  paint( g ) ;
}
```

Now for the fun part. When paint gets called by the system, either because the applet area has just been exposed by scrolling the document or in response to a repaint call in our run routine, we first compose the applet area image in the off-screen memImg area. Note that to draw in memImg, we first have to get a Graphics object which is appropriate for it. We can't use the Graphics object which is passed to paint because that is attached to the on-screen area of our applet.

We repeatedly draw the background image into memImg until it is completely tiled. This code will work with any size background image.

```
public void paint( Graphics g) {
    int x = 0 ;
    int y = 0 ;
    int shift = 1 ;
    Graphics memg = memImg.getGraphics();
    // now we completely tile the memory image with the bkg image
    while( y < size().height ) {
      x = 0 ;
      while( x < size().width ) {
        memg.drawImage( bkgI, x,y, this );
        x += bkgWidth ;
      } // end while over width
      y += bkgHeight ;
    } // end while over height
    memg.setFont( myFont );
    memg.setColor( Color.black );
    // note that the x and y in drawString refer to the type
    // baseline
    //  which is on the lower left
    memg.drawString( hText, 5, fontSize + 4 + shift );
```

```
memg.setColor( light );
memg.drawString( hText, 5 - shift , fontSize + 4  );
// only now do we draw to the screen
g.drawImage( memImg, 0,0, this );
}
```

Finish off the GHeadline.java code with a final closing curly bracket:

```
} // end class GHeadline
```

Now compile with the usual command line:

```
javac Gheadline.java
```

If it compiled without error, run the applet viewer with your example HTML code, you should see your color cycling headline over a background of "Hound" images. If that worked, on to the big test: using your browser to look at the complete Web page.

When we did this, we got Figure 7-1. Sharp-eyed Web-page composers will see that we have a problem! The Web page's background images and our applet's background images are not aligned the same way. If you are using a subtly colored background, you might find the colors are rendered more crudely in the applet.

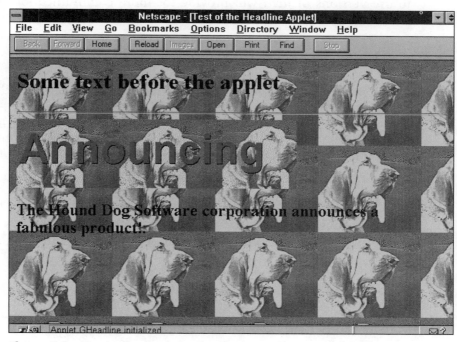

Figure 7-1   Here's what happens when backgrounds are out of synch.

Alignment

Alignment problems are caused by the fact that the browser tiles its background independently of the placement of our applet. At the present state of Java development, there is no way for an applet to find out exactly where on the browser page it has been placed. By experimentation, we can determine an initial horizontal and vertical offset which will result in correct alignment. These offsets are negative numbers which are used to modify the drawing routines in the paint routine:

```
int y = -10 ;
  while( y < size().height ) {
    x = -10 ;
    while( x < size().width ) {
      memg.drawImage( bkgI, x,y, this );
      x += bkgWidth ;
    } // end while over width
    y += bkgHeight ;
  } // end while over height
```

Hard-coding the offsets is very bad programming style. Ideally, offsets would become parameters in the HTML code just as we did with font size. Hopefully, future versions of Java will provide for more communication of page details between browser and applet.

Colors

You may also see color differences between the Web page's background and the applet's background, particularly if your background is more subtly colored than "Hound." This is due to Java's graphics routines being independent of the browser's. The present (1.0) version of Java uses a color palette limited to 256 colors and uses dithering to try to match the original image colors.

Further developments

You now know the basics for all Java animation tricks, threads and off-screen graphics composition. With these basic concepts, you can build truly dramatic and striking effects.

Summary

In this chapter, we considered two ways of extending the functionality of applets. In one example, we were able to add significant new functionality to an existing Java class by deriving a new class with just a few new added variables and routines. The more complex example required a rewrite of the original code, but we ended up with an applet that demonstrates all of the principles of Java animation.

In the next chapter, we introduce you to a full-blown Java application. Unlike the applets used in this chapter, an application is a stand-alone program that doesn't require a browser or applet viewer.

In this final part of the book, we examine full-blown Java applications. We begin with a discussion of designing, building, and using Java applications, as compared and contrasted with applets. Then, we proceed to discuss how Java applications may best be managed, both from the standpoint of handling class libraries and source code, but also from the standpoint of compilation, execution, and packaging issues. This part of the book includes step-by-step instructions on how to complete this process and what to do with the results. Next, we discuss how existing applications may be extended or enhanced, both from a design and implementation standpoint, and also cover software distribution, update, and patching mechanisms.

The book concludes its formal coverage of Java with a rumination on the future of this technology, an assessment of its potential security problems, and a jaundiced view at its platform-independent status. It includes pointers to resources and information to establish a more permanent relationship with Java.

Zilker Internet Park is a full-service, business-oriented Internet Service Provider based in Austin, TX (http://www.zilker.net). In addition to a wide range of connectivity options, Zilker offers custom programming, Web site design and management, and other highly focused programming business solutions to its customers.

DJ: What are you using Java for right now?

SC-M: Many of Zilker's existing Web extensions are Perl-based CGI programs. They're mostly written in Perl 5, but we do have some older code that's still in Perl 4. For that reason, switching to Java's object orientation has been pretty straightforward for us. In fact, Zilker is planning to switch all of the code that handles user interaction and on-the-fly page building to Java to help overcome any of our own platform dependencies. Although we have a pretty homogeneous computing environment in-house, we need to understand what our customers have to deal with.

And since we also offer a Java development environment to those customers, we have to be able to put ourselves in their shoes. At present, we're primarily developing on Solaris 2.51 with JDK 1.0, but we plan to move to the 1.1 JDK as soon as it firms up, probably in mid-1997.

DJ: What are the most interesting applications you've used Java for?

SC-M: We've got some message thread archives for several mailing lists, the beginnings of a customer billing system, and some pretty interesting animation widgets, all of which are Java-based. For us, what makes Java interesting is not so much what it looks like, but that it enables us to interact with customers through a Web browser. To typical end-users, our code would probably be dull and boring, but for our own purposes, it makes us able to do our jobs more quickly and cheaply.

In this business, anything that helps provide better service and control costs at the same time is a Godsend, and it helps to explain our enthusiasm for Java. In fact, we call Zilker a "Java Green Belt," because we're trying to encourage its growth and proliferation, as a way of improving our own efficiency, and helping our customers to do the same.

DJ: Where is Java taking Zilker Internet Park?

SC-M: We see Java as a way of attracting and retaining customers who want to customize or enhance their Web capabilities. In fact, we view Java as a must-have ingredient for our continued business involvement with our customers as a value-added ISP. It still remains to be seen whether Java is going to emerge as the standard language for Web development, but for us it's no longer a matter of "Java or not" but rather a matter of "how to use Java."

WRITING A JAVA APPLICATION

IN THIS CHAPTER YOU LEARN THESE KEY SKILLS

In this chapter, we show you how to write a standalone Java application, which is a different kind of bird from the applet we wrote earlier. An applet's execution is controlled by the browser initiating execution from the Java runtime system after the HTML document passes the URL included in the <APPLET> tag back to a Web server. A stand-alone Java application controls its own execution, communicating directly with the Java runtime system.

The Java interpreter executes Java applications from the command line. The interpreter operates much like a C program, loading the runtime library of standard classes and your application classes before starting the "main" routine. Java command-line arguments can also be passed like a C program.

Throughout this chapter, we step through the code to create a simple but powerful stand-alone Java application, called RenderImageApp, that takes advantage of the extensive image processing functions in the Java standard library. It is designed to let you quickly examine GIF and JPG image files without having to resort to a paint program. This application offers only limited functionality, but it is extendable.

RenderImageApp illustrates the concepts Java uses to organize a graphical user interface that is not tied to a specific operating system, using a platform-independent LayoutManager to control a graphic window layout. Our Java application also makes use of Button controls and the standard Java FileDialog.

Writing a Java Application, Step by Step

We will now guide you step by step through the creation of RenderImageApp. As each new concept is introduced, we explain its meaning and purpose.

Step 1: Creating the file "RenderImageApp.java" and importing required system packages

In this step, you create a file named RenderImageApp.java in the /html/ classes directory; the full path for your new application is /html/classes/ RenderImageApp.java.

You need to specify the system classes your application will incorporate from the java.awt package using the import keyword. The java.lang package, which has the other classes you'll use, is automatically imported by the compiler. Here's the code:

```
// -- An Image rendering Application
import java.awt.*;
```

Step 2: Declaring the new class RenderImageApp

The next step is to declare a new class, named RenderImageApp, that is an extension to the standard library class, Frame. The declaration looks like this:

```
public class RenderImageApp extends Frame {
   ... body of class goes here ..
}
```

You can see that your new class is an extension to the existing Frame class, which makes Frame its superclass. This means your application inherits all Frame's public and protected class variables, constructors, and methods.

Step 3: Declaring instance and class variables

Having declared your new class, you now need to declare your class and instance variables. You can use static Class variables when you know they are not going to change. Static Class variables are visible to all class instances; instance variables pertain only to a particular instance of a given class. Here are the declarations:

```
// these are the strings we'll use for button labels
final String GET_GIF = "Display a GIF Image";
final String GET_JPG = "Display a JPG Image";
final String EXIT    = "Exit" ;

ImagePanel imgPanel ;   // a new class we define later
Panel ctrlsPanel ;      // a standard Java Panel
```

Step 4: The main method

A main method occupies an unusual position in the Java object system. In this case, although it is declared inside the RenderImageApp class definition, it is not actually used as a method of that class. When the application is executed, the Java interpreter turns control over to the main method which is responsible for creating the objects used by the application. The main method is always declared as public and static. Here is the code for creating the main method for the new RenderImageApp class:

```
// main procedure of RenderImageApp class
public static void main(String args[]) {
RenderImageApp window = new RenderImageApp();
  window.setTitle("Render Image Application ");
  window.pack();
  window.show();
}
```

Any parameters typed after the class name on the command line are passed to the main method in an array of Strings. The first parameter is found in args[0], the second in args[1], and so on. In this particular case, we get input from a dialog box; however, an obvious extension of this code is passing a file path on the command line. The call to pack causes the LayoutManagers to adjust the size and position of the window components. The call to show causes the window to become visible and in front of other windows in the system.

Step 5: Creating the constructor

Here, you declare the constructor for the new RenderImageApp class, the purposes of which are:

* to create the panel and buttons used for controlling the Application.
* to create the ImagePanel that is used for display.
* to create the LayoutManager that controls the placement of the button and ImagePanels.

```
// constructor
RenderImageApp() {
 imgPanel = new ImagePanel();
 ctrlsPanel = new Panel(); // panel for buttons at the top

 // add buttons for the functions needed
 ctrlsPanel.add(new Button( GET_GIF ));
 ctrlsPanel.add(new Button( GET_JPG ));
 ctrlsPanel.add(new Button( EXIT ));
 // the default layout is "FlowLayout" so we have to:
 setLayout(new BorderLayout()); // change the LayoutManager
 add("North", ctrlsPanel);   // place ctrlsPanel at top
 add("Center", imgPanel);    // the imagePanel fills the remainder
 }
```

This is the first time we have used Panels and LayoutManagers, so let's look at them more closely. The java.awt.Panel class is descended from the abstract java.awt.Container class, which is in turn descended from the java.awt.Component class. Panels can contain a number of graphic components and have LayoutManagers that arrange the components. The default LayoutManager for a new Panel is a "flow" manager that simply adds components from left to right. The first button added to the ctrlsPanel ends up on the left side, with the others following it. The size of each button is determined by the space needed to display the label.

The Frame class from which RenderImageApp is derived is also derived from Container and can use a LayoutManager. By adding a BorderLayout (a kind of LayoutManager) to the new RenderImageApp object in the constructor, we allow for placing panels according to the BorderLayout syntax that lets us place components on the "North," "South," "East," and "West" edges, or in the "Center."

Step 6: Creating the EventHandler

 X-REF The EventHandler class handles user input like mouse clicks and key presses. It is described in the Chapter 8 Discovery Center section at the end of this book (page 287).

Step 7: Creating the ImagePanel class

The ImagePanel class contains the Canvas on which we display the image and the TextField that we use to report the true size of the image and to read the image. This code can be added conveniently to ImageRenderApp.java after the closing brace of the ImageRenderApp class definition. The code for the class definition and declaration of instance variables for ImagePanel follows:

```
class ImagePanel extends Panel {
  ImageCanvas iCanvas ;  // which we define later
  TextField   info ;  // a standard java.awt.TextField object
}
```

In the ImagePanel constructor, we create an ImageCanvas (a new class defined later) and an ordinary TextField. TextField objects are normally editable, but we use the setEditable method with a false input, because we don't want the user to be able to edit it in this case. We assign a BorderLayout type of LayoutManager (as we did with the RenderImageApp object), so we can place the ImageCanvas in the center with the TextField below.

```
ImagePanel() {
    setLayout( new BorderLayout() ) ;
    iCanvas = new ImageCanvas();
    info = new TextField();
    info.setEditable( false );
    add("Center", iCanvas );
    add("South", info );
    show();
  }
```

Because ImagePanel is only a container, it does not need to respond to any events; however, we need a method to get an image and pass it to the ImageCanvas for display. This is done in the ShowImage method. Note that although in the applet examples we were able to call the applet method getImage directly, in an application, we have to use the code:

```
getToolkit().getImage(fileloc) ;
```

The Toolkit contains the hardware- and operating system-specific routines necessary for interfacing with the local file system. In applets, this is supplied by the browser; but here, we have to request it specifically. Note that we have provided for a Boolean return from ShowImage to indicate success or failure. This is not used in the present application, but may be nice to have in place if we reuse this class for some other application.

```java
public boolean ShowImage( String fileloc ){
Image tmp ;
  String s ;
  MediaTracker trk = new MediaTracker(this) ;
  tmp = getToolkit().getImage(fileloc);
  trk.addImage( tmp, 1 );
  try {
   trk.waitForID( 1 ); // after this, image is resident
   iCanvas.setImage( tmp );
   iCanvas.repaint();
   int w = tmp.getWidth( this );    // will be -1 if no image
                                    // found
   int h = tmp.getHeight( this );
   if( w == -1 ) s = "File not found or not an image file" ;
   else s = "Image is " + w + " wide X " + h + " high"   ;
   info.setText( s );
   return true ;
  } catch(InterruptedException e ){
    info.setText("Interrupted loading");
    System.out.println("Image load " + e );
  }
  return false ;
}
```

Step 8: Creating the ImageCanvas class

As the last step in our application's code, we need to create the class that will actually display the image using the Canvas class as a convenient starting point. The only necessary instance variable is to hold the Image. We initialize myImg to null so that the paint routine can tell if an image has been loaded. Remember that paint routines are called by the system both in response to a repaint request and whenever it thinks the component area has been newly exposed.

```java
class ImageCanvas extends Canvas {

Image myImg = null ;
```

```
public void setImage( Image I ) { myImg = I ; }

public void paint(Graphics g) {
  if( myImg == null ) { // alternate display if no Image yet
    g.setColor(Color.white );
    g.fillRect(0, 0, size().width -1, size().height -1 );
    g.setColor(Color.black);// set the color to black
    g.drawString("Ready",15, 15);
  }
  else {
    // note that this drawImage method fits the image into a
    // preset space by stretching or compressing.
    g.drawImage( myImg, 0,0, size().width, size().height, this);
  }
}

// a minimumSize routine is needed so the LayoutManager can
// determine how much space to allocate.
public Dimension minimumSize() {
  return new Dimension(250,250);
}

public Dimension preferredSize() {
  return minimumSize();
}
}
```

Step 9: Saving RenderImageApp.java and Compiling

X-REF We hope that you have been saving frequently as you enter the code! Now we will compile the same way we compiled the applet in Chapter 4.

```
javac RenderImageApp.java
```

When the code has compiled, the following class files should be in your working directory:

* RenderImageApp.class — the application
* ImagePanel.class — the container for the image and text field
* ImageCanvas.class — the object that draws the image

The other classes that the Java interpreter requires for completion of the application will be drawn from the class library file, "classes.zip" in the \java\lib subdirectory.

Step 10: Run and Test

Finally, we can run the application. Note that in the command line for the Java interpreter, we give only the class name (without the ".class" file type):

```
java RenderImageApp
```

When you run the application, you should see a window with three buttons across the top. Clicking the "Display a GIF Image" button, should give you the normal file dialog for your operating system. Select a GIF file and it should appear after a short pause, adjusted to fit your window size. Resize the window and the image is redrawn to fit. When the window is resized, the LayoutManagers for the imgPanel, ctrlsPanel, and main app window resize their components, so when the paint routine in the ImageCanvas starts to draw the image, it finds the current window dimensions. If you reduce the width of the window, the LayoutManager for the ctrlsPanel will ignore buttons that can't be completely displayed.

Summary

n this chapter, we have covered the basics of creating applications with various graphic interface widgets and LayoutManagers. In the process, we have found that a Java application differs from an applet in that

* A main method controls overall execution.
* The windows created behave just like normal program windows.
* We are not constrained by browser security restrictions and can access any local file.

JAVA APPLICATION MANAGEMENT

9

IN THIS CHAPTER YOU LEARN THESE KEY SKILLS

Because Java is an OO programming language, among its major virtues are its extensibility and its reusability. Reusability is implicit in good OO programming, offering the dazzling possibility of reusing code easily and repeatedly. Unfortunately, both these virtues can cause major project-management headaches.

A library of core elements can be a saving grace in the headache area, and in Java, this library comes as a collection of Java packages. A package, you'll remember, is just a named collection of classes similar in functionality, data, or interface interaction. For example, the Java system library's java.net package contains classes related to distributed networking, and the java.io package contains classes that deal with Java input and output constructs. In this chapter, you'll learn why it's important to develop a robust library of classes upon which you can build, and how to use libraries effectively. You'll also learn about the Java compiler in even more glorious detail. Finally, we show you how to create and install an application wrapper script that provides a straightforward, simple interface to your Java applications.

Managing Class Libraries and Java Applications

I n this section, you'll discover why it's so important to effectively manage and organize your Java applications, and we propose a hypothetical organization for structuring your class library.

The system class library is located in a particular place in the file system in the Java runtime environment. It may have been put there automatically by the install script, or you may have placed it there explicitly. For example, the root directory for the system class library of the 1.0 distribution is defined as:

```
<my_path>/java/lib/
```

<My_path> is where you put the distribution in your file system.

There is a large "classes.zip" file in this directory. Each Java class occupies a single ".class" file when compiled. To avoid the hard-disk clutter and high disk overhead of hundreds of class files, Java1.0 designers provided for putting all 581 class files in a single file, using an approach similar to the familiar zip compressed file directory. The Java class files are not compressed, but are collected into the zipped directory that includes the package subdirectory scheme. The Java compiler, interpreter, and other utilities regard classes.zip as an extension of your hard disk file system.

You should note that browsers, such as Netscape Navigator, have their own zipped file of classes. For Netscape 3.0, this file is java_30, which contains 307 class files.

Obviously, it would be advantageous to combine your application's many class files into a single file for more efficient downloading and storage. Unfortunately, as this is written, conflicting browser approaches have been taken by Netscape and Microsoft. Sun is expected to release a standard for collecting class files; maybe this will let the industry settle on a single approach.

If you want to create a collection of classes that others can use, you'll have use the hard disk's subdirectory to organize your package. If you want to create such a collection of classes, you should first make sure that you're not duplicating classes and methods already provided in the system class library. If you're sure that you need a library of new classes, design it carefully. Judicious design and organization of classes into packages will pay off handsomely in the long run.

The first step in creating your own library of classes is to determine which package-naming convention you will use. The language designers intended that with dozens of vendors selling Java toolkits and development programs, package naming will prevent names "colliding." A company name is a good starting point for package naming; you will find classes in packages that start with "netscape" in the Netscape class library.

Next, you need to design the overall scheme of your new library. As an example, let's assume you're building a library of classes for a simulator that requires input, output, controls, and utilities. The following associated packages would be a reasonable point of departure:

```
MyCorp.Simulator.input
MyCorp.Simulator.output
MyCorp.Simulator.controls
MyCorp.Simulator.utils
```

You must define classes, each with its own distinct methods and variables within each of the packages, bearing in mind that each class is a direct or indirect descendent of a single super class, java.lang.Object.

For a real-world example of a nice collection of Java packages, look at the Web site which follows. WebLogic Technologies, a San Francisco-based company, has developed a tool called WebScript that facilitates the integration of the Web and existing business applications and databases. They've developed these three packages:

* webscript.dblayer

* webscript.html

* webscript.utils

Each package contains classes, their methods, and their variables, and each provides a specific capability. For instance, the webscript.dblayer package contains classes such as Database, DataSet, Column, Record, and Table that represent typical objects (or structural equivalents) that are found in most relational database systems.

 WEB PATH **For more information about WebLogic, go to the following URL:**

`http://www.weblogic.com/`

WebLogic's packages are an excellent example of how to organize the classes in your packages. To follow in those footsteps, you first need to determine the real-world and abstract objects your applications require.

In the example Simulator class library, you can look at the simulator as a real-world object and choose other real-world objects that either complement or make up a simulator. This is a classical approach to object-oriented design and is called decomposing an object. It involves breaking an object into smaller constituent objects. The decomposition approach can be very useful in developing a comprehensive library of classes.

You also need to consider including abstract classes when decomposing your classes. Abstract classes provide a unifying structural commonality. This can be especially important if your project involves more than one programmer. The container class of the java.awt package, for example, is an abstract class that provides common variables and methods for the Panel, Applet, Window, Dialog, and Frame classes.

Finally, you should provide a package declaration on the first noncomment line for each class in the package. Here's an example:

```
package MyCorp.Simulator.input;

import java.lang.*;

public class getData {
   ... body of class ...
}
```

The class getData is made a member of the Simulator.input package by the declaration in the preceding Java code fragment.

Compiling Java Applications

In this section, you'll learn more about compiling Java applications; much of this information can also be applied to Java applets. The Java compiler, javac, compiles each class specified in Java code into its bytecode representation. It compiles any file with a .java extension into a binary object file with a .class extension. The resulting new binary object can then be interpreted by the Java interpreter, java.

Although your Java-source-code files can contain more than one class declaration or implementation, only one can be declared public. Javac creates a byte-code binary object for each class definition and stores each object in a separate file with the .class extension.

Let's say your Java-source-code file declares three new classes called NewClassA, NewClassB, and NewClassC in a file named NewClassA.java. Javac would create three new files, NewClassA.class, NewClassB.class, and NewClassC.class, which are created in the same directory as the source code files — unless the -d command-line option is specified. In that case, the default will be overridden by the directory you specify.

When compiling several classes, if a referenced class doesn't exist in the source code file, javac searches for it based on values specified within the CLASS-PATH environment variable. If the referenced class is not found in either the source code file or in the class path, a compile-time exception occurs, resulting in an error message.

Javac_g

Javac_g is a nonoptimizing version of javac designed to be used with a debugger like jdb. Using a debugger is a usually a good idea, especially when you're trying to decipher the occasionally cryptic run-time error messages that javac issues.

The command for the nonoptimizing compiler is:

```
javac_g RenderImageApp.java
```

This command produces a binary object that a debugger can use in tracing variables and their values, or in stepping through the execution of your source code. It can even find where that bomb in your code exploded when you referenced a class that couldn't be found!

Compilation options

Both Java compilers accommodate the same set of command-line options that control the bytecode compilation and placement of the output files. The "classpath" option designates a path in the file system that either compiler uses to find referenced classes.

```
-classpath <path>
```

If this option is used, it overrides the CLASSPATH environment variable. Directories in <path> are colon-separated paths in UNIX and semicolon-separated in Windows. The period that starts the string in the following example is a context indicator that indicates the current working directory. When the compiler in this example is looking for a class, it looks first in the current directory.

```
javac -classpath .:/home/classes:/export/classes Spam.java
```

-d <directory>

The -d <directory> option defines the root directory for the class hierarchy and is used when you want the resulting compiled class file to be saved in a directory other than the one containing the source code file. For example:

```
javac -d /home/apps/classes Spam.java
```

In this example, the class file named Spam.class is saved in the /home/apps/classes directory rather than in the same directory as the source code.

-g

The -g option enables the generation of debugging tables necessary when you are using external debuggers. The tables contain information about variables, methods, and line numbers in the Java source code file. For example:

```
javac -g Spam.java
```

-nowarn

The -nowarn option turns off compiler warnings so the Java compiler sends no compile-time errors to STDERR. Here's an example:

```
javac -nowarn Spam.java
```

-O

The -O option optimizes your compiled class by compiling all static, final, and private methods inline. The danger with this option is that it can result in a larger bytecode representation of your compiled class. The upside is that the class should execute faster in Java's run-time environment. You'll have to decide which you prefer: speed or space. Here's an example:

```
javac -O Spam.java
```

-verbose

The -verbose option tells the compiler and linker to echo all compile and link messages to STDERR. These messages contain information about all the Java source files compiled and classes loaded. Here's an example:

```
javac -verbose Spam.java
```

This would produce the following sample output, echoed to SDTERR:

```
[parsed Spam.java in 2352ms]
[checking class Spam]
[loaded /html/classes/browser/Applet.class in 813ms]
[loaded /html/classes/java/lang/Object.class in 124ms]
[loaded /html/classes/awt/Graphics.class in 461ms]
[wrote Spam.class]
[done in 9479ms]
```

Verbose may be an understatement!

Installing Java Applications

 X-REF After successfully compiling a new application, you need to define a location for that application and its associated compiled classes. Refer to the Chapter 9 Discovery Center for an in-depth look at this issue (page 289).

Stepping Through Compilation and Installation

In this section, we take you step by step through the compilation and installation of the RenderImageApp application that you created in the previous chapter. You'll also create a wrapper script for UNIX use or a BAT file for Windows use of RenderImageApp.

Step 1: Compile RenderImageApp.java

In the first step, you compile the Java source code file named RenderImageApp.java in the /html/classes directory. Invoke the Java compiler with the -g option to enable debugging table generation and the -verbose option to echo compiler and loader information. On the command line, enter:

```
javac -g -verbose RenderImageApp.java
```

A successful compilation results in the creation of class files RenderImageApp.class, renderWindow.class, inputWindow.class, and urlField.class created in the /html/classes directory, without encountering warnings or compilation error messages.

Compilation warnings can result in an interpretable class, but the resulting bytecode should be considered unsafe. The one exception is when your code contains dusty corners that may never be reached by the executing thread. For example, the implementation of the system class named NetworkServer contains a while loop that will not terminate unless the process is explicitly killed. The next line after this while block is a close() statement.

The Java compiler prints a warning message that this statement is never reached. This is not harmful, and the compiled class is safe; execution will not result in any side effects that could wreak havoc on your local system.

Compilation error messages are a sure sign of an unsuccessful compile. Error messages are verbose and provide a good deal of information about the problem, including where in the source code file it originates. The compilation of a Java source code file named TC.java resulted in the following error messages:

```
chevelle:/html/classes[] javac TC.java
TC.java:48: Class tc not found in type declaration.
        public void ReadObj(tc tcnew) {
                            ^
TC.java:49: Undefined variable: tcNew
        inObject = tcNew;
                   ^
2 errors
```

Notice that each error message lists the file name, the line number in the source code, and an explanation of the error. In our example, the first error occurs in the TC.java file on line 48. The compiler couldn't find the class tc referenced in the argument list of the method named ReadObj. The second error message is related to the first; it's in the same file, but on line 49. The compiler found an undefined variable because the argument list for the method on line 48 specified an incorrect variable name (tcNew instead of tcnew).

Continue working through the error messages until all errors are fixed; it's the only way to get your code into working order.

Step 2: Recompile for optimization

Your next step is to recompile the RenderImageApp application for optimization and to disable debugger table generation. On the command line, enter:

```
javac -O -ng -verbose RenderImageApp.java
```

This creates an optimized bytecode representation for the RenderImageApp application and also disables the creation of debugging tables that increase the size of the resulting bytecode class file. (Note: The -ng option may not be necessary; it depends whether your site enables debugging table generation as a default.)

Step 3: Write a UNIX wrapper script or DOS BAT

This is where you write a wrapper script that provides a simple interface to the RenderImageApp application. Several site-independent environment variables are set in this script; alter these lines of the script accordingly.

The wrapper script can become a template for similar scripts for any Java applications you develop. To reuse the script, all you need to alter are the application location and name in the script. You may also need to adjust the class path to include specific classes required to run your applications. You can also add additional options to the Java interpreter.

In your text editor, enter this Bourne-shell wrapper script for the RenderImageApp application:

```
#! /bin/sh

############################################################
# Modify these variables
############################################################
# The directory where your java application is stored
APPDIR=/u/markg/java/classes/
# The name of your java application
APP=RenderImageApp
```

```
# java compiler options
OPTS='-classpath "$CLASSPATH"'
# the java compiler
PROG=$JAVA_HOME/bin/java

# make sure the JAVA_HOME environment variable is set
if [ -z "$JAVA_HOME" ]
then
  echo "Please set your JAVA_HOME environment variable"
  exit
fi
export JAVA_HOME

# If the location of your application is not found in your current
# class path, either change your CLASSPATH environment variable
# or append the location to this shell environment variable. The
# latter method makes the change to this variable local in scope.
# Outside this shell, this variable reverts back to its original
# value.
if [ -z "${CLASSPATH}" ]
then

  CLASSPATH=".:$JAVA_HOME/classes:$JAVA_HOME/lib/classes.zip:$APP
  DIR"
else
  CLASSPATH="$CLASSPATH:$APPDIR"
fi
export CLASSPATH

# change to the directory where your java application is stored
if [ ! -d "$APPDIR" ]
then
  echo "Unable to change to the application directory $APPDIR"
  exit
else
  cd "$APPDIR"
fi

# run the java interpreter with input of your java application
if [ -f "$PROG" ]
then
  eval exec $PROG $OPTS $APP
else
  echo "Could not find the java interpreter"
```

```
        exit
fi
```

When creating and debugging your application, you may have relied on the java interpreter finding class files in the current directory, but if you are going to use this application from any directory, the java interpreter needs to be able to find your application class files and the standard library files. By creating a "BAT" file with the correct classpath, you can run without worrying about the current directory. Here is an example one-line RenderImage.bat file for running the RenderImage application assuming the class files are in "d:\JDK\Image."

```
java -classpath d:\JDK\Image;d:\JDK\java\lib\classes.zip
    RenderImageApp
```

Step 4: Save the script (UNIX)

Save the Bourne-shell script as a hidden file named .render_image_app_wrapper in a place in your file system where other scripts are located. We recommend /usr/local/bin for most UNIX implementations, making the absolute name of the wrapper script /usr/local/bin/.render_image_app_wrapper. You use a hidden file so that when your users list the directory, the script will be invisible. If users can't see the script, they'll be less likely to change it.

Step 5: Install the wrapper script (UNIX)

You now install the wrapper script and make a symbolic link from RenderImage to the wrapper script. The link is intended to simplify invocation of the RenderImageApp application.

First, change to the /usr/local/bin directory. You'll need at least write permission for this directory. If you don't have the proper permissions, contact your site's system administrator.

On the command line, enter (or have the administrator enter):

```
ln -s .render_image_app_wrapper RenderImage
```

This creates a symbolic link named RenderImage in the /usr/local/bin directory. To invoke the RenderImageApp, enter the following on the command line:

```
./RenderImage &
```

This implicitly runs the wrapper script, sets the correct environment variable, and invokes the Java interpreter on the RenderImageApp application. Users can invoke RenderImage anywhere in the file system if /usr/local/bin is on their path.

> **TIP** Tip for csh and tcsh Users Only!
>
> You'll need to rehash the shell so it can find the new script!

Step 6: Test your new application

You're now ready to test your new RenderImageApp application, bearing in mind that RenderImage is the command-line interface to this application. This is the command your users will invoke, rather than the more obscure command RenderImageApp.

To test your new application, change to your home directory and enter the following on the command line:

```
./RenderImage &
```

If the shell returns an error message to the effect that the command cannot be found, check the permissions for the wrapper script. The permissions on .render_image_app_wrapper should be executable by world, group, and user for UNIX implementations. If the shell returns an error message to the effect that the RenderImageApp class cannot be found, check your CLASSPATH environment variable to make sure you entered the application's directory correctly.

Summary

Java's extensibility and reusability are valuable strengths, but they require careful management and organization. The design and installation of a class library should be the result of an intense and thorough process of analysis of existing classes, methods, and constructors.

The Java compiler offers numerous command-line options for controlling the handling of source code. Installation of Java applications can be greatly simplified by creating a wrapper script that controls the required environment and provides a simple execution interface. Wrapper scripts should be installed in well-known or common system locations.

EXTENDING JAVA APPLICATIONS

10

A Java application can be extended in much the same manner as a Java applet. In this chapter, we present a new Java application, written by William B. Brogden (wbrogden@bga.com), named HierApp. HierApp allows browsing in hierarchically organized text data and demonstrates a number of Java features not previously covered in this book, such as command line arguments, using scroll bars, and organizing data with linked lists. After introducing the application, we show you how it can be extended with various features.

Examining the HierApp Application

The Java application called HierApp reads a text file containing hierarchically organized categories and presents a graphical interface for browsing the data. The example data we use is a small subset of the Java standard library specification that has been reformatted from the original. This browser would also be useful for catalogs and corporate organization charts.

HierApp is derived from `java.awt.Frame` and consists of three new classes, `HierApp`, `HierCanvas`, and `NodeMem`. The application provides the basic window framework and the main routine. `HierCanvas` is derived from `java.awt.Canvas` and provides for drawing hierarchical elements and responding to user input. NodeMem is derived from the base class Object and allows you to keep track of the properties of a single entry in the hierarchical data.

Figure 10-1 shows the application in action, so to speak. The left panel shows the organization of the hierarchy, and the right panel offers a text description of the selected item. As a Java student, you will recognize that our test data represents part of the hierarchy of standard Java classes.

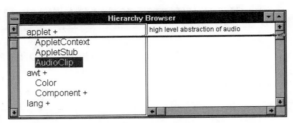

Figure 10-1 The HierApp application in action.

The HierApp class

HierApp is an extension of the Frame class and provides both a graphical user interface window appropriate to the operating system and the main routine that is called by the Java interpreter. The main routine expects to find a filename, which it passes to the constructor in the command line. The constructor creates all user interface elements, then calls getData to open the data file and build the data structure. After the initial display of the data, HierApp simply responds to user inputs — such as keystrokes, scrollbar movement, and mouse clicks — until a WINDOW_DESTROY event is received.

User input events are processed in the handleEvent method, an illustration of how Java treats keyboard and scrollbar inputs. Key presses, which involve function keys and cursor control keys, are turned into "Event.KEY_ACTION" type events. HierApp uses cursor control keys to move the highlighted areas through the data hierarchy. Ordinary keystrokes become "KEY_PRESS" events, which HierApp uses in toggling the expansion or contraction of the display. Control key presses are passed on to the system because Ctrl+C is used by the TextArea object as a signal to copy selected text.

WEB
PATH

We recommend that you create a new subdirectory for this application and put the source code for HierApp in a file named HierApp.java. Alternatively, you can download the source for all three classes from:

http://www.webtechs.com/java60/

```
/* HierApp is copyright 1996 by William B. Brogden.
 * It is released for all commercial or noncommercial uses,
 * provided this copyright notice is attached.  Enjoy! */
```

```java
import java.awt.*;
import java.io.* ;
import java.util.Vector ;

public class HierApp extends Frame {

   String hierfile ;
   Vector nlist = null ;
   Panel lPanel  ; // left side, canvas and scroll bar
   Panel rPanel  ; // right side, text display
   GridLayout layout ;
   Scrollbar scB ;
   TextArea  txT ;  // std text area

   int appHeight = 200 ;
   int appWidth  = 500 ;
   int state ;

   HierCanvas hc ;
   int      nLines = 10 ; // target number of lines in display
   int      nodect ;
   int      depth = 6 ; // maximum number of layers in hierarchy


   public static void main( String args[] ) {
     HierApp window ;
     if( args.length == 0 ) {
       System.out.println(
        "HierApp requires an input filename in the command line."
);
       System.out.println(
          "The input file must contain the hierarchy
information");
       System.out.println(
          "in a specific text format.");
       System.exit(1);
     }
     window = new HierApp( args[0] );
     window.setTitle("Hierarchy Browser");
     window.pack();
     window.show();
   }

   public HierApp(String file) {
```

```
        hierfile = file;
        layout = new GridLayout( 1,2 ) ; // for two panels side-by-side//
        setLayout( layout ) ;     // for the Frame
        hc = new HierCanvas( appHeight );
         // build panels built & add to Frame
        lPanel = new Panel() ; // left panel for canvas & scrollbar
        lPanel.setLayout( new BorderLayout() );
        scB = new Scrollbar( Scrollbar.VERTICAL,0,10,0, 100 ) ;
        lPanel.add("West", scB ) ;
        lPanel.add("Center", hc ) ;
        add( lPanel ) ; // to frame - grid layout
        rPanel = new Panel() ;
        rPanel.setLayout( new BorderLayout() ) ;
        txT = new TextArea("Text Area") ;
        txT.setEditable( false ) ;
        txT.setBackground( Color.white );
        // Connect components to the HierCanvas
        hc.AddParent( this ) ;  // so canvas can notify us of text chg//
        hc.AddScrollbar( scB ) ; // so canvas can make scB track
        // right panel has only a single TextArea in this version but
        // we could add specialized components here
        rPanel.add("Center", txT ) ;
        add( rPanel ) ;             // to Frame
        show();
        getData();
        repaint();
    }   // end constructor


public void getData() {
    int ret, nc ;
    FileInputStream inS = null ;
    BufferedInputStream BinS = null ;
    NodeMem nm ;
     // node list vector starts with 50 elements, grows by 10
     // if your hierarchy is larger, create vector with larger
     // initial number of elements.
    nlist = new Vector(50, 10 ) ;
    nc = 0 ; // to count NodeMem objects added to list
    try {
        inS = new FileInputStream( hierfile) ;
```

```
        BinS = new BufferedInputStream( inS );
        StreamTokenizer st = new StreamTokenizer( BinS ) ;
        // the StreamTokenizer will take apart the input lines
        // according to the following settings
        st.eolIsSignificant( true ) ;  // end of line is special
        st.whitespaceChars( 44, 46 ) ; // period, dash & comma
        st.whitespaceChars( 58, 59 ) ; // colon and semicolon
        st.wordChars( 32, 32 ) ; // space allowed in phrases
        st.wordChars( 95, 95 ) ; // underscore allowed in words
        st.quoteChar( 34 ) ;
        ret = StreamTokenizer.TT_EOL ;
        while( ret != StreamTokenizer.TT_EOF ) {
          nm = new NodeMem( depth, st ) ;
          ret = st.ttype ;
          if(( ret != StreamTokenizer.TT_EOF) && ( nm != null )) {
            nlist.addElement((Object) nm ); nc++ ;
          }


        }
        inS.close();  // close the input stream
      } catch(Exception e ) {
        System.out.println("Problem with input file " +
                       e.toString());
      }
      if( nc > 0 )
      { nodect = nc ;
        System.out.println("List has " + nodect + " items" ) ;
        // we have a vector of data, pass it to canvas
        hc.SetVector( nlist, nc, depth, nLines  );
        scB.setValues( 0,10,0, nodect + 10 ) ;
        hc.calculateHier() ;
        hc.repaint();   //  repaint with hc state = 1  after
                        //  calculation
      }
      else
      { System.out.println("No data found");
      }
    } // end getData()

// this method is called from HierCanvas when selection has
// changed, resulting in new text to be shown in the text area
// could do specialized processing of URLs or other data types
// here
```

```java
    public void TextChange( String newtx ) {
       txT.setText( newtx ) ;
    }


// handle all keyboard and scrollbar events
   public boolean handleEvent( Event evt ) {
     boolean ret = false ;
     switch( evt.id ) {
      case Event.KEY_ACTION : // just control keys
          // enable the following to watch what the events contain
          // System.out.println( "Key action" + evt.toString() ) ;
        switch( evt.key ) {
          case Event.UP :     hc.upSel( 1 ) ; ret = true ; break ;
          case Event.DOWN :   hc.dnSel( 1 ) ; ret = true ; break ;
          case Event.RIGHT : hc.expand()   ; ret = true ; break ;
          case Event.LEFT : hc.contract() ; ret = true ; break ;
          case   Event.F1 :  // testing

            break ;
         }
         break ;
       case Event.KEY_PRESS  :
          if(evt.controlDown()) { ret = false ;
            // let TextArea see ctrl-C for copy
          }
          else {
            hc.toggle(); ret = true ;
          } // normal key press toggles the current selection
         break ;
       case  Event.GOT_FOCUS :
        hc.setFocus( true ) ; hc.repaint(); // don't set ret = true
        break ; // because we want system to see
       case  Event.LOST_FOCUS :              // the focus change
        hc.setFocus( false ) ; hc.repaint();
        break ;
       case  Event.SCROLL_LINE_DOWN : hc.dnSel( 1 ) ; ret = true ;
        break ;
       case  Event.SCROLL_PAGE_DOWN : hc.dnSel( 2 ) ; ret = true ;
        break ;
       case  Event.SCROLL_LINE_UP   : hc.upSel( 1 ) ; ret = true ;
        break ;
       case  Event.SCROLL_PAGE_UP   : hc.upSel( 2 ) ; ret = true ;
        break ;
       case   Event.SCROLL_ABSOLUTE  : hc.absSel( scB.getValue() ) ;
```

```
        ret = true ; break ;
      case  Event.WINDOW_ICONIFY : hide();
       ret = true ; break ;
      case  Event.WINDOW_DESTROY : System.exit(0);
      }
    if( ret ){ hc.repaint(); return ret ;}
    return super.handleEvent( evt ) ;
  }

  public void update( Graphics g ) {
    if( state == 0 ) super.update( g ) ;
    else {  // avoid extra clear after first one
      paint( g ) ; state = 1 ;
    }
  }

  public Dimension minimumSize() {
      return new Dimension( appWidth, appHeight);
  }

  public Dimension preferredSize() { return minimumSize(); }

} // end class Hier
```

The NodeMem class

Each line in the data input file becomes a NodeMem object. The NodeMem construc-tor uses a StreamTokenizer, which was created in HierApp with an open file, and which recognizes the data tags by special punctuation. Tags are separated by periods or colons in the sample data and by double quotes enclosing strings that can have other punctuation.

The following are example lines from the test case that is drawn from the Java standard library hierarchy, followed by a description of the NodeMem objects that will be built:

1. awt: "Another Windowing Toolkit\nAbstract Window Toolkit"

2. awt.Color: "java.awt.Color.html"

3. awt.Component: "java.awt.Component.html"

4. awt.Component.Button: "java.awt.Button.html"

Notice that the data lines start with "awt." (The numbering used in the pre-ceding list is for convenience in the following description of how the lines are treated.)

The first line is a level 1 entry: it has no parent, and its child is 2. The string enclosed in double quotes becomes the "desc" variable.

Line 2 is a level 2 entry with 1 as the parent, no child, nxsib = 3, and no prevsib.

Line 3 is a level 2 entry with 1 as the parent, child = 4, and prevsib = 2. Whether or not it has a nxsib depends on the lines following line four.

Line 4 will be a level 3 entry with 3 as the parent and no prevsib. Whether or not it has a nxsib or a child depends on the following lines.

When NodeMem objects are first created, the relationship pointers are zero; it is up to HierCanvas to determine the relationships later. The following is the source code for the NodeMem class, which should go into a file named NodeMem.java:

```
import java.awt.Rectangle ; // the only class in awt we need
import java.io.StreamTokenizer;
import java.io.InputStream;
import java.io.IOException;
import java.util.Vector ;

// an object to represent a member of the hierarchy
public class NodeMem {
  public boolean visible ;  // in current display - calc by canvas
  public boolean exposed ;  // due to hierarchy selections
  public Rectangle sRect ;  // set when displayed
  public int level  ; // level values range 1 -  depth
// these pointers to other members of the hierarchy are
// implemented
// as integers for ease of debugging, they could just as easily
// have been NodeMem object pointers
  int parent ;  // if not level 1
  int child  ;  // n of first child, or 0 if none
  int nxsib, prevsib ;    // n of next or previous sib or 0 if
  none
  public String tags[] ;  // names appearing in hierarchy
  public String desc   ;  // long text description

  // Note that setting the way the StreamTokenizer recognizes
  // chars is extremely important
  //
  // number of tags, StreamTokenizer reading input file
  NodeMem( int Ntag,  StreamTokenizer st )  throws IOException {
    int tagct  = 0 ;
    tags = new String[ Ntag ] ;
```

```java
        sRect = new Rectangle() ;
        exposed = false ;
        nxsib = prevsib = -1 ; parent = -1 ;
        desc = null ;
        boolean inline = true ;
    while( inline ) {
        switch( st.nextToken() ) {
          case StreamTokenizer.TT_EOL :
           // System.out.println("End of line");
           inline = false ; break ;
          case StreamTokenizer.TT_EOF :
           // System.out.println("End of file");
           inline = false ; break ;
          case StreamTokenizer.TT_WORD :
           // System.out.println("Word: " + st.sval );
           tags[ tagct++ ] = st.sval ; break ;
          case StreamTokenizer.TT_NUMBER : // not supposed to find
any
           System.out.println("Number: " + st.nval ) ; break ;
          case 34 :  // parsed string in quotes
           // System.out.println("String: " + st.sval ) ;
           desc = st.sval ;  break ;
          default :
           System.out.println("Unknown token" + st.ttype );
        } // end switch
    } // end while loop
    if( tagct == 1 ) exposed = true ;
    level = tagct ;  // 1 to ?
    while( tagct < Ntag ) { tags[ tagct++ ] = "" ; }
    if( desc == null ) desc = "" ;
} // end constructor

// a useful routine for debugging
public void dump() {
    int i ;
    if( visible ) System.out.print("Vis ");
    else System.out.print("Not ");
    for( i = 0 ; i < level ; i++ ) {
       System.out.print(  tags[i] + " " );
    }
    System.out.println( "level " + level );
}

}
```

The HierCanvas class

The HierCanvas class organizes the vector of NodeMem objects into a hierarchy and displays it. The initial display shows only the first level of the hierarchy; the level of detail shown at any point in the hierarchy changes with user inputs in the form of key presses, scrollbar movements, or mouse clicks. The following is the code for the HierCanvas class, which should go into a file named HierCanvas.java:

```java
import java.awt.*;
import java.io.StreamTokenizer;
import java.io.InputStream;
import java.io.IOException;
import java.util.Vector ;


//  a class to contain a java.util.Vector of elements and display
//  it based on Canvas
public class HierCanvas extends Canvas {
    int state ;  // 0 = no vector resident

    Vector nodelist ;  // which we get from HierApp
    int     nodect ;
    int     topnode ;  // displayed on first line
    int     selnode ;  // always a visible selection
    int     level ;
    int      depth ; // number of layers in hierarchy
  // display related
  boolean gotFocus ;
  int insets[]  ; // x position for starting display line
  int hCheight ; // canvas height as initialized
  Dimension   sizeC ;
          // canvas size.height, size.width - as seen by paint
        // which could be affected by resize
  int nLines ;            // desired number of lines in the canvas
  int c_height, c_ascent ; // reset every paint
  int fontsize ;            // point size, smaller than height
  FontMetrics fmtr ;
  Font      curFont ;
  HierApp  parent ; // so we can inform of text change
  Scrollbar scB ;   // on left edge of panel which we update
```

```java
    // constructor - takes initial window height
    public HierCanvas(   int hi ) {
       state   = 0 ;
       nodect  = 0 ;
       topnode = 0 ;
       selnode = 0 ;
       level   = 1 ;
       hCheight = hi ;
       gotFocus = false ;
       setBackground( Color.white );
    } // end constructor

  // send the descriptive text attached to selnode to parent
  void updateTx() {
    NodeMem thisN = (NodeMem) nodelist.elementAt( selnode );
    if( parent != null ) {
      parent.TextChange( thisN.desc );
    }
  }

// selnode may have changed, recalculate topnode to ensure
// display
 void calcTop() {
    int i, nlines, posct ;
    NodeMem thisN ;
    if( state == 0 ) return ;
    int poss[] = new int[ nodect ] ;
    nlines = sizeC.height / c_height ;
    if( nlines < 2 ) nlines = 2 ;
    if( selnode <= topnode ) { topnode = selnode ; return ; }
    if( selnode <  topnode + nlines ) return ;
    // make list of possibles (exposed lines) until we hit selnode
    posct = 0 ;
    for( i = 0 ; i < nodect ; i++ ) {
      thisN = (NodeMem) nodelist.elementAt( i );
      if( thisN.exposed ) poss[ posct++ ] = i ;
      if( i >= selnode ) break ;
    }
    i = 1 + (posct - nlines ) ;
    if( i < 0 ) i = 0 ;
    if( topnode < poss[i] ) topnode = poss[ i ] ;
 }
```

```
// Action mouseDown is generated by clicking in the Canvas
// area. The sRect rectangles of every visible node were set
// in the most recent paint operation so we simply look through
// all the visible nodes to see if there was a hit. Mouse clicks
// just toggle the state of the selected node.
public boolean mouseDown( Event evt, int x, int y ) {
    NodeMem thisN ;
    int i ;
    for( i = topnode ; i < nodect ; i++ ) {
        thisN = (NodeMem) nodelist.elementAt( i );
        if( thisN.visible ) {
            if( thisN.sRect.inside( x, y ) ) {
                if( selnode == i ) { toggle();
                }
                else selnode = i ;
                repaint();
                return true ;
            }
        }
    }
    return false ;
}


// absolute selection - only from a scrollbar move as
// detected in HierApp and turned into a call to absSel
// since the n value may not correspond to an exposed node,
// we have to hunt
public void absSel( int n ) {
    int target, del, prev ;
    target = n ;
    if( n >= nodect ) target = nodect - 1 ;
    if( n < 0 ) target = 0 ;   // may not be possible, check anyway
    del = target - selnode ;   // neg means up, pos down
    if( del == 0 ) return ;
    if( del < 0 ) {
        while( target < selnode ) upSel( 1 ) ;
    }
    else {   // target may not be exposed
        prev = selnode ;
        while( target > selnode ) {
            dnSel( 1 ) ;
            if( prev == selnode ) break ;
// unable to go further down
            prev = selnode ; // try for another
```

```
        }
      }
    }

    // move up n exposed nodes if possible
    // upSel and dnSel are called from the HierApp handleEvent
    // routine on cursor key and scrollbar events
    public void upSel( int n ) {
      int ct ;
      NodeMem thisN ;
      ct = n ;
      while( ct > 0 )
      { if( --selnode <= 0 ){ selnode = 0 ; break;} //at top already
        thisN = (NodeMem) nodelist.elementAt( selnode );
        if( selnode < topnode ) topnode = selnode ;
        if( thisN.exposed ) ct-- ;  // found another exposed
      }
      calcTop();
    }

    public void dnSel( int n ) {
      int i, ct ;
      NodeMem thisN ;
      ct = n ;
      while( ct > 0 )
      { if( selnode + 1 == nodect ) break ;  // at bottom
        for( i = selnode + 1 ; i < nodect ; i++ ) {
          thisN = (NodeMem) nodelist.elementAt( i );
          if( thisN.exposed ) {
            ct-- ; selnode = i ; break ;
          }
        }
        // i == nodect if we got to end with no more exposed
        if( i >= nodect ) break ;
      }
      calcTop();
    }

    // toggle state of selnode, if children exposed, contract, and
    // so on called due to keypress or mouse click
    public void toggle() {
      NodeMem thisN = (NodeMem) nodelist.elementAt( selnode );
      int n ;
      n = thisN.child ;
```

```
    if( n == 0 ) return ;
    thisN = (NodeMem) nodelist.elementAt( n ) ;
    if( thisN.exposed ) contract() ; // already expanded
    else expand();
  }

// expose any children attached to selected node
public void expand() {
  NodeMem thisN = (NodeMem) nodelist.elementAt( selnode );
  int n ;
  n = thisN.child ;
  if( n <= 0 ) return ; // no child, can't expand
  thisN = (NodeMem) nodelist.elementAt( n ) ;
  if( thisN.exposed ) return ; // already expanded
  thisN.exposed = true ;
  selnode = n ;
  while( thisN.nxsib > 0 ) { // do all the sibs
    thisN = (NodeMem) nodelist.elementAt( thisN.nxsib ) ;
    thisN.exposed = true ;
  }
  calcTop();
}

// hide any children of this n - then itself & sibs - recursive
void hideNChild( int n ) {
  int chn ;
  NodeMem thisN = (NodeMem) nodelist.elementAt( n );
  chn = thisN.child ;
  if( chn > 0 ) hideNChild( chn ) ;
  thisN.exposed = false ;
  if( thisN.nxsib > 0 ) {
      hideNChild( thisN.nxsib ) ;
  }
}

// contract is tricky because we may be at a node
// with exposed  children
// or on a node without any, but with a parent
public void contract() {
  int n ;
  NodeMem thisN = (NodeMem) nodelist.elementAt( selnode );
  n = thisN.child ;
  if( n <= 0 ) return ;
  if( ((NodeMem) nodelist.elementAt( n )).exposed ) {
```

```
        hideNChild( n ) ;
    }
    calcTop();
}


// here is where we get the initial list of nodes
//  nc = count of nodes, dp = max depth,
//  nln = try for this number of lines in display
public void SetVector(  Vector nlist, int nc, int dp, int nln )
{
    int prevS, tmpN ;
    nodelist = nlist ;
    nodect  = nc ;
    topnode = 0 ;
    selnode = 0 ;
    state  = 1 ;
    level  = 1 ;
    nLines = nln ;
    depth  = dp ;
    gotFocus = false ;
    insets = new int[ depth ] ;
        // the inset from left edge, for each level
    for( int i = 1 ; i <= depth ; i++ ) {
      insets[ i - 1 ] = i * 15 ;
    }
    curFont = getFont();
    fmtr = getFontMetrics( getFont() ) ;
    fontsize = curFont.getSize() ;
    prevS = fontsize ;
    tmpN = hCheight / fmtr.getHeight() ;
    if( tmpN != nLines ) {
      if( tmpN < nLines )while( decrFont());
      else while( incrFont());
      }
  } // end SetVector

  public void AddParent( HierApp p ) { parent = p ; }
  public void setFocus( boolean flg ) { gotFocus = flg ; }
  public void AddScrollbar( Scrollbar s ) { scB = s ; }

// decrease font size to meet nLines target, min size is 8 point
// return true if latest decr fails to meet target
  boolean decrFont() {
    int tmpN, prevS ;
```

```
        if( fontsize <= 8 ) return false ;
        setFont( new Font( curFont.getName(),
                         Font.PLAIN, fontsize - 1 ));
        curFont = getFont();
        fontsize = curFont.getSize() ;
        fmtr = getFontMetrics( getFont() ) ;
        tmpN = hCheight/ fmtr.getHeight() ;
        return ( tmpN < nLines ) ;
    }

    // similar to increase font size - max 40
    boolean incrFont() {
        int tmpN ;
        if( fontsize >= 40 ) return false ;
        setFont( new Font( curFont.getName(),
                         Font.PLAIN, fontsize + 1 ));
        curFont = getFont();
        fontsize = curFont.getSize() ;
        fmtr = getFontMetrics( getFont() ) ;
        tmpN = hCheight/ fmtr.getHeight() ;
        return ( tmpN > nLines ) ;
    }

    public void paint(Graphics g) {
        NodeMem  thisN ;
        int i, x, y, txwid, pluswid ;
        x = 1 ;
        if( state == 0 ) {
            g.drawString("Working", 10,10 ); return ;
        }
    // NOTE: the check above prevents the initial paint from trying
    // to work with an incomplete data structure.
    // state is set to 1 after data read and structure built
        sizeC = size() ;   // current size of canvas
        fmtr = getFontMetrics( getFont() ) ;
        c_height = fmtr.getHeight() ;
        c_ascent = fmtr.getAscent() ;
        pluswid = fmtr.stringWidth( " + " ) ; // indicator of more
        // calculate visibility & layout
        calculateVis() ;
        // update text area in right panel from selnode
        updateTx() ;
        // the following draws a border in red if canvas has focus
        if( gotFocus ) g.setColor( Color.red ) ;
```

```
          else g.setColor( Color.black ) ;
          sizeC.width -= 4 ; sizeC.height -= 4 ;
          g.draw3DRect( 1,1, sizeC.width ,sizeC.height, true ) ;
          scB.setValue( selnode ) ;
          // prepare to show nodes until we run out of canvas or nodes
          i = 0 ; y = c_height + 1 ;
          while(( y < sizeC.height) && ( i < nodect )) {
            // thisN = (NodeMem) nodelist.elementAt( i );
            if( thisN == null ) {
              System.out.println("null thisN from list") ; break ;
            }
            // useful debugging statement at this point =
            // thisN.dump();
            if( thisN.visible ) {
              x = insets[ thisN.level - 1 ] ; // level 1 - depth
              if( i == selnode )
              { g.setColor( Color.darkGray ) ;
                txwid = fmtr.stringWidth( thisN.tags[ thisN.level - 1]);
                g.fillRect( x, y - c_ascent, txwid + pluswid, c_height
   );
                g.setColor( Color.white ) ;
              }
              else { g.setColor( Color.black ) ; }
              if( thisN.child > 0 ) {
               g.drawString(thisN.tags[thisN.level - 1] + " +", x, y ) ;
              }
              else {
               g.drawString( thisN.tags[ thisN.level - 1 ], x, y ) ;
              }
              thisN.sRect.reshape(x, y - c_ascent,sizeC.width
              ,c_height);
              y += c_height ;
            } // from visible test
            i++ ;
          }
      } // end paint

// enter with n = possible parent node, 0 based, check for
// children
// NOTE: any child would be following immediately and have next
// level as well as matching tags - print errors
   // IF there is a child, fill in child slot in element n,
   //    fill in parent slot in element n + 1,  return true
   boolean childCheck( int n ) {
     int i ;
```

```
         if( n >= nodect ) return false ;
         NodeMem thisN = (NodeMem) nodelist.elementAt( n );
         thisN.child = 0 ;      // default
         if( ( n + 1 ) >= nodect ) return false ; // at end of list
         NodeMem nextN = (NodeMem) nodelist.elementAt( n + 1 );
         nextN.parent = 0 ;
         if( nextN.level <= thisN.level ) return false ;
         // probably a child but check tags in case of error
         for( i = 0 ; i < thisN.level ; i++ ) {
           if( thisN.tags[i].compareTo( nextN.tags[i] ) != 0 ) {
             System.out.println("Err in tag order " + n +
                             thisN.tags[i] + nextN.tags[i] );
             return false ;
           }
         }
         thisN.child  = n + 1 ;
         nextN.parent = n ;
         return true ;
       }

     // link siblings with n - known to be a first child
     // return count of sibs found
     int sibCheck( int n ) {
       int i, j,ps, ct, mtch ;
       NodeMem nextN ;
       if( n + 1 >= nodect ) return 0 ; // no sibs possible
       NodeMem thisN = (NodeMem) nodelist.elementAt( n );
       if( thisN.prevsib > 0 ) {
         return 1 ;
       }
       ps = n ;   // use for prevsib pointer
       i = n + 1 ; ct = 0 ;
       // a sib could occur anywhere in remainder of the list
       while( i < nodect ) {
         nextN = (NodeMem) nodelist.elementAt( i );
         if( thisN.level == nextN.level ) {         // level must match
           if( thisN.level == 1 ) mtch = 0 ; // all level 1s are sibs
           else {
             mtch = 1 ;
             for( j = 1; j < thisN.level ; j++ ) { // tags must match
               mtch = thisN.tags[j - 1].compareTo( nextN.tags[j -
               1]);
                 if( mtch != 0 ) break ;
             }
```

```
        }
      if( mtch == 0 ) {   // i is sib to n and ps
        thisN.nxsib = i ;
        nextN.parent = thisN.parent ;
        nextN.prevsib = ps ;
        ps = i ;
        thisN = nextN ;
        ct++ ;
      }
      else break ;   // tested tags[], no match
    }
    i++ ;
  }  // end while( i < nodect)
  return ct ;
}


public void calculateHier()   // calculate hierarchy structure
{ int i  ;
  NodeMem thisN ;
  i = 0 ;
  while( i < nodect )
  { thisN = (NodeMem) nodelist.elementAt( i );
    if( childCheck( i ) ) {
      // childCheck sets Child in n, Parent in n + 1
      // if you have problems with hierarchy, use following
      // statement to help debug
      // System.out.print("has child ") ; thisN.dump();
    }
    sibCheck( i ) ; // set sib pointers
    i++ ;
  }
}


// calculate visibility of nodes based on current top, etc.
void calculateVis()
{ int i, j, y  ;
  NodeMem thisN ;
  i = 0 ;
  while(i < topnode)
      ((NodeMem)nodelist.elementAt(i++ )).visible = false ;
  y = c_height + 1 ;  // first line painted here
  for( i = topnode ; i < nodect ; i++ ) {
    thisN = (NodeMem) nodelist.elementAt( i );
    if( thisN == null ) break ;
```

```
      if( thisN.exposed ) {
       thisN.visible = true ;
       y += c_height ;
      }
      else thisN.visible = false ;
      if( y >= sizeC.height ) break ;
    }
  }

  public Dimension minimumSize() {
    return new Dimension( 100,100 ) ;
  }
}
```

The sample data

The hierarchy data file format uses one line per item, with each line having one
or more tags separated by commas, periods, semicolons, or colons. There is a
string enclosed in quotes after the final tag which is displayed in the right-hand
text area when the item is selected. Line breaks are inserted in the display by
embedding the character sequence "\n" in the string. The order of lines in the
data file must be that of a fully expanded hierarchy listing. Here is the sample
data that describes part of the Java standard library object hierarchy. Type this
into a text file and save it "javatree.lst" or download the file from our Web site.
For your convenience, the descriptive strings have been kept short; however,
there is no actual limit on the length of descriptive strings except that it must be
completed on one line.

```
applet:"Classes related to Applet services"
applet.AppletContext:"corresponds to an applet's environment"
applet.AppletStub:"not normally used by applet programmers"
applet.AudioClip:"high level abstraction of audio"
awt:"Another Windowing Toolkit\nAbstract Window Toolkit"
awt.Color:"A class to encapsulate RGB Colors"
awt.Component:"generic Abstract Window Toolkit component"
awt.Component.Button:" produces a labeled button component"
awt.Component.Canvas:"another generic component"
awt.Component.Checkbox:"GUI element that has a boolean state"
awt.Component.Choice:" a pop-up menu of choices"
awt.Component.Container:" a component that can contain others"
awt.Component.Container.Panel:" a generic container"
awt.Component.Container.Panel.Applet:"Applet objects"
awt.Component.Container.Panel.Window:"top level window"
```

```
awt.Component.Container.Panel.Window.Dialog:"creates dialogs"
awt.Component.Container.Panel.Window.Frame:"windows with borders"
awt.Component.Label:"displays a single line of read-only text"
awt.image.ColorModel:"abstract class for translating pixel values"
awt.image.ColorModel.DirectColorModel:"uses alpha, red, green
   blue"
awt.image.ColorModel.IndexColorModel:"indexes into a fixed
   colormap"
lang:"Basic Java language"
lang.Boolean:"only true or false values\nNot convertible from int"
lang.Math:"contains many standard math functions"
lang.Object:"all classes descend from Object"
util:"Utility classes\nnot always needed\nthus not included in
   lang"
util.Dictionary:"is the abstract parent of Hashtable"
util.Dictionary.Hashtable:"maps keys to values"
```

Compilation and installation

You should now have three Java source code files and one test data file in your project subdirectory. Compile the Java code in the usual way:

```
javac NodeMem.java
javac HierCanvas.java
javac HierApp.java
```

Assuming you got a clean compile, you are now ready for the big test!

```
java HierApp javatree.lst
```

Try moving around in the hierarchy with cursor keys and mouse clicks and resize the window with your normal operating system methods. We hope that applications in your own field are already occurring to you, such as catalogs, company directories, and help systems. Stay with us as we examine possible extensions of the HierApp classes.

Extending HierApp

By now you have learned many of the techniques that can be applied to extending this basic application. In the following sections, we suggest approaches while leaving the details of coding to you.

Add a file dialog

The basic `HierApp` constructor requires a filename that comes from the command line. You could create an alternate constructor that main would call when no file was on the command line. This constructor would use the file dialog technique we used in `RenderImageApp`, and goes something like this:

```
public HierApp() {
FileDialog dlog ;
dlg = new FileDialog(this, "Get Data",FileDialog.LOAD);
dlog.setFile("*.lst");
dlog.show();    // when this dialog exits, we may have a filename
if( dlog.getFile() == null  ) System.exit(0);
hierfile = dlog.getFile();
... body of constructor as before
} // end constructor
```

The main routine can now be modified to use the appropriate constructor depending on whether or not there is a file name in the command line.

```
public static void main( String args[] ) {
    HierApp window ;
    if( args.length == 0 ) {
      window = new HierApp() ; // uses file dialog
    }
    else {
      window = new HierApp( args[0] ); // uses command line
    }
    window.setTitle("Hierarchy Browser");
    window.pack();
    window.show();
  }
```

Add a RenderImage function

Astounding as it may appear, you can convert `HierApp` from showing descriptive text to showing pictures by using classes from the `RenderImageApp` you created earlier — and changing a few lines of code in HierApp.java. Put the `ImagePanel.class` and `ImageCanvas.class` files in the same directory as `HierApp`. Change the `HierApp` variable `rPanel` from a `Panel` to an `ImagePanel`. Change the `HierApp` constructor to look like this:

```
public HierApp(String file) {
    hierfile = file;
    layout = new GridLayout(1,2 ) ;
    setLayout( layout ) ; // for Frame
```

```
        hc = new HierCanvas( appHeight );
         // build panels built & add to Frame
        lPanel = new Panel() ; // for canvas
        lPanel.setLayout( new BorderLayout() );
        scB = new Scrollbar( Scrollbar.VERTICAL,0,10,0, 100 ) ;
        lPanel.add("West", scB ) ;
        lPanel.add("Center", hc ) ;
        add( lPanel ) ;
        rPanel = new ImagePanel() ;
        add( rPanel ) ;              // to frame
        // Connect components to the HierCanvas
        hc.AddParent( this ) ;  // so canvas can notify us of text chg
        hc.AddScrollbar( scB ) ; // so canvas can make sc track
        show();
        getData();
        repaint();
    }  // end constructor
```

Change the TextChange method in HierApp as follows:

```
public void TextChange( String newtx ) {
rPanel.ShowImage(newtx);
}
```

Create a data file that has complete filenames for GIF image files instead of for descriptive text — that's all there is to it. HierApp will now show images in the right panel — a great feature for a catalog application.

Limitations on applications

In the current state of Java language development, there are some functions that have been developed for Applets but that are not available for applications; for instance, version 1.0 does not allow applications to create or play AudioClip objects.

There are also other unexpected limitations on both Applets and applications. A good example of what we mean is the absence of a print function to allow a browser to print the graphic contents of an Applet or to allow an application to print text or graphics.

Summary

Extending Java applications is similar to extending Java applets. Basically, it is a matter of taking existing functionality and adding new classes and methods to provide the new behavior.

TEXT MANIPULATION IN JAVA, USEFUL APPLICATIONS

IN THIS CHAPTER YOU LEARN THESE KEY SKILLS

I n this chapter, we build a flexible set of classes for performing useful functions on text and put these classes to work in two example Java applications. This topic has been chosen to illustrate practical use of the Java "interface" concept and some of the Java standard library classes which we have not covered in previous chapters. We will be creating classes of "text widgets" which can be combined in a variety of ways.

Design considerations

The design of the Java standard library was heavily influenced by the need for network communication, which emphasizes input and output as streams of bytes as opposed to (for example) fixed-length records. The java.io package provides us with ideal starting points for text manipulation widgets. The classes derived from the abstract `java.io.InputStream` and `java.io.OutputStream` classes give us simple methods for getting text in and out of widgets.

The basic design philosophy of the Text Widgets is that each text-manipulating object must operate independently. Each widget must turn input into output as fast as it can, without regard for other things happening elsewhere in the program. This is accomplished by giving each widget its own thread of execution using the `java.lang.Thread` class.

The `PipedOutputStream` and `PipedInputStream` classes are a matching pair which form a "pipe" suitable for transferring bytes between objects when connected. The Thread writing a byte to a `PipedOutputStream` blocks other thread execution until the byte can be written, and the Thread reading a byte from a `PipedInputStream` blocks other thread execution until a byte is available or the pipe is closed.

We will be manipulating ASCII characters which Java handles as bytes, but there is no reason these widgets could not be modified to handle the 16-bit Unicode characters. The designers of Java clearly had the international world of the Internet in mind, support for 16-bit characters is designed into many standard classes. Unfortunately, display and printing Unicode font support is not available in the initial releases of the language.

The Interface construct in the Java language lets us define an abstract set of methods which can be implemented by one or more classes. The beauty of this construct is that connections between objects can be defined entirely in terms of interfaces. If we get the Interface definition right, we will never have to worry about changes in one class wrecking an entire program.

Inventing the Interfaces

It turns out that we will need only three interfaces, one for text sources, one for filters, and one for text output. As shown in Figure 11-1, an object implementing the `TWidgetSource` interface will feed a stream to a `TWidgetFilter` which can feed another filter or an object implementing a `TWidgetSink` interface.

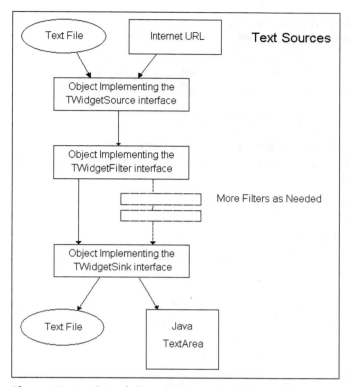

Figure 11-1 Flow of characters through objects implementing the Twidget interfaces.

THE TEXT SOURCE INTERFACE

Here is the definition for the TWidgetSource interface, which must be in its own file.

```
//  interface for text sources          TWidgetSource.Java
import java.io.* ;
abstract public interface TWidgetSource extends Runnable {
   static final int BUFSIZE = 512 ;
   abstract boolean OpenSource( String src, int type );
   abstract PipedOutputStream TWOutput() ;
   abstract void start();
   abstract boolean atEofQ();
}
```

When programming a class which implements this interface we will need to provide a method for opening a source, which might be a file, a URL, a serial port, or piped output from another program. The OpenSource method gets a String which in our example will be a file name; it must return true if the open was successful. The integer type is in the OpenSource method in case we need to provide an extra flag. The `TWOutput` method provides the connection a filter will use to get text input. We obviously need a `start` method to start the processing thread once connections have been made. Finally, we need `atEofQ` to determine if the text source has been exhausted. The constant BUFSIZE is available in case a source object needs a suggested buffer size but does not have to be used.

THE TEXT FILTER INTERFACE

Here is the definition for the filter interface, you can see that we have defined constants for many of the standard types of text filtering that we expect to be dealing with:

```
// interface for text filters        TWidgetFilter.java
import java.io.* ;
public interface TWidgetFilter extends Runnable{
  static final int BUFSIZE = 256 ;
  static final int UPPERCASE = 1 ;
  static final int LOWERCASE = 2 ;
  static final int CRLFTOLF  = 3 ;   // a standard replace
  static final int LFTOCRLF  = 4 ;
  static final int CHARSUBS  = 5 ; // char by char substitute
  static final int WORDSUBS  = 6 ; // word by word substitute,
  static final int SEQNSUBS  = 7 ; // arbitrary sequence
  substitute

  abstract boolean setTWidgetSource( Object Src );
  abstract PipedOutputStream TWOutput(); // source for next stage
  abstract boolean setFilterType( String info );
        // returns true if type is supported
  abstract void setSubstitute(String inS, String outS, String puncS );
  abstract void start();
}
```

Filter widgets will get a source when `setTWidgetSource` is called and provide a source for the next widget when `TWOutput` is called. The `setFilterType` method lets us use the same basic object for many simple filter operations. For those filters which need additional input instructions, we provide the `setSubstitute` interface. Naturally we need a `start` method to start the processing thread once the filter has been set up.

THE TEXT OUTPUT INTERFACE

The interface for final output of processed text is `TWidgetSink`:

```
import java.io.* ;

public interface TWidgetSink extends Runnable {
```

```
static final int BUFSIZE = 512 ;
abstract boolean setTWidgetSource( Object Src );
abstract boolean ReadySink( Object sink );
abstract void start();
}
```

The kinds of text output we want to support include a file, a printer, a Java
TextArea or just a bit bucket. An object implementing TWidgetSink will get its
input set by the setTWidgetSource routine and output method set by ReadySink.
As with the other interfaces, we will use start to start processing once the widget
has been set up correctly.

Example Input and Output Classes

Here are some Input and Output classes that you can look at to gain an understanding of how they work.

TWFILESOURCE

In order to keep the example programs simple, we will be using input from files.
The TWFileSource class is defined as follows:

```
// simple text source reading a single file TWFileSource.java
import java.io.* ;

public class TWFileSource implements TWidgetSource {
  PipedOutputStream outS ;
  BufferedInputStream BinS ;
  String fileName ;
  boolean eofFlg ;

  TWFileSource() { outS = null ; eofFlg = false ;
  }

public PipedOutputStream TWOutput() { return outS ;}

  // returns true if source opened ok
  // type could be used to alternately open a URL
  public boolean OpenSource( String src, int type ) {
    boolean ret = true ;
    try {
      FileInputStream inS = new FileInputStream( src );
      BinS = new BufferedInputStream( inS ) ;
      // don't create output stream unless file opened ok
      outS = new PipedOutputStream();
    }
```

```
      catch(FileNotFoundException ex) {
        System.out.println("Problem opening " + src );
        ret = false ;
      }
      catch(IOException e) {
        System.out.println("Error " + e );
        ret = false ;
      }
      return ret ;
    }

  public void start() { new Thread(this).start() ;
    }

  public void run() {
      byte[] buffer = new byte[ BUFSIZE ] ;
      int rdbytes ;
      try {
        while( !eofFlg ) {
          rdbytes = BinS.read( buffer ); // this blocks until rd
          if( rdbytes == -1 ) eofFlg = true ;
          else  outS.write(buffer,0, rdbytes );
        }
        outS.close();
      } catch(IOException e ) {
          if( e instanceof EOFException ) {
            try { outS.close();
            } catch(Exception ex) {}
            eofFlg = true ;  return ;  // good finish
          }
          System.out.println("Source error " + e );
      }
    }

    public boolean atEofQ() { return eofFlg ; }
    }
```

As you can see, once the file is opened, all the action takes place in the run method which simply reads bytes from the file and writes them to the `PipedOutputStream`. Although we can detect the -1 returned by the file read call when the end of the file has been reached, we still have to provide for catching possible `IOExceptions` which might include a normal end of file (`EOFException` is a subclass of `IOException`).

TWFILESINK

This class can output text to a Java TextArea object or to a file if a filename is supplied. In the absence of a call to ReadySink, output defaults to the standard System.out stream. Output to a Java TextArea should only be used when the size of the output text will be less than 32K characters due to TextArea limitations.

Note that in setTWidgetSource, the source input can be either an object implementing the TWidgetFilter or the TWidgetSource interface. Although one would not normally connect a file source to a file output, we might want to use a TWidgetSource connection to check the operation of more complex text sources.

```java
//   TWFileSink.java
import java.io.* ;
import java.awt.TextArea ;

public class TWFileSink implements TWidgetSink {
  PipedInputStream   PinS ;
  FileOutputStream   Fout ;
  TextArea           TAout ;
  int BytesOutCt ;

  TWFileSink() {
     PinS = null ; BytesOutCt = 0 ; Fout = null; TAout = null ;
  }


  // can be called with either filter or source
  // return true if we were able to create input stream
  public boolean setTWidgetSource( Object src ){
     boolean ret = false ;
     if( PinS != null ) return ret ; // already have one
     try {
        if( src instanceof TWidgetSource ) {
           TWidgetSource TWS = (TWidgetSource) src ;
           PinS = new PipedInputStream( TWS.TWOutput() );
           ret = true ;
        }
        else {
         if(src instanceof TWidgetFilter ) {
            PinS = new PipedInputStream(
            ((TWidgetFilter)src).TWOutput() ) ;
            ret = true ;
         }
        }
     }catch(IOException e ) {
```

```java
            System.out.println("TWFileSink set err " + e );
        }
        return ret ;
    }

    // if this is not called, System.out is assumed
    public boolean ReadySink( Object sink ) {
        boolean ret = false ;
        if( sink instanceof String ) {
            String fname = (String) sink;
            try {
                Fout = new FileOutputStream( fname ) ;
                ret = true ;
            } catch(IOException e ) {
                System.out.println("Unable to open " + fname ) ;
                System.out.println("Err " +  e );
            }
        }
        if( sink instanceof TextArea ){ TAout = (TextArea) sink ;
        }
        return ret ;
    }

    public void start() {
        new Thread(this).start();
    }

    public void run() {
        byte[] buffer = new byte[BUFSIZE] ;
        int rdbytes ;
        boolean runflg = true ;
        try {
            while( runflg ) {
                rdbytes = PinS.read(buffer, 0, BUFSIZE ) ;
                if( rdbytes == -1 ) { runflg = false ;
                }
                else {
                    if( TAout != null ){
                        String tmpS = new String( buffer,0,0,rdbytes);
                        TAout.appendText( tmpS );
                    }
                    else {
                        if( Fout == null ) System.out.write( buffer, 0,
                        rdbytes) ;
```

```
          else Fout.write( buffer,0, rdbytes );
        }
      BytesOutCt += rdbytes ;
    }
  }
  if( Fout != null ) Fout.close();
  if( TAout != null) TAout.appendText("\n****END***\n");
} catch(IOException e ) {
    System.out.println("Sink error " + e );
}
finally {
  if(Fout == null ) System.out.flush();
  System.out.println("Total bytes = " + BytesOutCt );
}
}

}
```

The operation of the run method is similar to that of the file source: bytes are accepted from a `PipedOutputStream` by a `PipedInputStream` and then written to either the `System.out` stream, a file, or a `TextArea`. Note that when the input is exhausted and the last byte's written, we can simply close the output file, but if output is to the `System.out` stream, we have to call `System.out.flush`. This is because `System.out` does not write to the screen until a linefeed byte is written; however, we can't count on a linefeed being the last byte in a stream.

Example filters

An important device in input and output is the filter. By looking at the following examples, you should be able to get a handle on how they work and how you can use them.

A SIMPLE CASE CONVERSION FILTER

We will describe the simplest filter in detail first. `TWSimpleFilter` can only perform case conversions but can do them rapidly because the conversion is done all in one buffer. Here is the source code:

```
import java.io.* ;

public class TWSimpleFilter implements TWidgetFilter {
  int type ;
  PipedInputStream  inS ;
  PipedOutputStream outS ;
  byte[] buffer ;
```

```java
  TWSimpleFilter() { inS = null ; outS = null ; type = 0 ;
    buffer = new byte[BUFSIZE] ;
  }

  // can be called with either filter or source
  // return true if we were able to create input stream
  public boolean setTWidgetSource( Object src ){
    boolean ret = false ;
    if( inS != null ) return ret ; // already have one
    try {
      if( src instanceof TWidgetSource ) {
        PipedOutputStream Ptmp = ((TWidgetSource)src).TWOutput() ;
        inS = new PipedInputStream( Ptmp );
        outS = new PipedOutputStream();
        ret = true ;
      }
      if( src instanceof TWidgetFilter ) {
        PipedOutputStream Ptmp = ((TWidgetFilter)src).TWOutput() ;
        inS = new PipedInputStream( Ptmp );
        outS = new PipedOutputStream();
        ret = true ;
      }
    }catch(IOException e ) {
        System.out.println("setTWidgetSource err " + e );
    }
    return ret ;
  }

  public void setSubstitute(String inS, String outS, String puncS ){
    System.out.println("Simple Filter cant substitute");
  }

  public PipedOutputStream TWOutput() { return outS ;
  }

  public boolean setFilterType( String info ) {
    boolean ret = false ;
    if( info.equals("UPPER")   ){type = UPPERCASE ;ret = true;}
    if( info.equals("LOWER")   ){type = LOWERCASE ;ret = true;}
    return ret ;
  }

  public void start() {
    new Thread(this).start();
```

```
    }

    // enter with ct of bytes in buffer
    // return number written or -1 if err
int filterAndWrite( int ct ) throws IOException {
    int i ;
    int outCt = 0 ;
    switch( type ) {
        case UPPERCASE :
            for( i = 0 ; i < ct ; i++ ) {
                if((buffer[i] >= 'a' ) && (buffer[i] <= 'z') ) {
                    buffer[i] -= 32 ;
                }
            }
            outCt = ct ; // number doesn't change;
            break ;
        case LOWERCASE :
            for( i = 0 ; i < ct ; i++ ) {
                if((buffer[i] >= 'A' ) && (buffer[i] <= 'Z') ) {
                    buffer[i] += 32 ;
                }
            }
            outCt = ct ; // number doesn't change;
            break ;
        default :
            System.out.println("Bad filter type");
            return -1 ;
    }
    outS.write(buffer,0, outCt ) ; // simple write
    return outCt ;
}

public void run() {
    int rdbytes ;
    int BytesOutCt = 0 ;
    boolean runflg = true ;
    try {
        while( runflg ) {
            rdbytes = inS.read(buffer, 0, BUFSIZE ) ;
            if( rdbytes == -1 ) { runflg = false ;
            }
            else {
                filterAndWrite( rdbytes );
                BytesOutCt += rdbytes ;
```

```
          }
        }
        if( outS != null ) outS.close();
      } catch(IOException e ) {
          System.out.println("Simple filter error " + e );
      }
      finally { // following is useful for debugging
        System.out.println("Total bytes = " + BytesOutCt );
      }

  }


  }
```

Operation is similar to the source and sink widgets. Once set up and connected to an input and output, all the action takes place in the run method.
Every buffer of bytes that is read in is processed by the filterAndWrite routine
which converts upper-case characters to lower case or vice versa depending on
the filter type.

A MORE GENERAL FILTER

Now lets look at a more general filter. This filter is capable both of recognizing
one character sequence and converting it into another and doing simple character replacements. With this we can actually accomplish useful work such as
changing the linefeed-terminated text lines typical of UNIX- and Mac-generated
text files into the carriage-return/linefeed-terminated lines preferred by many
programs originating in the DOS world.

Here is a complete listing of TWGenFilter.java — you will note that the
setTWidgetSource and TWOutput methods are the same as those used in
TWSimpleFilter. This filter handles upper- and lower-case conversion as a special
case of character substitution. The common carriage-return/linefeed to linefeed
and vice versa are also handled as special cases of sequence substitution.

```
import java.io.* ;

public class TWGenFilter implements TWidgetFilter {
  static final String UCstring = "ABCDEFGHIJKLMNOPQRSTUVWXYZ" ;
  static final String lcString = "abcdefghijklmnopqrstuvwxyz" ;

  int type ;
  PipedInputStream  inS ;
  PipedOutputStream outS ;
  byte[] buffer ;   // read into this buffer
  byte[] outBuf ;   // will be writing from here with complex
                    // filters
  byte[] subsBuf ;  // substitute string as a byte array
```

```java
  int bufStart ;
  int bufCt ;

  String InString ;
  String OutString ;
  String PuncStr ;

  TWGenFilter() { inS = null ; outS = null ; type = 0 ;
    buffer = new byte[BUFSIZE] ;
  }

// BUFSIZE can be called with either filter or source
// return true if we were able to create input stream
public boolean setTWidgetSource( Object src ){
    boolean ret = false ;
    if( inS != null ) return ret ; // already have one
    try {
       if( src instanceof TWidgetSource ) {
        PipedOutputStream Ptmp = ((TWidgetSource)src).TWOutput() ;
        inS = new PipedInputStream( Ptmp );
        outS = new PipedOutputStream();
        ret = true ;
       }
       if( src instanceof TWidgetFilter ) {
        PipedOutputStream Ptmp = ((TWidgetFilter)src).TWOutput() ;
        inS = new PipedInputStream( Ptmp );
        outS = new PipedOutputStream();
        ret = true ;
       }
    }catch(IOException e ) {
        System.out.println("TWGenFilter set err " + e );
    }
    return ret ;
}

public PipedOutputStream TWOutput() { return outS ;
}

// note that outS could be empty to remove all instances of inS
public void setSubstitute(String inS, String outS, String puncS ){
   // leave the next two statements in for debugging
   System.out.println("GenFilter substitute:" + outS );
   System.out.println("                 for:" + inS );
```

```java
      InString = inS ;
      OutString = outS ;
      PuncStr   = puncS ;
   }

   public boolean setFilterType( String info ) {
      boolean ret = false ;
      if( info.equals("UPPER")   ) {
          type = UPPERCASE ;
          InString  = new String( lcString ) ;
          OutString = new String( UCstring );
          ret = true ;
      }
      if( info.equals("LOWER")   ) {
          type = LOWERCASE ;
          InString  = new String( UCstring );
          OutString = new String( lcString );
          ret = true ;
      }
      if( info.equals("CHARSUBS")) {
          type = CHARSUBS ;
          ret = true ;
      }
      if( info.equals("SEQNSUBS")) {
          type = SEQNSUBS ;
          ret = true ;          // strings must be set by later call
      }
      if( info.equals("CRLFTOLF" )) {
          type = SEQNSUBS ;
          InString = "\r\n" ;
          OutString = "\n" ;
          ret = true ;
      }
      if( info.equals("LFTOCRLF" )) {
          type = SEQNSUBS ;
          InString = "\n" ;
          OutString = "\r\n" ;
          ret = true ;
      }
      return ret ;
   }

   public void start() { new Thread(this).start();
   }
```

ADVANCED JAVA APPLICATIONS AND DEVELOPMENT TOPICS

```java
// enter with ct of bytes in buffer - simple filter style
// typically UPPERCASE, LOWERCASE or CHARSUBS
// return number written or -1 if err
int filterAndWrite( int ct ) throws IOException {
   int i ;
   int pos ;
   for( i = 0 ; i < ct ; i++ ) {
     pos = InString.indexOf( buffer[i] ) ;
     if( pos >= 0 ) buffer[i] =(byte) OutString.charAt(pos);
   }
   // number doesn't change;
   outS.write(buffer,0, ct ) ; // simple write
   return ct ;
}

private void SmplRun() {
   int rdbytes ;
   int BytesOutCt = 0 ;
   boolean runflg = true ;
   try {
     while( runflg ) {
        rdbytes = inS.read(buffer, 0, BUFSIZE ) ;
        if( rdbytes == -1 ) { runflg = false ;
        }
        else {
          filterAndWrite( rdbytes );
          BytesOutCt += rdbytes ;
        }
     }
     if( outS != null ) outS.close();
   } catch(IOException e ) {
      System.out.println("Sink error " + e );
   }
   finally {
     System.out.println("Total bytes = " + BytesOutCt );
   }
}

// recognize a sequence and substitute
private void SeqnRun() {
   int rdbytes ;
   int tmp, i ;
   int BytesOutCt = 0 ;
```

```
int sLen = InString.length();
int sMark ;
int outSlen = OutString.length() ;
outBuf = new byte[BUFSIZE] ;
if( outSlen > 0 ) {
 subsBuf = new byte[ outSlen ] ;
 OutString.getBytes( 0, outSlen , subsBuf, 0 );
}
bufStart = 0 ;
boolean runflg = true ;
try {
  while( runflg ) {
     rdbytes = BUFSIZE - bufStart ;
     rdbytes = inS.read(buffer, bufStart, rdbytes ) ;
     if( rdbytes == -1 ) {   rdbytes = 0 ; // fake it
     }
     // even at eof, may have bytes in buffer
     bufCt = bufStart + rdbytes ; // avail to examine
     if( bufCt == 0 ) { runflg = false ; break ;
     }
     // if here, we have bytes in buffer
     // construct string so we can use string search - string is
     // of chars with hi byte = 0, lo byte = ascii char from
     //  buffer[0] & with bufCt chars
     String tstr = new String( buffer, 0, 0, bufCt );
     if( bufCt < sLen ) { // only small chunk left, EOF assumed
       outS.write( buffer, 0, bufCt );
       BytesOutCt += bufCt ;
       bufStart = 0 ; continue ;
     }
     sMark = tstr.indexOf( InString );
     if( sMark == -1 ) { // not found
       tmp = bufCt - (sLen - 1 ) ; // can safely write this many
       outS.write( buffer, 0, tmp );
       BytesOutCt += tmp ;
       // now save the sLen -1 bytes at the end
       for( i = 0 ; i < (sLen - 1 ) ; i++ ) {
          buffer[i] = buffer[ tmp++ ] ;
       }
       bufStart = sLen - 1 ;
     }
     else { // found - sMark may == 0
       if( sMark > 0 ) {
          outS.write( buffer, 0, sMark ) ;
```

```
                    BytesOutCt += sMark ;
                }
                if( outSlen > 0 ) outS.write( subsBuf,0,outSlen ) ;
                BytesOutCt += outSlen ;
                sMark += sLen ; // points to a char to save
                tmp = bufCt - sMark ;  // number to save
                for( bufStart = 0 ; bufStart < tmp ; ) {
                    buffer[bufStart++] = buffer[sMark++ ] ;
                }
            }
        }
        if( outS != null ) outS.close();
    } catch(IOException e ) {
        System.out.println("SeqnRun error " + e );
    }
}

    public void run() {
        switch( type ) {
            case UPPERCASE :
            case LOWERCASE :
            case CHARSUBS :
                SmplRun(); break ;
            case CRLFTOLF :
            case LFTOCRLF :
            case SEQNSUBS :
                SeqnRun() ; break ;
        }
    }

} // end TWGenFilter class
```

TWGenFilter can do two types of filtering. The first type of filtering is simple byte substitution in which the number of bytes written is the same as the number read. The second type of substitution, sequence substitution, is more complex. Here is a breakdown of the steps inside the main loop of SeqnRun.

FILLING THE BUFFER

We read characters from the `InputStream` into the byte array "buffer." On the initial read, the buffer is empty and bufStart = 0, but on subsequent cycles the buffer will likely be partially full.

CONSTRUCTING A STRING

Because we want to use the Java library's string search, the buffer of ASCII bytes must be turned into a Java String. Recall that a Java Character uses 16 bits to support Unicode. Normally we tend to ignore this because Java automatically takes care of converting ASCII bytes to characters, for example, in creating String constants. When constructing a string from a byte array, we have to specify zero fill of the high byte with the following:

```
String tstr = new String( buffer, 0, 0, bufCt );
```

Note that we have to check for the special case which may occur at the end of a file in which the remaining string is shorter than the string we are looking for.

MATCHING THE SEQUENCE

The code statement

```
sMark = tstr.indexOf( InSting);
```

will return the location of a match to `InString` within `tstr` or a minus one if no match was found. You might think we could write the entire buffer if no match was found, but we have to watch out for the case in which part of the match string occurs at the end of the buffer. We can safely write most of the buffer but have to save characters at the end.

UNIQUE WORD LIST BUILDER

Up to this point we have used filters which pass text through with some modification but in the original order, but we are not restricted to that style. Here is a filter which reads in all the words in a stream, sorts them, and discards duplicates. The output stream is a sorted list of all words in the input text. You might find this useful to check the size of your working vocabulary, sort part numbers, or help to build a book index.

The ideal input to the `TWUniqueFilter` is the output of a `TWSimpleFilter` set up to convert to upper case and replace punctuation with spaces. We could collect the words from the entire text in a Vector of Strings and then sort the whole vector, but because there is a lot of repetition of words in typical text, eliminating duplicates as soon as possible saves memory. The algorithm we are using gets words from a modest chunk of text, sorts them, and merges them with a growing list while eliminating duplicates.

```java
import java.io.* ;
import java.util.Vector ;

public class TWUniqueFilter implements TWidgetFilter {

  byte buffer[] ;

  PipedInputStream  inS ;
  PipedOutputStream outS ;
  Vector totalWV ;  // accumulate all words here in sorted order
  Vector tempWV ;   // accumulate words for sorting

  int wordCt = 0 ;
  int tempLim = 200 ;

  TWUniqueFilter() { inS = null ; outS = null ;
    totalWV = new Vector( 1000, 200 ) ;
    tempWV  = new Vector( 200, 10 ) ;
    buffer = new byte[BUFSIZE] ;
  }

  // can be called with either filter or source
  // return true if we were able to create input stream
  public boolean setTWidgetSource( Object src ){
    boolean ret = false ;
    if( inS != null ) return ret ; // already have one
    try {
      if( src instanceof TWidgetSource ) {
        PipedOutputStream Ptmp = ((TWidgetSource)src).TWOutput() ;
        inS = new PipedInputStream( Ptmp );
        outS = new PipedOutputStream();
        ret = true ;
      }
      if( src instanceof TWidgetFilter ) {
        PipedOutputStream Ptmp = ((TWidgetFilter)src).TWOutput() ;
        inS = new PipedInputStream( Ptmp );
        outS = new PipedOutputStream();
        ret = true ;
      }
    }catch(IOException e ) {
        System.out.println("TWUniqueFilter set err " + e );
    }
    return ret ;
  }
```

```java
public PipedOutputStream TWOutput() {
    return outS ;
}

// these have to be here to satisfy the TWidgetFilter interface
public boolean setFilterType( String info ) { return true ; }
public void setSubstitute( String inS, String outS, String puncS
){
    return ; }

public void start() {
    new Thread(this).start();
}

public void run() {
    boolean eof = false ;
    int tmpCt = 0 ;
    while( !eof ) {
        tmpCt = getWords();
        wordCt += tmpCt ;
        System.out.println("Word ct " + tmpCt + " total " + wordCt );
        if( tmpCt == 0 ){ eof = true ; break ;}
        sort( tempWV );
        System.out.println("Unique " + merge());
    }
    // final sort merge goes here
    // dispose of sorted words to output
    if( tmpCt > 0 ) {
        sort( tempWV ) ;
        System.out.println("Final Unique " + merge());
    }
    try {
        System.out.println("totalWV has " + totalWV.size() );
        dumpOut( totalWV ); // writes to outS
        outS.close();
    } catch(Exception ex ) {
        System.out.println("Unique output err " + ex );
    }
}

// accumulate words in tempWV until tempLim or input eof hit
// assumes tempWV empty on entry
int getWords() {
    int cCt = 0 ;
```

```java
        int ch ;
        boolean eof = false ;
        try {
        while( !eof && (tempWV.size() < tempLim )){
            do {
              ch = inS.read();
              if( ch == -1 ) { eof = true ; break ; }
            } while( ch <= ' ' ) ;
            // here either eof or ch is a character at start of word
            while( !eof ) {
              buffer[ cCt++ ] = (byte) ch ;
              ch = inS.read();
              if( ch == -1 ) { eof = true ; break ; }
              if( ch <= ' ' ) break ;
            }
            if( cCt > 0 ) { // have a word in buffer
              String nS = new String( buffer, 0,0, cCt ) ;
              tempWV.addElement( nS );
              cCt = 0 ; // reset for next
            }
        }
        } catch(Exception ex ) {
            System.out.println("getWords " + ex );
        }
        return tempWV.size();
}


// alphabetic sort of the Vector of strings
//  using the "Shell" sort algorithm
void sort( Vector V ) {
    int j ;
    int gap = V.size() ;
    int ct = gap ;
    if( gap <= 1 ) return ;
    while((gap = gap / 2) > 0 ) {
        for( j = gap ; j < ct ; j++ ) OneShell( j, gap, V ) ;
    }
}

void OneShell( int j, int gap, Vector V ) {
    int res ;
    Object tS ;
    while( (j - gap ) >= 0 ) {
        // res <0 if first str < 2nd etc.
```

```java
            res = ((String)V.elementAt( j - gap)).compareTo(
                    ((String)V.elementAt( j )) ) ;
            if( res <= 0 ) return ;
            // if here, must exchange
            tS = V.elementAt( j - gap );
            V.setElementAt( V.elementAt(j), j - gap ) ;
            V.setElementAt( tS, j );
            j -= gap ;
        }
    }


    // return number of unique words
    int merge(){
        if( totalWV.size() == 0 ) return simpleMerge();
        String tS ;
        String wS ;
        Vector tV = new Vector( 1000,200 );
        int res ;
        tS = (String)tempWV.firstElement();
        wS = (String)totalWV.firstElement();
        do {
            // now remove dups in tempWV
            while((tempWV.size() > 0 ) &&
                    tS.equals((String) tempWV.firstElement() )) {
                tempWV.removeElementAt(0) ;
            }
            // no more dups of tS in tempWV, tempWV may be empty
            // but wS still in totalWV, totalWV known to have at least 1
            res = wS.compareTo( tS ) ;
            if( res == 0 ) {
                tV.addElement( wS ) ;
                totalWV.removeElementAt(0);
                if( !totalWV.isEmpty() ) {
                    wS = (String) totalWV.firstElement(); // new wS
                }
                if( !tempWV.isEmpty() ) tS = (String)tempWV.firstElement();
            }
            if( res < 0 ) { // wS comes before tS
                tV.addElement( wS ) ; totalWV.removeElementAt(0) ;
                if(totalWV.size() > 0) wS = (String)totalWV.firstElement();
            }
            if( res > 0 ) { // tS comes before wS
                tV.addElement( tS ) ;
```

```
         if( tempWV.size() > 0 ) tS = (String)
tempWV.firstElement();
      }
      //
   } while((tempWV.size() > 0 ) && (totalWV.size() > 0 )) ;
   // reached end of one or both vectors
   if( tempWV.size() > 0 ) { // tS must have new string
      tV.addElement(tS) ; // not the same as new lead str in
                          // tempWV
      while( tempWV.size() > 0 ) { // while more
         tS = (String)tempWV.firstElement();
         tempWV.removeElementAt(0);
         while((tempWV.size() > 0 ) &&
               tS.equals((String) tempWV.firstElement() )) {
            tempWV.removeElementAt(0) ;
         }
      }
   }
   else { // wS must have new string
      tV.addElement( wS ) ; totalWV.removeElementAt(0) ;
      while( totalWV.size() > 0 ) {
         tV.addElement( totalWV.firstElement() );
         totalWV.removeElementAt(0) ;
      }
   }
   totalWV = tV ; // temp becomes working total
   return totalWV.size() ;
}


int simpleMerge( ){
   String tS ;
   tS = (String)tempWV.firstElement();
   totalWV.addElement( tS );
   tempWV.removeElementAt(0);
   // now tS = previous string, all we have to do is avoid dups
   while( tempWV.size() > 0 ){
      if( !tS.equals( ((String)tempWV.firstElement()) )) {
         tS = (String)tempWV.firstElement() ;
         totalWV.addElement( tS ) ;
      }
      tempWV.removeElementAt(0);
   }
   return totalWV.size();
}
```

```
        // enter with Vector of strings - output to outS and discard
    void dumpOut( Vector V ) {
        PrintStream Prs = new PrintStream( outS );
        String tS ;
        // System.out.println( "Vector " + V );
        while( V.size() > 0 ) {
            try {
             tS = (String) V.firstElement();
             // Note -
             // Prs.println( tS ) outputs string plus a line feed char
             // Prs.println( tS ) ;  // use for UNIX or Mac
             // the following outputs string plus <cr><lf>
             Prs.print( tS ) ; Prs.write( 0x0D ) ; Prs.write( 0x0A ) ;
             V.removeElementAt( 0 ) ;
            } catch(Exception ex) {
                System.out.println("dumpOut Err " + ex ); break ;
            }
        }
    }

} // end   TWUniqueFilter.java
```

STATISTICS FILTER

If you have ever wondered how many words or lines of text were in a file, here is the filter for you. It counts words, lines, and sentences and also tracks the number of times each ASCII character appears. As with the unique word filter, no output is generated until the entire input has been read. We have stretched the concept of a filter considerably since none of the input actually appears in the output, but our TWidgetFilter interface still does everything we need.

```
import java.io.* ;

public class TWStatFilter implements TWidgetFilter {
    int type ;
    PipedInputStream  inS ;
    PipedOutputStream outS ;

    int senLeng,  senTotal,  senCt ;  // for sentence statistics
    int wordLeng, wordTotal, wordCt ;  // for word statistics
    int charCt[] ; // for individual character use

    String PuncStr = " .,<>;:'?!@#$%^&*()_-+=\"\\/" ;
        // default punctuation - can be replaced with a call to
        // setSubstitute()
```

```java
TWStatFilter() { inS = null ; outS = null ; type = 0 ;
   senLeng = senTotal = senCt = 0 ;
   wordLeng= wordTotal= wordCt = 0 ;
   charCt = new int[256] ;
   for( int i = 0 ; i < 256 ; i++ ) { charCt[i] = 0 ; }
 }


// can be called with either filter or source
// return true if we were able to create input stream
public boolean setTWidgetSource( Object src ){
   boolean ret = false ;
   if( inS != null ) return ret ; // already have one
   try {
     if( src instanceof TWidgetSource ) {
       PipedOutputStream Ptmp = ((TWidgetSource)src).TWOutput() ;
       inS = new PipedInputStream( Ptmp );
       outS = new PipedOutputStream();
       ret = true ;
     }
     if( src instanceof TWidgetFilter ) {
       PipedOutputStream Ptmp = ((TWidgetFilter)src).TWOutput() ;
       inS = new PipedInputStream( Ptmp );
       outS = new PipedOutputStream();
       ret = true ;
     }
   }catch(IOException e ) {
       System.out.println("TWStatFilter set err " + e );
   }
   return ret ;
 }


public PipedOutputStream TWOutput() { return outS ;
 }


// The only string we need to set is the punctuation,
// but we still have to match the interface definition.
public void setSubstitute( String inS, String outS, String puncS ){
   PuncStr = puncS ; // replace the default punctuation list
 }


// We have to have this to fit the interface, but there is
// presently only one kind of Stat filter
public boolean setFilterType( String info ) { return true ;
 }
```

```java
public void start() { new Thread(this).start();
}

// read words, gathering statistics until a period indicating end
// of sentence is hit. Returns count of words in sentence or
//  -1 on end of file.
int readSen() {
  boolean eof = false ;
  int ch ;
  int wdsThis = 0 ;
  wordLeng = 0 ;
  try {
    while( !eof ) {
      ch = inS.read();
      if( ch == -1 ) {eof = true ; continue ; }
      charCt[ch]++ ;
      // check for word break at space, ctrl char or punctuation
      if((ch <= ' ') || ( PuncStr.indexOf( ch ) >= 0 )){
        if( wordLeng > 0 ) {
          wordTotal += wordLeng ; wordCt++ ;
          wdsThis++ ;
          // if we were creating a word length histogram,
          // here is where we would record data.
          wordLeng = 0 ;
          if( ch == '.') return wdsThis ;
        }
      }
      else wordLeng++ ;
    }
  } catch(Exception ex ){
      System.out.println("Error in readSen " + ex ) ;
  }
  return -1 ;
}


public void run() {
  boolean eof = false ;
  while( !eof ) {
    senLeng = readSen() ;
    if( senLeng == -1 ) break ;  // eof
```

```
        if( senLeng > 0 ) {
            senTotal += senLeng ; senCt++ ;
            senLeng = 0 ;
        }
    }   // after processing entire file, we write statistics to
        // the output stream
    PrintStream Prs = new PrintStream( outS );
    try {
     Prs.println("Total words " + wordCt );
     if((wordCt == 0 ) || (senCt == 0 )){
       System.out.println("No Data");
     }
     else {
      float avew = ((float) wordTotal) / wordCt ;
      Prs.println("Ave word size " + avew );
      Prs.println("Total sentences " + senCt );
      avew = ((float) senTotal) / senCt ;
      Prs.println("Ave sentence length " + avew );
      Prs.println("Lines as indicated by <lf> " + charCt[0x0A ] );
      Prs.println("Character counts");
      for( int i = 0 ;i < ' ' ; i++ ){
          if(charCt[i] > 0 ) {
              Prs.println("Ctrl Char " + i + " count " + charCt[i] );
          }
      }
      for( int i = ' ';i < 128 ; i++ ){
          if(charCt[i] > 0 ) {
              Prs.println("Printing Char " + i + " count " +
              charCt[i] );
          }
      }
      for( int i = 128 ; i < 256 ; i++ ){
          if(charCt[i] > 0 ) {
              Prs.println("High Char " + i + " count " + charCt[i] );
          }
      }
     }
     Prs.close();
    }catch(Exception ex){}
 }

} // end TWStatFilter.java
```

You might extend the basic statistics this code gathers by building histograms of word lengths or sentence lengths. This could lead to a calculation of relative "readability."

Complete Application Programs

You now have all the elements of a simple TextWidget program, so it's time to put them together.

COMMAND LINE DRIVEN APPLICATION USING THE CASE CONVERSION FILTER

CaseCvt.java is a command-line-driven Java application that converts a text input file to upper-case characters. As you may recall, Java applications must have a public static main routine similar to that required in a C program. The notable difference is that the parsed command line is passed to main as a String array with args[0] being the first command-line parameter, whereas in C the first parameter would be args[1].

```java
//    CaseCvt.java
import java.io.* ;

// a command-line-driven program to convert a text file to all
// upper-case characters
public class CaseCvt {
    TWFileSource Fsrc ;
    TWFileSink   Fout ;
    TWSimpleFilter  CFilter ;

  CaseCvt(String inStr, String outStr ){
    Fsrc = new TWFileSource();
    if( !Fsrc.OpenSource( inStr, 0 ) ){
       System.out.println("Unable to open " + inStr );
       System.exit(1);
    }
    CFilter = new TWSimpleFilter();
    CFilter.setFilterType("UPPER");
    CFilter.setTWidgetSource( Fsrc ) ; // gets output pipe from
                                       // Fsrc
    Fout = new TWFileSink();
    if( outStr != null ) { // a file for output has been supplied
      if( !Fout.ReadySink( outStr )){
        System.out.println("Unable to open " + outStr +
        " for output.");
```

```
                System.exit(2);
            }
        }
        Fout.setTWidgetSource( CFilter );
        Fsrc.start();
        CFilter.start();
        Fout.start();
    }

    public static void main( String args[] ){
        if( args.length == 0 ) {
            System.out.println("Requires input file on command line");
            System.exit(0);
        }
        if( args.length == 1 ) {
            new CaseCvt( args[0], null ) ;
        }
        else new CaseCvt( args[0], args[1] );
    }

}// end class CaseCvt
```

Now to run the program. The command line to execute CaseCvt with its own source code file as input and output to the console is:

```
java CaseCvt CaseCvt.java
```

If you wanted output to a file, the command line would look like:

```
java CaseCvt CaseCvt.java CCTEST.TXT
```

APPLICATION USING THE TWSTATFILTER WITH A FILE DIALOG INTERFACE

In this example Application, the text file selected by the user is opened and scanned to gather basic statistics which are sent to the TextArea which fills the window. The original was created using the Symantec "Cafe" development system - extra notation used by Cafe has been removed to shorten the listing.

```
// A Java AWT based Text Widget demo          TWidget.java
import java.awt.*;
```

```java
import java.io.* ;
import java.util.* ;

public class TWidget extends Frame {

    Menu fileMenu ;
    Menu aboutMenu ;
    TextArea results ;

    public TWidget() {
        super("TWidget window");
        MenuBar mb = new MenuBar();
        fileMenu = new Menu("&File");
        fileMenu.add(new MenuItem("&Open..."));
        fileMenu.addSeparator();
        fileMenu.add(new MenuItem("&Exit"));
        mb.add(fileMenu);
        aboutMenu = new Menu("&About");
        aboutMenu.add( new MenuItem("&About..."));
        mb.add(aboutMenu);
        setMenuBar(mb);
        results = new TextArea("");
        setLayout( new BorderLayout() );
        add("Center", results );
        addNotify();
        resize(insets().left + insets().right + 306,
                insets().top + insets().bottom + 254);
        show();
    }

    public synchronized void show() {
        move(50, 50);
        super.show();
    }

    public boolean handleEvent(Event event) {

        if (event.id == Event.WINDOW_DESTROY) {
          hide();             // hide the Frame
          dispose();          // tell windowing system to free
                              // resources
          System.exit(0); // exit
          return true;
        }
```

```
            return super.handleEvent(event);
    }

    public boolean action(Event event, Object arg) {
        if (event.target instanceof MenuItem) {
            String label = (String) arg;
            if (label.equalsIgnoreCase("&About...")) {
                selectedAbout();
                return true;
            } else if (label.equalsIgnoreCase("&Exit")) {
                selectedExit();
                return true;
            } else if (label.equalsIgnoreCase("&Open...")) {
                selectedOpen();
                return true;
            }
        }
        return super.action(event, arg);
    }

    public static void main(String args[]) {
        new TWidget();
    }

    // this is the routine that does all the work
    // If the user selects an input file from the file dialog
    // a file source is created and the chain of text filters
    // is assembled.
    public void selectedOpen() {
      FileDialog fdlg ;
      fdlg = new FileDialog(this, "Open...") ;
      fdlg.show();
      String fname = fdlg.getDirectory() + fdlg.getFile();
      System.out.println("File is " + fname );
      if( fname != null ) {
        TWFileSource Fsrc = new TWFileSource();
        if( Fsrc.OpenSource( fname, 1 ) ) {
          results.appendText("Opened " + fname + "\n") ;
          System.out.println("Opened " + fname );
          // ok, we have a source, now for a filter
          TWStatFilter Filter = new TWStatFilter();
          if( !Filter.setTWidgetSource( (Object) Fsrc ) ){
            System.out.println("err setting filter src");
          }
```

```java
                // The TWStatFilter outputs lines terminated with a line
                // feed, to get a file with the DOS convention of <cr><lf> we
                // add a filter with one of the preset types.
                TWGenFilter Fcrlf = new TWGenFilter();
                Fcrlf.setFilterType("LFTOCRLF");
                Fcrlf.setTWidgetSource( Filter ) ;
                // Final output goes to a TWFileSink using the TextArea
                // "results" for display.
                TWFileSink Fsink = new TWFileSink();
                Fsink.ReadySink( results );
                // note the method is defined in terms of an interface!
                if( Fsink.setTWidgetSource( (Object)Fcrlf ) ) {
                 Fsrc.start();
                 Filter.start();
                 Fcrlf.start();
                 Fsink.start();
                 }
             }
            else { System.out.println("NoGo");
             }
          }
       }


    public void selectedExit() {
        QuitBox theQuitBox;
        theQuitBox = new QuitBox(this);
        theQuitBox.show();
    }

    public void selectedAbout() {
        AboutBox theAboutBox;
        theAboutBox = new AboutBox(this);
        theAboutBox.show();
    }
} // end Twidget class


/* A simple About box as created by Symantec Cafe  */

class AboutBox extends Dialog {

    Label label1;
    Button OKButton;

    public AboutBox(Frame parent) {
        super(parent, "About", true);
```

```java
        setResizable(false);
        setLayout(null);
        addNotify();
        resize(insets().left + insets().right + 292,
               insets().top + insets().bottom + 89);
        label1=new Label("Java Text Statistics Application");
        add(label1);
        label1.reshape(insets().left + 15, insets().top +
        18,200,16);
        OKButton=new Button("OK");
        add(OKButton);
        OKButton.reshape(insets().left + 50,insets().top +
        48,73,23);
    }

    public synchronized void show() {
        Rectangle bounds = getParent().bounds();
        Rectangle abounds = bounds();

        move(bounds.x + (bounds.width - abounds.width)/ 2,
             bounds.y + (bounds.height - abounds.height)/2);

        super.show();
    }

    public boolean handleEvent(Event event) {
        if (event.id == Event.ACTION_EVENT && event.target ==
            OKButton) {
                clickedOKButton();
                return true;
        }
        else

        if (event.id == Event.WINDOW_DESTROY) {
            hide();
            return true;
        }
        return super.handleEvent(event);
    }

    public void clickedOKButton() {
        handleEvent(new Event(this, Event.WINDOW_DESTROY, null));
    }
}
```

```java
class QuitBox extends Dialog {
    Button yesButton ;
    Button noButton ;

    public QuitBox(Frame parent) {

        super(parent, "Quit Application?", true);
            setResizable(false);

          setLayout(null);
          addNotify();
          resize(insets().left + insets().right + 261, insets().top
          + insets().bottom + 72);
          yesButton=new Button("Yes");
          add(yesButton);
          yesButton.reshape(insets().left + 68,insets().top +
          10,46,23);
          noButton=new Button("No");
          add(noButton);
          noButton.reshape(insets().left + 135,insets().top +
          10,47,23);
    }

    public synchronized void show() {
        Rectangle bounds = getParent().bounds();
        Rectangle abounds = bounds();

        move(bounds.x + (bounds.width - abounds.width)/ 2,
            bounds.y + (bounds.height - abounds.height)/2);

        super.show();
    }


    public boolean handleEvent(Event event) {
        if (event.id == Event.ACTION_EVENT && event.target ==
            noButton) {
                clickedNoButton();
                return true;
        }
        else
        if (event.id == Event.ACTION_EVENT && event.target ==
            yesButton) {
```

```
                clickedYesButton();
                return true;
            }
            else

            if (event.id == Event.WINDOW_DESTROY) {
                hide();
                return true;
            }
            return super.handleEvent(event);
        }

    public void clickedYesButton() {
        System.exit(0);
    }
    public void clickedNoButton() {
        handleEvent(new Event(this, Event.WINDOW_DESTROY, null));
    }
}
```

Because using the `FileDialog` can change the "logged in" directory under Windows, the Twidget program should be run with the Java command line format which specifies the `ClassPath` as in the following example. Alternately, set your environment `ClassPath` to include the path to the `TextWidgets` classes.

```
java -classpath
```

```
d:\Cafe\TextWidgets;d:\Cafe\java\lib\classes.zip TWidget
```

Figure 11-2 shows the results of running TWidget on its own source code.

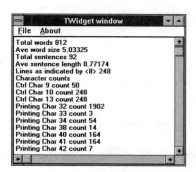

Figure 11-2   Twidget on its own source code.

BONUS

Text Sources, Filters, and Sinks

In this chapter we created a group of classes which constitute a "toolkit" for text manipulation. The ease with which we built a wide variety of classes which, because they all implemented the same interface, can be combined in a variety of ways should encourage you to consider inventing your own interfaces. Here are some possible text sources, filters, and sinks.

Text sources

You could read a file from an Internet site using the URL rather than the local file system.

Text filters

The following are some ideas for filters you could create.

NAME RECOGNITION

How about locating every paragraph your name was mentioned in.

ENCRYPTION

A filter could apply or remove an encryption to the text stream. You could use the setSubstitute() method to set the encryption keys.

HTML TAGS

A filter to detect HTML tags could locate all URLs and produce a sorted list, or just remove all HTML tags to produce plain text.

REFORMATTING WORD PROCESSOR TEXT

It would be easy to write a word-wrap filter to reformat those annoying long lines which result from output of text from word processors.

Text Output

You could add HTML tags to produce a complete formatted document.

Summary

n this chapter we created interfaces for text manipulation classes. In so doing, we also considered some design elements, explored Input and Output Classes, and studied some example filters. We then moved on to examine the Unique Word List Builder, and some complete application programs. Next, in the final chapter in the book, we explore Java's future.

## CHAPTER TWELVE

THE FUTURE OF JAVA

IN THIS CHAPTER YOU LEARN THESE KEY SKILLS

12

J ava is a fast-growing child with great potential. The initial enthusiasm shared by visionaries and Internet enthusiasts has spread to major players in the software industry. Part of this trend springs from an incredibly rapid rise in the perception that the Internet is central to the future of computing.

It's also clear from the enthusiastic reception that Java has received on the Web that a powerful demand exists for client-side interactivity and data manipulation (that is, applets). Likewise, it's clear that ample demand exists for a network- and Internet-aware, cross-platform application-development environment like that supplied by the Java compiler, interpreter, and runtime system. There are now many technologies competing to fill that demand, but Java seems to be holding its own.

As we close this investigation of Java, the real questions we'd like to tackle are:

* What is Java good for today?
* What are the important Java developments of late?
* What are Java's most serious limitations?

Learning What Java's Good for Today

To put it briefly, Java's good for lots of things! In the first Java book we wrote, our search for working applets and applications was centered around Sun's Web site and a few others. That search turned up more than 100 applets of interest.

Since then, a huge Java community has sprung up on the Net. Today, there are dozens of quality sites devoted to Java programming; and Java applets can be found on both commercial and enthusiasts' Web pages all over the Internet. As of this writing, the Gamelan Web repository of Java information (which JavaSoft has designated as the Official Directory for Java) lists 4,342 Java applets, applications, and documents.

Because the Internet currently occupies center stage in the software industry, Java has been thrust into the spotlight. When you see articles about a programming language in national business magazines and hear it discussed on National Public Radio, you know there has been a major change in public perception and focus.

On the Netscape front, Navigator's 2.01 release was Java-savvy, as all subsequent Navigator releases have been. Microsoft's Internet Explorer runs Java as well. Interestingly, Oracle's PowerBrowser Release 1.5 was the initial browser to offer support for both Java and Basic scripting. Furthermore, Java has been licensed by Novell, IBM, Microsoft, Borland, Symantec, and many other heavy-hitters in the software industry. There has also been a significant proliferation of Java tools; rather than designing Java with the rudimentary combination of a text editor and the JDK, you can now choose from a bevy of Java creation tools.

In this chapter, we take a look at what's available right now in the Java universe, and follow it up with some predictions about where Java development is going. Most of the Web addresses that follow are pretty stable, but if they've changed when you try to visit, check an Internet search engine like Yahoo — many search engines now index Java applets as a separate search category!

Examining Important Java Developments

Our first Java book was one of the earliest on the market; since its release, a great deal of Java development has occurred. In the upcoming sections, we profile the most important happenings in the Java arena.

JDK 1.1

By the time you read this, Sun will undoubtedly have released its 1.1 version of the Java Developer's Kit. This updated JDK is expected to be much more reliable. Some of its anticipated features are as follows:

* Increased security features, including digital signatures and "signed" applets
* A standard programming interface for writing Java-native methods
* Greatly improved AWT, which aids performance and facilitates GUI development
* Internalization, which permits the creation of customizable applets
* Ameliorated networking abilities
* Simpler syntax for the creation of adapter classes through inner classes

JavaBeans

Sun's JavaBeans are component APIs for Java that enable developers to create reusable software components. One major advantage of JavaBeans is that its code runs in any application environment within every operating system. Although Java has always been touted as being portable, JavaBeans fully validate this claim.

JavaBeans' component-based essence means that different developers — and end users — can use application builders to construct parts of an application. The JavaBean components employed will engage in dynamic communication. As we go to press, JavaSoft was preparing to release a JavaBeans Developers' Kit. The JavaBeans API and other JavaBeans documentation are available here:

`http://splash.javasoft.com/beans/index.html`

Java Enterprise API: JDBC, RMI, and IDL (eek!)

Sun developed Java Enterprise APIs to provide connectivity to enterprise databases and legacy applications. Corporate developers can use these APIs to create distributed Java applications and client/server applets that are both hardware- and software-neutral. There are three parts to the Java Enterprise API: JDBC, Java IDL, and Java RMI. (Those names make it seem as if Sun is as tired of the lame, caffeine-inspired monikers as we are!)

JDBC

JDBC stands for Java Database Connectivity; this is the primary API for SQL database access. The JDBC's uniform interface connects to a variety of relational databases and endows developers with a fundamental base to create higher-level tools and interfaces. When JDBC is available, it will be possible to access databases from a server-based application, or from an applet. In the JDBC, Java classes are defined to represent database data, SQL statements, database connections, and result sets. Unlike IDL or RMI, JDBC is fully included in the JDK 1.1 release.

JAVA IDL

Through Java IDL (Interface Definition Language), Java clients can be transparently connected to a network server. Because Java IDL adheres to the OMG Interface Definition Language specification, it creates a language-neutral interface between an object on one platform and a client on a different platform.

JAVA RMI

Java RMI (Remote Method Invocation) similarly permits transparent connectivity between Java clients and network servers, but the Java RMI mechanism is used when both ends of an application are written in Java. Through RMI, you can invoke the methods of remote Java objects from other Java virtual machines. The machines can even be on different hosts. See this site for additional information:

```
http://chatsubo.javasoft.com/current/rmi/index.html
```

A Java-based operating system

We had speculated that a Java-based OS could emerge. It has: In May, 1996, JavaSoft released JavaOS, an operating system designed to run Java on a wide range of microprocessors. JavaOS is small and compact, and can run Java on pagers, printers, game machines, PDAs, cell phones, and many more devices (oh, right, on computers, too).

The JavaOS architecture is layered, and each layer can be individually updated. When an application is written for the JavaOS, it can also be read by Java-friendly browsers and operating systems. JavaOS's commendable portability and extensibility allow it to remain timely in a way that traditional operating systems cannot. In addition, it's remarkably undemanding in terms of processing power and space; it requires only 4 MB of disk space and 4 MB of RAM.

JavaStation

Don't let JavaStation's slick look fool you into thinking that it's greedy, demanding hardware. Sun's JavaStation was designed as "thin client" hardware, which means that, unlike a "fat client," it doesn't have its own storage, operating system, or peripherals. Instead, JavaStation almost takes users back to the day of the mainframe; centralized servers hold all applications and data, giving the JavaStation the appropriate Java applications upon request. The low-cost possibilities for JavaStation's intranet and networking use are quite attractive to many companies.

Java Chips: Java goes silicon

Sun has announced a family of three microprocessors designed to directly execute Java opcodes. At the time of writing, the least expensive chip of the three, the simple picoJava I, was the only one available. PicoJava is designed for use in PDAs, network computers, Java-savvy phones, and other low-cost/low-power consumer appliances. The chip family will eventually include microJava and ultraJava processors. The target market for ultraJava is the network computer — currently a highly-hyped concept for a low-cost Internet connection in households without a computer. UltraJava is primed for general entertainment use, as well as 3-D graphics/imaging applications. MicroJava, based on the picoJava core, is geared toward functions that fall between the other two chips, including low-end games and telecom equipment.

Exploring Java's Limitations

In our first book we identified three major problem areas for Java:

* Not enough documentation
* Lack of broad platform support
* Slow performance

With a flood of new books, more documentation is now available for Java, including some from the Sun Java team. Even so, many of the language's details remain obscure. Fortunately, Sun has pursued an open approach, and made the source code for Java available to those willing to dig into the details. Unfortunately, there's often no other recourse than to dig into the source code — at length — and to experiment with features and functions to figure out how they really work!

Broad platform support is also coming along nicely. Compilers, interpreters, and browsers are available for a number of operating system and hardware combinations. Some of these compilers have been created using Sun-licensed code, and some have been developed under "clean room" conditions using only the Java language specification.

Concerns about performance remain unresolved. The widely promised just in time (JIT) compilers are starting to appear for stand-alone applications, but they have yet to appear within any Web browsers, where they'll make the biggest difference. Because Java is still perceived as too slow for computation-intensive applications, the application of JIT technology to browsers is critical to ensure Java's future success. Sun has predicted that Java applications could run up to 50 times faster with JIT compilers, and if this is true, then Java should become even more ubiquitous when JIT compilers unite with Web browsers.

As you can see, some of our earlier concerns continue to remain problematic. In the meantime, we've also developed a new list of Java limitations:

* Security — The Internet-using public is rightfully concerned about inviting unknown programs to execute on their machines, which is essentially how any Java applet behaves. Sun has taken an open approach to the security problem by publishing all the details of the Java virtual machine. When Java was initially released, two flaws in the execution (not the design) of Java were found by academic investigators. Both were immediately tackled by Sun and Netscape, and fixes were quickly released. Java appears to be more secure than all other technologies that have been proposed for network clients, but applications may continue to be hampered by security considerations. Look for a set of planned security extensions to emerge; these extensions will furnish signed code and encryption keys, thereby furthering Java's security. Sun is also working on a registry of Java applets that will authenticate and authorize applets.

* User Interface Technology — As Java moves to more and more different platforms, the limitations of the AWT standard library are becoming apparent (not surprising considering it was written in two months). When they're moved to multiple platforms, Java applets don't always end up looking like the designer planned. In fact, there are still major inconsistencies in behavior among platforms. Advances and refinements in the AWT will be essential to the wider use of Java. Thankfully, Sun addressed this issue and made the AWT much stronger, but we expect further progress in this area in the next year or so.

* Asynchronous I/O — To create applications that are sufficiently powerful to work for large user bases, Java needs to have asynchronous I/O. Sun can't expect Java to be thoroughly accepted until it executes as well as whatever languages it's replacing. Native database support will help to solve this quandary.

Java is by no means a perfect language; nor is it a mature development environment. Nevertheless, it remains appealing to programmers, and delivers a level of networking capability and reach that have kept its promise unbroken. Time will tell if it really takes the Internet by storm, and remakes the online universe in its image. We think the potential is there and remain hopeful that this promise will be fulfilled. Our ideas in the next section, about Java applications we expect to see in the relatively near future, should help to explain our enthusiasm.

Looking Ahead to Java's Future

While we're not one-hundred percent sure that all of these applications will be coded in Java, we're pretty sure that they'll partake of much of its approach and capabilities, albeit with significant extensions. Nevertheless, we expect Java and related development efforts to spawn a whole new class of interactive applications right away, and into the foreseeable future. And we expect it to be pretty exciting stuff, not just for entertainment, but for all kinds of practical uses, too.

For one thing, it's clear that current research is aimed at remedying the most obvious deficiencies in Java's current implementation. Significant efforts are already underway to

* Beef up the user interface with better tools and widgets
* Expand current foundation classes and class libraries with a broader, more useful set of tools
* Improve performance, system documentation, and developer support
* Broaden the base of suitable developer platforms

The question of whether Java will become ubiquitous is difficult to answer specifically (since we don't have a crystal ball, virtual or otherwise), so prior to hazarding an educated guess, we'd like to restate our question as "What kind of applications will Java make possible?"

For one thing, we'd certainly expect to see more powerful capabilities for users to interact with large collections of data. Right now, a request for database access through Java still tops Sun's list of requested Java enhancements — this points to the strong perceived need for users to be able to formulate queries and process results at their own workstations. Likewise, the ability to search, sort, and report on the results of such queries is important, as applets for statistical analysis, graphing, charting, and sorting also already indicate.

In a similar vein, we'd expect to see the delivery of complete text search engines at the user level. Today, one limitation that's hampering widespread use of HTML as a format for static documents, like those published on CD-ROMs, is the lack of a client-side search engine to help users query and interact with local data quickly and effectively. A full-blown Java search engine would allow multiple users with access to a Web browser and a Java run-time system to read the same CD-ROM, irrespective of platform.

Java applets

At a far finer level of detail, Java applets could help to organize data received on the fly and let users interact with it immediately. Once data collections are downloaded to the user's workstation, it could also be manipulated locally, without having to wait on background processing of server requests. This could not only improve the kinds and quality of interaction possible, it would definitely help to speed such things up! Although prototypes for such applets do exist, they definitely haven't fulfilled their potential. For example, analyses of a subset of a product information database could be performed on a local version, downloaded once at the beginning of a session, and manipulated locally thereafter (with only occasional checks to make sure the data's still fresh).

In short, we expect this kind of technology to have a sweeping impact on the way we view and use the Web, from the basic interactive behavior of what are now static documents, to the ability to localize and interact with online databases, either in whole or in part. Likewise, we also believe that Java-enabled Web browsers can deliver cross-platform access to large collections of textual, graphical, and other kinds of information that today require platform-specific hypertext and search engines.

From a broader point of view than our own, here's a sampling of proposed future applications of Java as drawn from the flurry of Java-related hype, press releases, gee-whiz extrapolations, and prognostications from computer industry savants:

* *Intranet applications* — Many corporations are discovering the power of Web browsers for information distribution within internal networks. Hardware independence means that Macs, UNIX workstations, and Windows systems can share the same Java applications. We expect to see Java become the language of choice for corporate networks that need platform independence.

* *Hybrid network applications* — Java may become the programming language of choice for specialized Net applications supported by custom driver software. An example of this is the "Liquid Reality" package for creating virtual worlds. The developers of this package found Java ideal for adding behavior to objects rendered by their 3-D graphics software. You may soon be able to define the behavior of objects in a 3-D virtual reality by writing Java code.

* *Multimedia browser extensions* — Although Java is still limited in respect to image and audio formats, Sun is known to be working on multimedia extensions, such as full-motion video. It seems likely that those capabilities that currently require browser plug-ins will be integrated into browser technology through Java.

Upcoming Java API releases

Sun's JavaSoft site contains a listing of impending API releases, with corresponding dates. The subjects of these APIs give an interesting indication of the direction that Sun intends to push Java. These are some of the APIs scheduled for release:

* *Java Media Framework* — This framework will contain media players for MIDI, audio, and video, as well as clocks for synchronizing.
* *Java 3D* — This API will furnish an abstract, interactive imaging model to determine the behavior and control of 3-D objects.
* *Java Telephony* — The Java Telephony API will apply Java to computer-based telephone functions; caller ID, teleconferencing, call transfer, and DTMF decode/encode will all be included.
* *Java Animation* — This API will enable motion and transformations of 2-D objects. It will operate in conjunction with the Java Media Framework to include proper timing, synchronization, and composition.

For more information about Java's future directions, you can surf the Web or consult a computer industry trade magazine, but you'll also find it hotly debated in your local newspaper, national news magazines, and even on mass media like news radio and national television! There is no shortage of opinion on the subject, nor paucity of projections to consider. The only real problem remains separating the wheat from the chaff, or rather, the shameless hype from the remotely possible!

BONUS

Additional Java Resources

This section lists a few additional Java resources.

General Java resources

Here are some of the most significant resources to be found at Sun, which remains the ultimate repository of Java-related information.

* Main documentation page:

   http://java.sun.com/doc.html

* Frequently asked questions, with topics including the latest JDK release, how to obtain the source, licensing, trademark, and copyright for Java and tools, Java security, and the HotJava browser:

   http://java.sun.com/faqIndex.html

* Gamelan, the premier resource for Java on the Net, has sections on: Arts and Entertainment, Business and Finance, Educational, JavaScript, Multimedia, Network and Communications, and News. A search facility will let you find just what you need to spice up your Web page. Every entry has a note indicating the availability of source code:

   http://www.gamelan.com/

* JARS, the Java Applet Rating Service, maintains lists of top applets from all over the Web, rated by Java experts. (Warning! At least one of the authors of this book belongs to this rag-tag assemblage of Java enthusiasts and developers.) Maybe an applet you write will get a top one-percent rating from JARS! Includes topic search capability:

   http://www.jars.com/

* The Java book site lists all Java-related books, and contains scoop on forthcoming guides as well:

   http://lightyear.ncsa.uiuc.edu/~srp/java/javabooks.html

* Online Magazine's Caffeine Connection is a frequently updated site with searchable applet and consultant indices, and includes articles on featured applets, Java news, Java product reviews, and links to interesting sites:

  `http://www.online-magazine.com/cafeconn.htm`

* Java World is IDG's online magazine for the Java community. It includes technical articles by Java experts, Java news, and applet reviews:

  `http://www.javaworld.com/`

* Finally, on CompuServe, GO JAVAUSER for extensive libraries and on-going discussions. CompuServe also has interest groups for other aspects of the Internet.

Consultant resources

* TeamJava HQ's mission is to promote and advance Java and assist Java consultants the world over in locating and completing contract work. The site includes a professional registry, a collection of resources, and some interesting Java demos:

  `http://teamjava.com/`

* The Java Developers Organization was created to promote and protect the interests of Java developers. Consequently, it's attracted quite a bit of useful and interesting information about Java developers, development tools, and other Java esoterica:

  `http://www.jade.org/`

Programming resources

* The newsgroup comp.lang.java is extremely busy, with over 200 messages a day. A FAQ is maintained at:

  `http://sunsite.unc.edu/javafaq/javafaq.html`

* Information on a Java special interest group (SIG) for Sun User Group members can be found at:

  `http://www.sug.org/java-sig.html`

* Java Optimization is an extremely helpful Web page with hints and tips to optimize Java programs, and to make your code smaller and faster:

  `http://www.cs.cmu.edu/~jch/java/optimization.html`

* The official online Java Tutorial is an HTML-based tutorial that you can download or browse online:

  `http://www.javasoft.com/tutorial/index.html`

* Visit "How Do I?" for an extensive collection of Java-related questions and answers from the extremely simple, to the blisteringly complex. This list also includes links to Java-related job opportunities:

  `http://www.digitalfocus.com/digitalfocus/faq/howdoi.html`

* Check out The World Wide Web Virtual Library: the Java Programming Language, which includes a language overview and reference material:

  `http://www.acm.org/~ops/java.html`

* Thingtone's Java Workshop, by Russ Ethington, is a collection of instructive Java programs and annotated source code examples. It was written especially to help experienced programmers become productive with some of the less obvious aspects of Java. Its many examples include lots of source code:

  `http://users.aol.com/thingtone/workshop/index.htm`

* Cyba Java Main Page is a showcase for an easy-to-use shareware library of pixel-based graphics and Java functions for image processing, games, and off-screen image manipulation:

  `http://www.demon.co.uk/cyba/javamain.html`

* Jim Buzbee's Hershey Font Page is a spectacular demo of methods for loading a specified Hershey font, setting the rotation, horizontal alignment, vertical alignment, character width, character height, font-line width, italics, and slant specification. A *tour de force* illustration of using font information within the Java environment, this site is well worth a visit:

  `http://www.nyx.net/~jbuzbee/font.html`

* Liquid Reality is a package consisting of a browser for viewing, and a toolkit for creating dynamic, interactive VRML worlds that can be extended with the Java language. According to its developers, "Liquid Reality is based upon Ice, our 3-D graphics package for use with Java-enabled browsers." Check out:

  `http://www.dimensionx.com/products/index.html`

Entertainment

The last time we checked, the Gamelan site had information on 818 entries in the Arts and Entertainment section. Obviously, games (with 683 entries) occupy a lot of Java programmers' minds:

```
http://www.gamelan.com/
```

Education

* Some of the examples at Sun include 3D Chemical Model, fractal demonstrations, and animated sorting algorithms:

```
http://java.sun.com/applets/applets/MoleculeViewer/example1.html
http://java.sun.com/applets/applets/Fractal/example1.html
http://java.sun.com/applets/applets/SortDemo/example1.html
```

* One of the most dramatic educational applets on the Web is VisibleHuman. This Java applet allows you to select and view high-resolution images of two-dimensional slices of a human body, using image data taken from the National Library of Medicine's Visible Human Project:

```
http://www.npac.syr.edu/projects/vishuman/VisibleHuman.html
```

We hope we've given you the information you need to get familiar with Java, or maybe even to start some Java applet or application construction on your own. Whatever your objectives, we hope you achieve them!

Summary

Throughout this book, we've explored Java's current structures and capabilities, while trying to understand its motivation and technical limitations. In this chapter, we've extended our scope to speculate on what Java could mean to the future of networking and computing in general. We've extended Java's potential impact from widgets in HTML documents to multimedia and corporate database applications. We hope we haven't compromised your enthusiasm or understanding along the way.

There's no question that Java's capabilities are thoroughly exciting. There is still, however, a certain amount of question surrounding Java's future, and Java's branching into hardware leaves even more room for speculation. If Intel ends up wiring its microprocessors with Java, Java's chance of becoming a standard is much more powerful. However, how would Microsoft react to such power? Would it want to fully acquire Java for its domain? Or simply attempt to submerge it with ActiveX?

Alas, we're not sufficiently omniscient to answer such probing questions. But perhaps this annotated list of Web sites will lead you to someone who is; at the very least, you can use these resources to extend your own studies of Java and related phenomena and technologies. We sincerely hope that you've found our coverage useful and illuminating, and that you'll continue your investigations.

In an area as new and fluid as Web-based interactivity, there's no substitute for staying current with emerging theories, technologies, and implementations. Our concluding list of Web resources should help you keep track of the companies, technologies, and people that are making Java happen. And while you're out there trolling for enlightenment, remember to enjoy yourself!

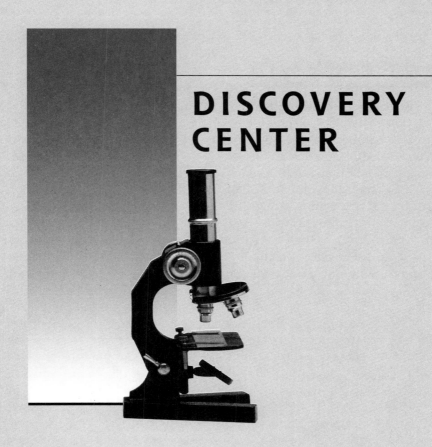

DISCOVERY CENTER

The *Discovery Centers* were pulled from selected chapters and placed in a section all their own to provide a handy review of some of the important elements covered in those chapters. One *Discovery Center* might be a code fragment that is crucial in the development of a Web page; another may provide helpful background information that clarifies the reasoning behind the steps you're asked to perform. Refer to this section any time you need a kick in the memory, or to review a key concept.

CHAPTER 1

Java's Aromatic Past (page 7)

Java was created by the fecund Sun Microsystems, Inc. It started like this: In 1990, Patrick Naughton was a Sun employee who was thinking about leaving Sun to go to NeXT Computer, Inc., where he thought more interesting work was taking place. When Naughton told Scott McNealy, Sun's CEO, about his plans, McNealy (who's regarded as somewhat of a renegade visionary) requested that Naughton create a list of suggestions for Sun before he left. The Sun execs were impressed with Naughton's suggestions; they gave him, along with a carefully selected team of other Sun employees, the go-ahead to put his ideas into action. It was from this team that Java, then code-named "Green," emerged. The goal behind Green was to design a simple, compact language that could run on a variety of devices. The Green team spent their time searching for a way to build a device that would be able to control everyday consumer appliances and electronics.

Green begat "Oak," which took its predecessor's work into the realm of cyberspace. Oak's development was headed by Bill Gosling, whose intention was to build a visual gateway to a virtual world. Frustrated with C++'s unreliability, Gosling decided to create his own language, which he named after the tree outside his office. Oak had many similarities to Java: it worked in a highly distributed manner, it was a hard-core OOL, and it incorporated security issues into its core. The team decided that building a small hand-held, battery-powered box through which Oak's programs would run was the best way to market the new language. The prototypes were prohibitively expensive, however, and there was doubt whether they were marketable. Sun's management was getting antsy about what its years of funding were producing, and pressured the developers to produce some more impressive results. Ironically, the development team initially turned to the very technology that Java had been trying to surpass: the personal computer market. Sun executives weren't particularly taken with the suggestion, and development was basically tabled in 1994.

The Oak development team had been so preoccupied trying to solve the project's pitfalls that they weren't paying much attention to the Web explosion that was occurring simultaneously. Sun cofounder Bill Joy was already connecting the two entities in his mind, though. Although Joy hadn't been too involved with recent matters at Sun, the combination of Java and the Web intrigued him — so he lobbied Sun to resuscitate Java's development. Joy recruited Gosling and Naughton to make the language viable for Internet use. Naughton was responsible for creating the HotJava Web browser, while Gosling worked on the code.

By December 1995, the development team was ready for a little feedback. They acquired it by covertly sticking Java and HotJava in a deep corner of the Net and releasing its coordinates to a select group of the cyberati. The buzz was positive, and Java received its first rave reviews from insiders including Mark Andreesen, Mosaic's creator and Netscape VP.

In May of 1995, Java and HotJava were formally unveiled at the SunWorld '95 exposition. Banking on the idea that they'd turn a profit from Java's commercial licensing deals, Sun followed Netscape's Internet Play approach of building market share without profit, and agreed to make Java and HotJava available free of charge.

Netscape, having profited from Andreesen's inside information, already had its foot in the door on this hot new technology by the time the SunWorld exposition rolled around — they simultaneously announced their plans to license Java for Netscape Navigator 2.0. In doing so, Netscape was Java's first commercial client. A plethora of other illustrious clients soon followed, including: Adobe, Borland, IBM, Macromedia Inc., Metrowerks, Mitsubishi Electronics, Spyglass, Sybase, and Symantec. In addition to the list of these early licensees, some of Java's more recent licensees include: Dimension X, Microsoft, Novell, and Pierian Spring Software.

Sun was very smart to garner such powerful industry support early on — it increased Java's ubiquity and cemented its placement in the rosters of programming languages. To obtain a license, licensees have to pass conformance tests and receive branding from Sun; this testing ensures that applets will work on all products that carry the brand.

Sun teamed with Netscape in 1995 and released JavaScript, an easier, more accessible version of Java that opened the language to nonprogrammers. In May 1996, Sun also released an updated version of the HotJava browser that allayed questions about whether it, the initial Java browser, was going to become obsolete.

CHAPTER 2

Playing with Blocks of Java (page 43)

Java code is structured in sections, or blocks. The beginning and end of its code is always indicated by curly braces, like this:

```
{
// This is a steaming hunk of Java code
}
```

It doesn't matter how much code comes between the pearly — whoops, make that *curly* — gates. It's all recognized as Java code. Every single executable statement in the Java language exists within a block or more of code, and almost everything that exists between the braces exists independent of what's outside the braces. Braces are an extremely crucial part of the Java syntax, because they're responsible for showing the compiler exactly where code begins and ends. Braces are important for *humans*, too — it would be hard to look at your own code and see where it began and ended if you didn't have braces, and much harder to evaluate someone else's.

Although everything that falls between matching braces is executed as a single statement, blocks can contain one or more nested subblocks. Different blocks are identified by indentation. Every time you start a new block, indent your source code by a number of spaces (preferably two). In leaving a block, it's conventional to *unindent*, or move back, two spaces. This spacing is a generally accepted style, but isn't required for the language to work. It's really for the programmer that indentation exists, since it makes it much easier to read and follow code. If you don't believe the difference it makes, check out these two examples of applets. The first one has proper block indentation, the second doesn't.

```
/* File: GraphicsApplet.java */
import java.awt.*;
import java.applet.*;

public class GraphicsApplet extends Applet {
public void paint(Graphics g) {
    Dimension r = size();
    g.setColor(Color.green);
    g.drawLIne(0,0, r.width, r.height);
  }
}
/* File: GraphicsApplet.java */
import java.awt.*;
import java.applet.*;

public class GraphicsApplet extends Applet {
public void paint(Graphics g) {
Dimension r = size();
g.setColor(Color.green);
g.drawLIne(0,0, r.width, r.height);
}
}
```

Most people find it much harder to read the second block of code, since without the indentation, you can't derive any visual clues about the relationships between the blocks of code.

CHAPTER 3

Where to Find It! (page 67)

Here is a quick-reference list to find explanations of some of the more commonly used objects, classes, and methods — broken down by subject area.

Objects and threads

Standard language objects

CHAPTER 4

DocFooter Code (page 119)

In Chapter 4, we create a Java applet called DocFooter. Here's a listing of the complete DocFooter applet source code:

```
import java.applet.Applet ; // Import Applet system package.
import java.awt.* ;         // Import all items of awt system
   package.
import java.awt.image.* ;
import java.util.Date ;  // Import only the Date class from util
                         // package.
```

```java
import java.net.URL ;

public class DocFooter extends Applet {

/* declaration of instance variables */
URL     appletURL ;
private String date;     // date of last update
private Date   today ;   // date of this access
private String email;      // author's e-mail address
private String copyright;     // copyright blurb
private Image logo; /* GIF image of company logo */
    /* Make sure your logo is no larger than 80x80 pixels;
     * otherwise, you must adjust the canvas size. */

/* method invoked by Browser to initialize the applet */
public void init() {
  resize(500,100); /* 500 pixels wide & 100 pixels high  */
  logo = getImage(getDocumentBase(), "images/logo.gif");
    /* Retrieve GIF file from images, a subdirectory of the
     * location of our HTML file. */

    // Get applet parameters from <APPLET> tag as String objects.
    // Note that these will be null if the parameter is not found,
    // so we check before painting.
  date = getParameter("LAST_UPDATED");
  email = getParameter("EMAIL");
  copyright = getParameter("COPY_RIGHT_NOTICE");
  today = new Date();  // Create Date object with today's date.
}

// definition of the paint() method of the DocFooter class
// The system calls paint with a Graphics object appropriate
// for the particular operating system and hardware.
public void paint(Graphics g) {

  // Render the logo image in the canvas
  // for drawImage; x and y refer to upper-left corner of image.
  if( logo != null ) g.drawImage(logo,0,0, this);

  // Render string data into the canvas at specific spots.
  // Note that for drawString, x and y refer to lower-left
  // corner of text.
  if( date != null ) g.drawString(
        "Last modified: " + date ,110,15);
```

```
      g.drawString( "Accessed " + today,110,30);
      if( email != null ) g.drawString( email, 110, 45 );
      if( copyright != null ) g.drawString(copyright,110,60);

      // Get the URL of the document with the embedded <APPLET> tag.
      // Note that an error in creating the URL will result in a
      // MalformedURLException so the statements creating it are
      // enclosed in a "try" "catch" structure.
      try {
        appletURL = new URL(getDocumentBase(),"");

        // Convert the URL to a String.
        String urlstring = appletURL.toExternalForm();

        // Render the URL string to the canvas.
        g.drawString(urlstring,110,75);

      } catch(Exception e) {
        System.err.println("Problem with URL");
      }
    }
  }
```

CHAPTER 5

Designing for Debugging and Testing (page 147)

No kidding, it is possible to design your program with testing and debugging in
mind. This is particularly necessary in network applications and applets where a
problem could be due to browser or network errors. The Java language error and
exception reporting gives you very informative messages, but things will go
faster if you use some of the following techniques.

Using exceptions — the first line of defense

Exceptions signal abnormal conditions that need to be dealt with, but do not
necessarily prevent the program from functioning. If you don't catch an exception close to its source, the Java run-time system will eventually catch it, terminating the thread that triggered the exception. For an example of Exception
catching as a debugging aid, consider the following code for a method for creating a Point object from a String which is expected to have two integers in a fixed
format such as "123 456."

```
Point getPt( String s ){
   try{
      int X = Integer.parseInt( s.substring( 0,3 ) ) ;
      int Y = Integer.parseInt( s.substring( 4,7 ) ) ;
      return new Point(X, Y );

   }catch (StringIndexOutOfBoundsException sx ){
      System.out.println("String too short " + s + " " + sx);
   }catch( NumberFormatException nx ){
      System.out.println("Format error " + s + nx );
   }
   return null ;
}
```

By catching and reporting the error and showing the data which caused the error, you now have a lot more information — as opposed to the system reporting something like the following error message and stopping:

```
java.lang.StringIndexOutOfBoundsException: String index out of
   range: 3
```

Furthermore, if the routine that calls getPt is able to cope with a null return, your program might be able to continue without this data.

Temporary variables and System.out.println()

In the receding getPt example, the "s.substring(0, 3)" code causes the creation of a String object which has only a short existence during the call to Integer.parseInt. If we were having trouble debugging this code, we could assign the String to a local variable and print it out for examination:

```
String strX = s.substring(0, 3);
System.out.println("Parsed X as " + strX );
```

What good is a toString method?

As you look through the Java object methods, you come across toString methods. These methods are automatically used by the compiler whenever it thinks you are trying to build a string such as in System.out.println calls. The toString method is why you can stick any Java object into a string constructor and get something readable, at the least, you will get the string defined by the Object base class. If you are debugging a custom class, consider adding your own toString method which will be more informative than the default. With that in your custom class, getting a quick look at the status of one of your custom objects is just a matter of putting it in a System.out.println statement.

Testing with various browsers and hardware

At last! your applet works perfectly as a local file with appletviewer and your browser. It even works when you put it on your Web site. Are you finished debugging? Nope, at the present stage of Java development, there are plenty of applets which work fine with one browser, but fail with another. Maybe you should leave some of those debugging statements in there for a while and ask people to test your Web site. Of course, the error messages will appear on their browsers, but maybe they will remember to write them down before calling you.

CHAPTER 6

How a Browser Invokes an Applet (page 153)

Here's what a Java-enabled browser does on running across the `<APPLET>` tag in your HTML document:

1. The browser uses the `height` and `width` parameters to reserve space in the document display.

2. The browser uses `codebase` and `code` parameters to create an HTTP request for a class file and sends it to a Web server. While the request is pending, the browser continues working on the rest of the document.

3. The Java runtime system passes the input class file to a `classLoader` object.

4. The `classLoader` checks that the class byte codes make sense and do not violate security constraints; it also locates the names of other classes the applet will need and ensures that all classes have unique names.

5. At this point, all of the classes used by the applet are loaded — standard classes from the browser's local library of classes and custom classes from the codebase directory over the Net.

6. The `Applet` object is created, then its `init()` method is called.

7. If the applet implements the `Runnable` interface and has its own `thread`, the `start()` method is called, otherwise the `paint()` method will be called and your applet will display itself to the user in the document.

8. What happens next depends on the design of the applet and the actions of the user. In general, the browser gets events such as mouse actions and keyboard actions from the user and decides what to do with them. The applet only sees events that the browser passes to it.

9. Whenever the applet's display area is obscured and then re-exposed by movement of the browser window, the `paint()` method is called to regenerate the display.

10. If the user moves to another page, the applet's `stop()` method (if any) is called. This method should suspend any threads your applet uses.

11. When the browser decides to recover the memory the applet is using, the destroy() method is be called.

CHAPTER 7

Packages and Java Extensibility (page 165)

As described in Chapter 2, the Java language provides the package concept to organize classes, methods, and interfaces. This elaborate naming and importing convention may seem like overkill at the present stage of development, but when the number of vendors, toolkits, and libraries for Java starts to approach the number offered for C++, you'll be glad the language designers thought ahead. The Java import feature allows you to utilize and leverage functionality found in the system class library and in the libraries of other vendors without naming confusion.

The current Java class library contains collections of classes ranging in functionality from Java language specifics to networked socket applications. In the examples we have used so far, you have imported classes like the `Graphics` and `Image` classes found in the `java.awt.*` (abstract window toolkit) package and the URL class found in the java.net package.

Even if you start from scratch when building an application, you have a wide spectrum of system library classes to build upon at your fingertips. You can quickly develop applets and applications using extensions of existing system packages and their associated classes, variables, methods, and exceptions.

CHAPTER 8

Creating the EventHandler (page 185)

The sixth step in the step-by-step description of creating a Java application in Chapter 8 is described here.

Users interact with Graphical User Interface (GUI) operating systems by means of keystrokes and mouse operations. As discussed in Chapter 3 under "Events sent to Components," Java runtime code turns these raw system events into standardized Event objects and then looks for a component to handle each event. If a `handleEvent` method can process the event, it returns a Boolean true; if not, it returns false and the system continues looking for a handler. Standard codes for events are static constants in the Event class. Event handling can get quite complicated, but for this application, we are concerned with only three types.

ACTION_EVENT events

Clicking a mouse on a component creates a mouse event for which the system tries to find a handler by passing it to whichever component the mouse was on at the time. The mouse click is eventually turned into an Event with an ID of AC-TION_EVENT, with the button label string attached, so we can see where the event originated.

WINDOW_ICONIFY events

A WINDOW_ICONIFY event is produced when the user clicks on the part of the window frame that controls shrinking the window to an icon. Our code responds to that with the hide method.

WINDOW_DESTROY events

A WINDOW_DESTROY event is produced when the user clicks on the part of the window frame that creates a system menu and chooses "Close."

The event handler code for the RenderImageApp class follows:

```java
public boolean handleEvent(Event e) {
  FileDialog dlog = null ;
  if ((e.id == Event.ACTION_EVENT )  &&
      (e.target instanceof Button )) {
    // the event arg will be the button label
    String label = (String)e.arg;
    if( label.equals( EXIT )) {
      System.exit(0) ; // immediately close and exit
    }
    if (label.equals( GET_GIF )) {
     dlog  = new FileDialog(this, "Get Image ",FileDialog.LOAD);
     dlog.setFile("*.gif");  // preset file type
    }
    if (label.equals( GET_JPG )) {
      dlog = new FileDialog(this, "Get Image", FileDialog.LOAD);
      dlog.setFile("*.jpg");
    }
    // if dialog was created, show it
    if( dlog != null ) {
      dlog.show();
        // when this dialog exits, we may have a file name
      if( dlog.getFile() != null ) {
        imgPanel.ShowImage(dlog.getDirectory() + dlog.getFile() );
      }
    }
    return true; // to show we took care of the event
  }

  if (e.id == Event.WINDOW_ICONIFY) {
```

```
        hide();
        return true;
    }

    if(e.id == Event.WINDOW_DESTROY) {
      System.exit(0);  // terminates the application


    }
    return super.handleEvent(e);
  } // end handleEvent()


} // end RenderImageApp
```

The events `GET_GIF` and `GET_JPG` trigger the creation of a `FileDialog` — a stock class in the java.awt package. We call the `FileDialog` `show` method after setting the initial value of the File string in the dialog to control the type of file names that will be displayed. Execution after the show occurs only when the user has made a decision and selected a file. If no file is selected, a null is returned by the `getFile` method. If a file name is available, it is combined with the directory and the complete path is passed to the `ImagePanel` object.

CHAPTER 9

Installing Java Applications (page 194)

After successfully compiling a new application, you need to define a location for that application and its associated compiled classes. This may be in a well-known directory already defined in your `CLASSPATH` environment variable. In other cases (as when you're testing code that's not yet ready for prime time), the location can be new and private, and you will need to append the new location onto your `CLASSPATH` environment variable.

The `CLASSPATH` environment variable is specified by a colon-separated (UNIX) or semicolon-separated (Windows) list of directories that list the locations for bytecode representations of compiled classes in your runtime system.

Here's an example of a UNIX C shell definition of `CLASSPATH`:

```
setenv CLASSPATH .:/html/classes:/export/system/classes
```

In Windows 95 you would put the following in the AUTOEXEC.BAT file:

```
set CLASSPATH=.;\html\classes;\export\system\classes
```

In these examples, three locations are specified. The initial dot defines the current working directory. The second directory indicates that compiled classes may also be found in the directory /html/classes. The final entry specifies that compiled classes may also be found in the directory /export/system/classes.

UNIX Considerations

UNIX programmers who have installed the Java Developers Kit (JDK) should look in the directory where the Java tools are stored (for example, the compiler and interpreter). By default, this is "java/bin/" relative to where you have installed the JDK. If you do a long listing of this directory, you will see that all of the JDK tools are actually symbolic links to a single script named ".java_wrapper." Wrapper scripts are valuable because they provide a simple user interface to Java applications, while also providing complex setup and execution options to the Java runtime system.

For example, in the java/bin directory of the JDK distribution, the wrapper is a Korn shell script named .java_wrapper. This script sets several environment variables, determines the proper architecture of the binary to execute, and finally executes the program in the Java run-time system on the file or files specified on the command line. This one wrapper is used for java, javac, javadoc, javah, javap, and javaprof.

We recommend creating a wrapper script for your new Java applications. A wrapper script allows you to manage where the applications' compiled classes are stored and how they're referenced by users. If you install the wrapper script in your common tools directory, other users can begin to use your new applications.

CHAPTER 11

Using the Java Interface (page 225)

Java provides the "interface" concept as a way to let the program designer add common functionality to otherwise disparate classes. You have seen this discussed in Chapter 3 where the use of the "Runnable" interface to add a thread to a class was described. In this chapter we create interfaces for text manipulation classes in the following steps.

Through consideration of the type of problems to be solved, we isolate the key functions which will be required and formulate an interface definition. In Java, an interface is defined like an abstract class, it can have static constants but the methods must be abstract. Here is the interface for text sources as we will use it later in the chapter. Notice that our interface extends the Java standard library Runnable interface.

```
abstract public interface TWidgetSource extends Runnable {
    static final int BUFSIZE = 512 ;
    abstract boolean OpenSource( String src, int type );
    abstract PipedOutputStream TWOutput() ;
    abstract void start();
    abstract boolean atEofQ();
}
```

Adding an Interface to a Class

To incorporate interface functionality in a class, we declare it in the class definition as seen in the following code fragment. Note that this class extends `Object` which is the default parent of any class in the Java system. However, we could base it on any convenient class without changing the way the interface works.

```
public class TWFileSource implements TWidgetSource
```

The class definition must include complete "bodies" for the methods declared as abstract in the interface definition, or else the Java compiler will note an error.

Connecting objects using the Interface

Now wherever we have a `TWFileSource` object we can refer to it as a `TWidgetSource` object and connect it to any object expecting a `TWFileSource` (interface) object. This sort of modular approach results in tremendous flexibility.

CHAPTER 12

Java-Related Web Sites (page 263)

In this Discover Center, we're arming you with a plethora of Java-centered Web sites. This collection of resources is really just the tip of a huge volume of information. When we first got involved with this technology, using a search engine to look for Java resources would seldom turn up more than three or four screens' worth of information. Today, that number is in the hundreds. Therefore, while we've tried to pick the best of what's out there, we also feel compelled to warn you that our selections will inevitably reflect our tastes. In other words, to find what appeals to you best, use our recommendations as starting points, but don't be afraid to do a little searching — and winnowing — of your own!

Spicing up HTML documents with Java

This section details some valuable Java resources for adding functionality to your Java programming endeavors.

* Sun has an extensive collection of applets with source code; one starting point is:

  http://java.sun.com/applets/applets.html

* New Media Marketing's CAFE DEL SOL is an exhibition of Java applets for the Web (New Media Marketing is part of Sun Microsystems, Inc.):

  http://www.xm.com/cafe/

* Network Oriented Software's Noware "makes Java Web page enhancements accessible to non-programmers, and gives Java power-users a shortcut to super-productivity":

  http://www.noware.com.au/index2.htm

Compilers and development environments

The following resources are a great place to start when searching for the right Java compilers and development environments:

* IBM's Java environment includes alpha-level code and information on its VisualAge Java power tools. Visit the following site for the latest on IBM's support for the Java environment on OS/2 and AIX, information, news, discussion groups, cool links, downloadable goodies, and FAQs:

  http://ncc.hursley.ibm.com/javainfo/

* Diva for Java provides an Integrated Development Environment for editing, compiling, and testing Java, Perl, and HTML files. The beta test version download was free the last time we visited:

  http://www.qoi.com/javaside.html

* Symantec offers the Café Java Integrated Development Environment (IDE) for Windows 95 and Windows NT:

  http://cafe.symantec.com/

* Symantec Caffeine for Macintosh is Symantec's product for Java Development on the Power Macintosh platform:

  http://cafe.symantec.com

* Rogue Wave sells the Jfactory — a Visual Builder for Java. Jfactory is a rapid development environment for Java, based on Rogue Wave's zApp C++ development environment:

  http://www.roguewave.com/

* Borland's latest C++ compiler comes with Java support. This page covers the current status of all Borland Java-related products:

  http://www.borland.com/Jbuilder

* Natural Intelligence sells a product named Roaster, a Java development system for Macs with Power PC processors:

  http://www.natural.com/pages/products/roaster/index.html

TROUBLESHOOTING GUIDE

This appendix examines some common troubleshooting techniques when working with Java programming.

General

I can't find a way to . . .

* **Write a file to the server**. You can't write a file to a server without some kind of cooperating process on the server.

* **Write a file on an applet client system**. Generally, browser security prevents writing on the local hard disk. The client would have to run the applet viewer or a browser, which do allow writing local files. For access to small amounts of data, look into using JavaScript, which has access to "Cookie" information on the client.

* **Do IO to a port on a PC using Java**. You will have to write a "native method," presumably in C or C++, and link it to your Java program. This is the price we pay for the hardware independence of Java.

* **Let the background of my Web page show through**. You can't make an applet or a component transparent because the browser turns total control of the component area on the screen over to the component.

I keep getting a Null Pointer error

* **With an array of objects**. Recall that array creation proceeds in three steps. First, you declare that the variable will be an array; next, you create the array object; finally, you create the individual objects in the array.

```
String words[] ; // says words is an array of String
words = new String[100] ; // creates words as an array with 100
    slots
// at this point if you tried to use words[0] you would get a
    null pointer
```

```
for( i = 0 ; i < 100 ; i++ ) {words[i] = "" ; }// fill array
                                        // with empty strings
```

* **With a Graphics object**. If you try to create a Graphics object before anything has been shown on the screen, you will get a null object. This is because Java only finds out what kind of graphics hardware it is dealing with when the first window is displayed. People frequently get this error by trying to do too much in the `init` method of an applet.

I keep getting security exceptions

* **Reading a file from an applet**. Browser security won't let you use any of the "File" objects such as `java.io.File` or `java.io.FileDescriptor`. Use "Stream" methods instead.

The program locks up

* **Using threads**. If you are using threads, be sure not to use the `suspend()` method unless you are absolutely sure the thread is not executing a synchronized method. It is much safer to have a thread use wait and notify methods. Also check for the possibility that two threads are trying to access the same synchronized method.

* **The usual possibilities**. Check for loops that are not being exited because you forgot to increment the counter (Don't you just hate it when that happens?).

The program responds erratically

* **Using the wrong thread**. Be aware that the thread that executes `handleEvent`, `action` and `paint` methods is the only system thread communicating with your program. If you use this thread to conduct time-consuming calculations, it is not available for handling more mouse clicks, and so on, and the program will respond to new events erratically. The solution is to start your own thread for any time-consuming calculations or data downloads.

It's not doing what I expected

* **The mouse gets way ahead of my drawing**. The basic problem is that mouse movements can generate events much faster than Java can paint the screen. The result is that the image or whatever is supposed to track the mouse gets way behind. In your code that tracks the mouse, set a flag after you call `repaint`, and then clear this flag in the `paint` method. In your mouse event handler, don't call `repaint` if the flag is still set.

* **The GIF image keeps flashing**. Java starts a separate thread to download image files. If you are not using a `MediaTracker` to wait for the complete image, Java will repaint the image in various partial stages.

* **The GIF image looks horrible**. At the present state of development, Java can only display 256 color images. It attempts to represent colors by dithering, which sometimes looks really lousy. Particularly for applets, try to create images that use the standard Netscape colors.

* **Identical Strings test differently**. You can have two strings that print out with identical contents but that fail the "`stringA.equals( stringB)`" test. This may be due to the fact that strings use 16-bit characters but the printout routines drop the high byte. The other possibility is you are using "`stringA == stringB`," which will never work unless both `stringA` and `stringB` refer to the same object. Remember, "`==`" only works like what you expect with the primitive variable, not with objects.

* **When I resize the browser window it acts weird**. The Netscape browser calls your applet's `stop` method when you begin resizing the browser window and calls the start method when you finish resizing. You will need to design those methods so they can survive multiple calls.

Applets

My applet runs locally but I can't get it to work from my Web site

* **CompuServe**. As of this writing, CompuServe's Web maintenance utility does not correctly handle maintaining the class names, but truncates them to 8.3 style. Microsoft's WebPost (free download from www.microsoft.com) does support long class names correctly but requires Win95. Recall that Java requires an absolute match of class file names to the class contained therein.

* **Other ISPs**. Typically the reason has to do with having changed file names or transferred the class files in "text" mode. If you are using FTP software be sure to transfer all class files, sound files, and image files in "binary" mode.

* **Behind a firewall**. Many corporate networks have "firewall" programs which may have been configured to not pass Java class files. Talk to your network administrator.

My sound files play just fine but the applet won't play them

* **Format**. Java can only play mu-law encoded mono ".au" files. The sampling frequency must be 8000 hertz. Use a utility such as GoldWave to convert from Windows WAV and other formats, being sure to resample to 8000 hertz.

* **OK, I resampled but it clicks and pops**. You can reduce clicking and popping at the start and end of a sound file by using the GoldWave "offset removal" function. Selectively reducing volume at the start and end of a sound clip also helps.

Applications

* **Using a** FileDialog **crashes my application**. If your application is crashing with a "class not found" error right after you use a FileDialog, it is because, unless you specify otherwise, Java looks first in the current directory to find class files. We suggest creating a batch file that specifies the classpath option. Here is an example that runs the Twidget application.

```
java -classpath d:\ Cafe\TextWidgets;d:\
  Cafe\java\lib\classes.zip TWidget
```

* **I can't get a** FilenameFilter **to work**. Don't worry, neither can anybody else! Sun was not able to get this working for the 1.0 release of Java.

APPENDIX B

ABOUT THE CD-ROM

What You'll Find

Following is a summary of the software you will find on this CD-ROM.

JAVA DEVELOPMENT KIT 1.0.2

Five archived versions of this software are located on the CD-ROM in the \JDK102 directory:

Version	For
JDK-1_0_2-solaris2-sparc.tar.Z	Sun Solaris 2.3, 2.4, and 2.5 SPARC
JDK-1_0_2-solaris2-x86.tar.Z	for Solaris 2.5 x86
JDK-1_0_2-win32-x86.exe	Microsoft Windows NT (Intel) and Windows 95
JDK-1_0_2-MacOS.sea.hqx	Power Macs and 68030/25 Macs with at least System 7
JDK-1_0_2-MacOS.sea.bin	Power Macs and 68030/25 Macs with at least System 7

CODE AND EXAMPLES FROM THE CHAPTERS

You can find code and examples from the chapters in the \CODE directory, separated into unique subdirectories, namely: \CH04, \CH06, \CH07, \CH08, \CH10, and \CH11. These elements are for your convenience as a reader of this book. As items are needed in the chapters, you will be instructed to retrieve them from the CD-ROM.

Installation and Troubleshooting

We've included brief, general instructions at the back of this book that tell you where to find the documentation for the JDK; obtain and read that documentation before you try to install or use the JDK. We've also tried our best to collect materials that will work on most computers that meet the minimum system requirements. Alas, all computers are not identical and programs may not work properly for some reason. Before calling our technical support line, consider: The likeliest problem is that you have too little free RAM. If you are certain you've got enough memory, try these tips:

* Turn off any anti-virus software.

* Close all unneeded programs that are running. The more programs you have running, the less memory is available for other programs to use.

* Disable unneeded system extensions that eat up memory on Macs. System 7.5.*x* users can use the Extensions Manager to do this; users of System 7.1 or earlier will need to open the System Folder, open the Extensions folder, and then move the unneeded extensions out of the folder. Restart your computer afterwards.

If you have a problem when you run the programs from the CD-ROM and we haven't resolved it here, please call the IDG Books Worldwide Customer Service phone number: 1-800-762-2974.

INDEX

AT&T (American Telephone & Telegraph), 42

audio, 10, 37–38, 120–121, 138, 140–141, 223, 272

AudioClip class, 223

AUTOEXEC.BAT, 289

AWT (Abstract Windowing Toolkit), 26, 67, 129, 139, 171, 184, 201–202, 207, 265, 268, 287

    basic description of, 81–103

    graphics and, 91–103

    GUI components and, 81–83

    screen building and, 143–144

B

backslash (/), 50

backspace character, 50

base classes, 67–116

baselines, 95

Basic, 264

Bell Labs, 42

<blank> keyword, 64, 65

Boolean class, 72–73

Boolean data type, 22, 23, 56

boolean enabled variable, 82

boolean keyword, 59

Boolean literals, 49, 50

Boolean operators, 52–53, 56

boolean valid variable, 82

boolean visible variable, 82

BorderLayout, 90, 184

Borland, 26, 28, 147, 264, 279, 292

Bourne-shell scripts, 196–197

brackets ([]), 60

break keyword, 59

break statement, 63

Brogden, William B., 201, 202

browsers, 27–28

    multimedia extensions for, 271

    testing applets with, 162–163

BufferedInputStream class, 108

BufferedOutputStream method, 110–111

buffers, byte array, 242

Button class, 81, 86

Buzbee, Jim, 274

ByteArrayInputStream class, 108

ByteArrayOutputStream method, 109

bytecodes, 14–15, 17, 19, 25

byte data type, 23, 57

byte keyword, 59

byvalue keyword, 59

C

Cafe, 31–32, 41, 142, 145, 253, 292

Cafe Au Lait Web site, 41

Caffeine Connection, 273

Caffeine for Macintosh, 292

Canvas class, 81, 139, 201–202

capitalization, 49, 156, 242

CardLayout class, 90–91

Carl-Mitchell, Smoot, 180

carriage return characters, 50, 236

case conversion filter, 252–253

case keyword, 59

case-sensitivity, 49, 156, 242

casting. *See* conversion

cast keyword, 59

CatalogItem class, 140, 141

catch blocks, 65

catch keyword, 59

catch statements, 73

CD-ROMs, 269–270

character arrays, 44

character literals, 49, 50

char data type, 22, 23, 58, 74

char keyword, 59

CHeadline class, 173

CHeadline.java, 168–170

Checkbox class, 81, 86–87

CheckBoxGroup class, 86–87

chips, Java, 9, 34–35, 267

class(es)

    applet extension and, 165–176

    browsing, 144

java.io package, 26, 68, 225–226
isActive() method, 123
ISO 8859-1 character set, 58

J

Jamba, 34
JARS (Java Applet Rating Service), 272
Java Animation API, 271
java.applet package, 67, 129
java.awt (Abstract Windowing Toolkit)
    package, 26, 67, 129, 139, 171, 184,
    201–202, 207, 265, 268, 287
    basic description of, 81–103
    graphics and, 91–103
    GUI components and, 81–83
    screen building and, 143–144
java.awt.image package, 26, 67, 129
java.awt.peer package, 26, 68
Java Beans, 34, 265
Java Bugs Web site, 41
javac compiler, 120, 145, 193
javac_g compiler, 145, 193
Java Developers Organization, 273
Java Enterprise API, 265
Java forum, 147
Java History Web site, 12, 40
Java IDL (Interface Definition Language),
    265, 266
java.io (input/output) package, 26, 68,
    225–226
java.lang package, 68, 182, 191, 226
Java Licensee Web site, 12
Java Links Web site, 8
Java Media Framework, 271
Java Message Board Web site, 41
java.net package, 68, 111–112, 129
Java Optimization Web site, 273–274
JavaOS, 27, 266
Java RMI (Remote Method Invocation),
    265, 266
JavaScript, 16, 28

basic description of, 32–41
    Java and, differences between, 39–40
JavaSoft, 8, 36, 146, 264
JavaSoft Web site, 8
JavaStation, 267
Java Telephony, 271
Java Tools Web site, 8
Java Tutorial, 274
JAVAUSER forum, 273
Java User Group Web site, 41
java.util package, 68, 129
Java Virtual Machine, 14–15
Java Widgets Web site, 41
Java Workshop, 274
Java World Web site, 8, 41, 118, 273
JDBC (Java Database Connectivity), 265,
    266
JDK (Java Developer's Kit), 12, 15, 31,
    118, 141–142, 144–146, 180
    basic description of, 26
    downloading, 146
    embedding applets and, 158
    the future of Java and, 264, 265
    writing Java applets and, 118, 121,
        136
Jfactory, 292
JIT (just-in-time) compilation, 19, 25, 28,
    268
JPG images, 181

K

KC Multimedia Group, 118
keyDown method, 123
keywords, 46, 56, 58–60, 142. *See also*
    specific keywords

L

Label class, 82, 86
LaDue, Mark, 18
Latin-1 character set, 58

public void write method, 109
public write method, 109

Q

QuickCode Pro, 33

R

RAM (random-access memory), 266. *See also* memory
RandomAccessFile class, 110–111
Random class, 113
ReadySink, 229, 231
Record class, 191
Rectangle class, 91, 93–94
relational operators, 23
RenderImageApp, 181–186, 196–199, 222–223
RenderImageApp class, 182–187
repaint() method, 124
repaints, multiple, 150
requestFocus method, 122
requirements analysis, 137–141
reserved method names, 59–60
resize method, 124, 154, 162
rest keyword, 59
return keyword, 59
reusability, 13–14
RGBImageFilter, 101–102
RMI (Remote Method Invocation), 265, 266
Roaster, 33, 292
Rogue Wave, 26, 292
run() method, 70
Rusty Elliotte's Java tutorial, 8

S

scope, 48
screen building, 143–144

Scrollbar class, 82, 88–89
security, 16–18, 28, 268
SecurityManager, 157–158
semicolon (;), 48, 193, 220, 289
SequenceInputStream class, 108
setBackground method, 124
setFilterType method, 228
setFont method, 124
setSubstitute() method, 260
setTWidgetSource method, 228, 229, 236
short data type, 23
short keyword, 59
ShowImage method, 185, 186
showStatus method, 124
single quote ('), 50
slash (/), 46–47
sleep method, 149–150
Smalltalk, 25
Solar Vengeance Applet, 138
sound, 10, 37–38, 120–121, 138, 140–141, 223, 272
square brackets ([]), 60
Stack class, 105
start() method, 125, 127, 168, 228, 286
static keyword, 59, 64, 65
statistics filter, 248–252
stop() method, 125, 127
StreamTokenizer, 207
StringBuffer, 76–79
string data type, 58
String method, 157
String operator, 54
SubsFilter.java, 101–102
Sun Microsystems Web site, 264, 272
SunOS, 28
Sun User Group, 273
super keyword, 59
switch keyword, 59
switch statements, 62–63
Symantec Developers Tools forum, 147
symbols
  @(at sign), 47
  \(backslash), 50

W

wait method, 60, 69
Web servers, moving files to, 163
WebLogic Technologies, 191
WebScript, 191
WebWare Online, 118
while loops, 62
width attribute, 30
WIDTH parameter, 126, 154, 155, 162,
    286
Windows 3.1, 28, 68
Windows 95, 19, 26, 28, 161
Windows NT, 19, 26, 28, 161
word processor text, reformatting, 260
World Wide Web Virtual Library, 274
wrappers, 72–76, 196–198

X

Xerox, 35

Z

Zilker Internet Park, 180

Java™ DEVELOPER'S KIT VERSION 1.0.2 BINARY CODE LICENSE

This binary code license ("License") contains rights and restrictions associated with use of the accompanying software and documentation ("Software"). Read the License carefully before installing Software. By installing Software you agree to the terms and conditions of this License:

1. **Limited License Grant.** Sun grants to you ("Licensee") a nonexclusive, nontransferable limited license to use Software without fee. Licensee may redistribute complete and unmodified Software to third parties provided that this License conspicuously appear with all copies of Software and that Licensee does not charge a fee for such redistribution of Software.

2. **Java Platform Interface.** In the event that Licensee creates any Java-related API and distributes such API to others for applet or application development, Licensee must promptly publish an accurate specification for such API for free use by all developers of Java-based software. Licensee may not modify the Java Platform Interface ("JPI," identified as classes contained within the "java" package or any subpackages of the "java" package), by creating additional classes within the JPI or otherwise causing the addition to or modification of the classes in the JPI.

3. **Restrictions.** Software is confidential copyrighted information of Sun and title to all copies is retained by Sun and/or its licensors. Licensee shall not modify, decompile, disassemble, decrypt, extract, or otherwise reverse engineer Software. Software my not be leased, assigned, or sublicensed, in whole or in part. Software is not designed or intended for use in on-line control of aircraft, air traffic, aircraft navigation or aircraft communications; or in the design, construction, operation or maintenance of any nuclear facility. Licensee warrants that it will not use or redistribute the Software for such purposes.

4. **Trademarks and Logos.** Licensee acknowledges that Sun owns the Java trademark and all Java-related trademarks, logos and icons including the Coffee Cup and Duke ("Java Marks") and agrees to: (i) comply with the Java Trademark Guidelines at http://java.com/trademarks.html; (ii) not do anything harmful to or inconsistent with Sun's rights in the Java Marks; and (iii) assist Sun in protecting those rights, including assigning to Sun any rights acquired by Licensee in any Java Mark.

5. **Disclaimer of Warranty.** Software is provided "AS IS," without a warranty of any kind. ALL EXPRESS OR IMPLIED REPRESENTATIONS AND WARRANTIES, INCLUDING ANY IMPLIED WARRANTY OF MERCHANTABILITY, FITNESS FOR A PARTICULAR PURPOSE OR NON-INFRINGEMENT, ARE HEREBY EXCLUDED.

6. **Limitation of Liability.** SUN AND ITS LICENSORS SHALL NOT BE LIABLE FOR ANY DAMAGES SUFFERED BY LICENSEE OR ANY THIRD PART AS A RESULT OF USING OR DISTRIBUTING SOFTWARE. IN NO EVENT WILL SUN OR ITS LICENSORS BE LIABLE FOR ANY LOST REVENUE, PROFIT OR DATA, OR FOR DIRECT, INDIRECT, SPECIAL, CONSEQUENTIAL, INCIDENTAL OR PUNITIVE DAMAGES, HOWEVER CAUSED AND REGARDLESS OF THE THEORY OF LIABILITY, ARISING OUT OF THE USE OF OR INABILITY TO USE SOFTWARE, EVEN IF SUN HAS BEEN ADVISED OF THE POSSIBILITY OF SUCH DAMAGES.

7. **Termination.** Licensee may terminate this License at any time by destroying all copies of Software. This License will terminate immediately without notice from Sun if Licensee fails to comply with any provision of this License. Upon such termination, Licensee must destroy all copies of Software.

8. **Export Regulations.** Software, including technical data, is subject to U.S. export control laws, including the U.S. Export Administration Act and its associated regulations, and may be subject to export or import regulations in other countries. Licensee agrees to comply strictly with all such regulations and acknowledges that it has the responsibility to obtain licenses to export, re-export, or import Software. Software may not be downloaded, or otherwise exported or re-exported, (i) into, or to a national resident of, Cuba, Iraq, Iran, North Korea, Libya, Sudan, Syria, or any country to which the U.S. has embargoed goods; or (ii) to anyone on the U.S. Treasury Department's list of Specially Designated Nations or the U.S. Commerce Department's Table of Denial Orders.

9. **Restricted Rights.** Use, duplication or disclosure by the United States government is subject to the restrictions as set forth in the Rights in Technical Data and Computer Software Clauses in DFARS 252.227-7013(c)(1)(ii) and FAR 52.227-19(c)(2) as applicable.

10. **Governing Law.** Any action related to this License will be governed by California law and controlling U.S. federal law. No choice of law rules of any jurisdiction will apply.

11. **Severability.** If any of the above provisions are held to be in violation of applicable law, void or unenforceable in any jurisdiction, then such provisions are herewith waived to the extent necessary for the License to be otherwise enforceable in such jurisdiction. However, if in Sun's opinion deletion of any provisions of the License by operation of this paragraph unreasonably compromises the rights or increases the liabilities of Sun or its licensors, Sun reserves the right to terminate the License and refund the fee paid by Licensee, if any, as Licensee's sole and exclusive remedy.

IDG BOOKS WORLDWIDE, INC.
END-USER LICENSE AGREEMENT

Read This. You should carefully read these terms and conditions before opening the software packet(s) included with this book ("Book"). This is a license agreement ("Agreement") between you and IDG Books Worldwide, Inc. ("IDGB"). By opening the accompanying software packet(s), you acknowledge that you have read and accept the following terms and conditions. If you do not agree and do not want to be bound by such terms and conditions, promptly return the Book and the unopened software packet(s) to the place you obtained them for a full refund.

1. **License Grant.** IDGB grants to you (either an individual or entity) a nonexclusive license to use one copy of the enclosed software program(s) (collectively, the "Software") solely for your own personal or business purposes on a single computer (whether a standard computer or a workstation component of a multi-user network). The Software is in use on a computer when it is loaded into temporary memory (i.e., RAM) or installed into permanent memory (e.g., hard disk, CD-ROM or other storage device). IDGB reserves all rights not expressly granted herein.

2. **Ownership.** IDGB is the owner of all right, title and interest, including copyright, in and to the compilation of the Software recorded on the disk(s)/CD-ROM. Copyright to the individual programs on the disk(s)/CD-ROM is owned by the author or other authorized copyright owner of each program. Ownership of the Software and all proprietary rights relating thereto remain with IDGB and its licensors.

3. **Restrictions On Use and Transfer.**

   (a) You may only (i) make one copy of the Software for backup or archival purposes, or (ii) transfer the Software to a single hard disk, provided that you keep the original for backup or archival purposes. You may not (i) rent or lease the Software, (ii) copy or reproduce the Software through a LAN or other network system or through any computer subscriber system or bulletin-board system, or (iii) modify, adapt or create derivative works based on the Software.

   (b) You may not reverse engineer, decompile, or disassemble the Software. You may transfer the Software and user documentation on a permanent basis, provided that the transferee agrees to accept the terms and conditions of this Agreement and you retain no copies. If the Software is an update or has been updated, any transfer must include the most recent update and all prior versions.

4. **Restrictions on Use of Individual Programs.** You must follow the individual requirements and restrictions detailed for each individual program in [the shareware section] of this Book. These limitations are contained in the individual license agreements recorded on the disk(s)/CD-ROM. These restrictions include a requirement that after using the program for the period of time specified in its text, the user must pay a registration fee or discontinue use. By opening the Software packet(s), you will be agreeing to abide by the licenses and restrictions for these individual programs. None of the material on this disk(s) or listed in this Book may ever be distributed, in original or modified form, for commercial purposes.

5. **Limited Warranty.**

   (a) IDGB warrants that the Software and disk(s)/CD-ROM are free from defects in materials and workmanship under normal use for a period of sixty (60) days from the date of purchase of this Book. If IDGB receives notification within the warranty period of defects in materials or workmanship, IDGB will replace the defective disk(s)/CD-ROM.

   (b) IDGB AND THE AUTHOR OF THE BOOK DISCLAIM ALL OTHER WARRANTIES, EXPRESS OR IMPLIED, INCLUDING WITHOUT LIMITATION IMPLIED WARRANTIES OF MERCHANTABILITY AND FITNESS FOR A PARTICULAR PURPOSE, WITH RESPECT TO THE SOFTWARE, THE PROGRAMS, THE SOURCE CODE CONTAINED THEREIN, AND/OR THE TECHNIQUES DESCRIBED IN THIS BOOK. IDGB DOES NOT WARRANT THAT THE FUNCTIONS CONTAINED IN THE SOFTWARE WILL MEET YOUR REQUIREMENTS OR THAT THE OPERATION OF THE SOFTWARE WILL BE ERROR FREE.

   (c) This limited warranty gives you specific legal rights, and you may have other rights which vary from jurisdiction to jurisdiction.

6. **Remedies.**

   (a) IDGB's entire liability and your exclusive remedy for defects in materials and workmanship shall be limited to replacement of the Software, which is returned to IDGB at the address set forth below with a copy of your receipt. This Limited Warranty is void if failure of the Software has resulted from accident, abuse, or misapplication. Any replacement Software will be warranted for the remainder of the original warranty period or thirty (30) days, whichever is longer.

   (b) In no event shall IDGB or the author be liable for any damages whatsoever (including without limitation damages for loss of business profits, business interruption, loss of business information, or any other pecuniary loss) arising out of the use of or inability to use the Book or the Software, even if IDGB has been advised of the possibility of such damages.

   (c) Because some jurisdictions do not allow the exclusion or limitation of liability for consequential or incidental damages, the above limitation or exclusion may not apply to you.

7. **U.S. Government Restricted Rights.** Use, duplication, or disclosure of the Software by the U.S. Government is subject to restrictions stated in paragraph (c) (1) (ii) of the Rights in Technical Data and Computer Software clause of DFARS 252.227-7013, and in subparagraphs (a) through (d) of the Commercial Computer--Restricted Rights clause at FAR 52.227-19, and in similar clauses in the NASA FAR supplement, when applicable.

8. **General.** This Agreement constitutes the entire understanding of the parties, and revokes and supersedes all prior agreements, oral or written, between them and may not be modified or amended except in a writing signed by both parties hereto which specifically refers to this Agreement. This Agreement shall take precedence over any other documents that may be in conflict herewith. If any one or more provisions contained in this Agreement are held by any court or tribunal to be invalid, illegal or otherwise unenforceable, each and every other provision shall remain in full force and effect.

Alternate Disk Format Available.
The enclosed disks are in 3 1/2" 1.44MB, high-density format. If you have a different size drive, or a low-density drive, and you cannot arrange to transfer the data to the disk size you need, you can obtain the programs on (5-1/4" 1.2 MB high-density disks or 3-1/2" 720K low-density disks or 800K low-density disks] by writing to the following address: Disk Fulfillment Department, Attn: [Title of Book], IDG Books Worldwide, Inc., 7260 Shadeland Station, Indianapolis, IN 46256, or call 1-800-762-2974. Please specify the size of disk you need and allow 3 to 4 weeks for delivery.

IDG BOOKS WORLDWIDE REGISTRATION CARD

Visit our Web site at http://www.idgbooks.com

Title of this book: DISCOVER JAVA™

My overall rating of this book: ❏ Very good [1] ❏ Good [2] ❏ Satisfactory [3] ❏ Fair [4] ❏ Poor [5]

How I first heard about this book:

❏ Found in bookstore; name: [6]

❏ Advertisement: [8]

❏ Word of mouth; heard about book from friend, co-worker, etc.: [10]

❏ Book review: [7]

❏ Catalog: [9]

❏ Other: [11]

What I liked most about this book:

What I would change, add, delete, etc., in future editions of this book:

Other comments:

Number of computer books I purchase in a year: ❏ 1 [12] ❏ 2-5 [13] ❏ 6-10 [14] ❏ More than 10 [15]

I would characterize my computer skills as: ❏ Beginner [16] ❏ Intermediate [17] ❏ Advanced [18] ❏ Professional [19]

I use ❏ DOS [20] ❏ Windows [21] ❏ OS/2 [22] ❏ Unix [23] ❏ Macintosh [24] ❏ Other: [25]_____

(please specify)

I would be interested in new books on the following subjects:

(please check all that apply, and use the spaces provided to identify specific software)

❏ Word processing: [26]

❏ Data bases: [28]

❏ File Utilities: [30]

❏ Networking: [32]

❏ Other: [34]

❏ Spreadsheets: [27]

❏ Desktop publishing: [29]

❏ Money management: [31]

❏ Programming languages: [33]

I use a PC at (please check all that apply): ❏ home [35] ❏ work [36] ❏ school [37] ❏ other: [38] _____

The disks I prefer to use are ❏ 5.25 [39] ❏ 3.5 [40] ❏ other: [41]_____

I have a CD ROM: ❏ yes [42] ❏ no [43]

I plan to buy or upgrade computer hardware this year: ❏ yes [44] ❏ no [45]

I plan to buy or upgrade computer software this year: ❏ yes [46] ❏ no [47]

Name: _____ Business title: [48] _____ Type of Business: [49] _____

Address (❏ home [50] ❏ work [51] /Company name: _____)

Street/Suite# _____

City [52]/State [53]/Zipcode [54]: _____ Country [55] _____

❏ **I liked this book!** You may quote me by name in future IDG Books Worldwide promotional materials.

My daytime phone number is _____

IDG BOOKS
WORLDWIDE

THE WORLD OF COMPUTER KNOWLEDGE®

❑ YES!

Please keep me informed about IDG Books Worldwide's
World of Computer Knowledge. Send me your latest catalog.